Harris

wort: ochsenblutrot
nie: schwefelgelb
ahl: tintenschwarz
äche: knochenweiß
edanke: fliederfarben
aum: smaragdgrün

15. August
2014

andreas uebele
material
monograph volume 3
2003 – 2016

unit editions

foreword

kai bierich
terreno comune uebele

when i first met andreas uebele 20 years ago i thought: how could anyone who produces such good work have a name with such negative connotations (in german, uebel = bad). at the time i didn't know this was the beginning of a long friendship, one which has influenced me greatly, personally and professionally, through to the present day. the thinking in shared categories and the added value that comes from interdisciplinarity are things i wouldn't want to be without now – quite apart from the sheer quality and standard of his work.

what i've learned is that we as architects have to stop thinking solely in terms of categories of buildings – it's an overly restrictive definition of the environments we have to create together. architecture is just one means of communication; it tells stories, shapes consciousness and memory, and can sometimes impart sensory and emotional well-being – but this shouldn't be all it does. a building, when it's a good one, can have a message – and yet at the same time the architecture is just a framework for other media: graphic displays, texts, wayfinding aids and inscriptions. it doesn't have to be the three-dimensional space constructed by the architect, the structural outcome, that formulates a concept – the non-material signs can play an equal part in supporting an implicit idea or indeed conveying it themselves.

a key challenge, arguably, for a practice like this one is combining its own high standards, its specific stratum, with the signature styles, the intellectual enterprise, of the architects it partners with. that this succeeds time and again in our collaborations – and in a different way each time – is something exceptional and precious. we all know well enough that partnerships like this aren't always "happy ever after".

the visual appearance of our joint projects resonates deeply with a connection that's both formal and definitely also intellectual: in every case the signs and lettering become an autonomous and important visual element of our architecture. it's similar to the approach we see in giorgio vasari's writings on design: vasari describes a drawing – and he was a keen collector of other artists' drawings – as a "concetto", a concept, which already contains within itself the essence, the expressive substance, of the intended work. "design," he writes, "the parent of our three arts, architecture, sculpture, and painting, having its origin in the intellect, draws out from many things a general judgement …". this awareness of drawing's pre-eminent importance, nowadays almost entirely lost, is given renewed, poetic life by andreas uebele. he is someone who works challengingly, provocatively on and across the borderline between word and image. he draws all kinds of things – forms, structures, typefaces – producing sketches which, when paired with his powerful statements, have found resonance not only with us but also with many of our clients.

i would perhaps compare our terreno comune – our common ground – and our collaboration with rowing a boat: each rower has their own style, their role, their way of doing things. but success is always the result of joint enterprise.

85 projects

with contributions by

joachim blüher andreas uebele on a 2015 scholarship at villa massimo · lxxxvi
hannes böhringer sweeping · lxxxv
matthew carter verdana and georgia · lv
andreas cukrowicz cape nordkinn · cxii
adrian frutiger alphabet métro · viii
durs grünbein cvi
hans hansen xl
klaus klemp typography becomes architecture and more · lxxviii
norbert lammert lvi
jórunn ragnarsdóttir natural beauty and artificial beauty · lxvi
thomas ruff xix
karin sander kitchen pieces · xxxix
manfred schmalriede lxv
klaus schmiedek andreas uebele – playfully serious, seriously playful · cxvii
eva-maria schön gebiet geknittert · cxi
massimo vignelli cv
hermann zapf melior antiqua · liii
peter zizka lxxvii

higher, faster, further

smarter and brighter and better, that's the walls of the new adidas gym. colourful decorations made up of numbers and letters get the rooms in the company's own gym into shape, boosting energy, pulse and power. up to ten metres tall, the graphic elements are more than just feel-good wallpaper, instead communicating actively with the gym's users as they warm up or chill. because the numbers and letters are also signs, holding coded messages that can be deciphered or ignored at will. at first sight they are numbers and colours like the ones that appear on sportswear. the colours are indeed taken from the world of sport but all jumbled up. a closer look reveals – through the beads of sweat – the number 13, once worn, for example, by gerd müller, plus the 10 and 23, which starts one wondering who they could stand for. just what "om bliss" and "relax" are all about is revealed by a visit to the bar.

numbers (left) from top to bottom: derrick rose, cafu, ronaldo, lionel messi, thomas müller, david beckham and michael jordan, kareem abdul jabbar, year the company was registered, "trefoil", launch of the "reebok step"

adidas gym
spatial design
herzogenaurach, 2014

what design means to me

design is an opportunity to shape the world. design strikes deep inside us as human beings. we are surrounded by items forged by human endeavour: spectacles, cars, houses, dresses, cups, knives, chairs or pencils are all tools that expand our existence or render us human in the first place. a violin can provide a means of expressing our personality. such articles are cultural entities that, like an artificial limb, are extensions of our inner selves, allowing us to live dignified and fulfilling lives. and graphic design forms another module of human culture. all these things have a soul, because we breathe into them what we are or what we aspire to become. which is why they merit our attention and appreciation. this is what design and being a designer mean to me.

**at what point in decision-making should
we listen to our intuition?**

our inner voice is a reliable partner. it never lies to us. we should trust it.

what does responsibility mean?

seriousness
lightness
simplicity
recalcitrance
beauty

grey

associating colours with specific qualities results in meaningless rules. grey comes out of this systematic approach especially badly, forever linked with dull days, sadness, tedium and unhappy faces. the new year is going to be grey, too, if the colour of the sky is anything to go by. then — suddenly, unexpectedly — you notice the motion of the grey storm clouds. and as the light fades the wall that had been brightly illuminated becomes a stage for shadowy figures. are they grey? blue-grey? grey-green? greyish yellow? reddish grey? grey is a fine interplay of light and colour, grey is softer than the hard white of the wall and calmer than a colour. grey is beautiful.

in some rooms there are bright ideas to be found in the shape of huge illuminated numbers on the ceiling: 54 ... now wasn't that the year of germany's miraculous world cup win?

black and white and read all over

deutsche? werkbund? exhibition? deutsche we can deal with. but few people will know what this "werkbund" thing is or what its original purpose was. which is why the exhibition poster is designed to illustrate precisely what this honourable institution stands for: bringing together the interests of the arts and business across multiple disciplines. that may sound simple enough these days, but when the organisation was founded exactly 100 years ago, it was nothing less than revolutionary. so this poster is a sign of change in more ways than one – because this captivating collection of 598 words invites you to do just that: change them around, mix and merge them to form amusing or insightful combinations and collocations, reading left to right or top to bottom. the outcome is a series of self-made crossfunctional phrases and thought-flows like: "passion swarm" or "beyond consistency". they spread the word that every nascent notion begins with language and that a diversity of disciplines will enrich any task and its outcome. just like the 41 authors from 14 specialist fields who contributed to this visionary vocabulary of the changing times.

authors:
2xgoldstein
joachim baldauf
olaf barski
ruedi baur
lothar bertrams
kai bierich
hannes böhringer
christian boros
jürgen braun
bazon brock
andreas cukrowicz
timo gaessner
brigida gonzález
martin grothmaak
wolfgang hartauer
frank höhne
peter ippolito
holger jacobs
jehs+laub
axel kufus
arno lederer
sindri lederer
sarah maier
nils holger moormann
harald f. müller
julia münzing
uwe münzing
sandro parrotta
frank philippin
sybille philippin
jórunn ragnarsdóttir
arno ritter
daniel rothaug
karin sander
gerwin schmidt
eva-maria schön
werner sobek
oliver sorg
tobias wulf
diane ziegler
peter zizka

deutsche werkbund exhibition
exhibition poster
venice, 2014

	pain	twinkle	focus	angst	wagram	principles	programm-änderung	renditeerwart
nus	time	curiosity	alive	beständigkeit	die	things	rückmeldung	masterplan
ert	power	identity	coherence	reise	fly	explain	anpassung	nordseite
	system	beyond	consistency	wunder	suze	twelve	entwicklungs-schritt	fristgerecht
	faith	respect	relaxation	klarheit	genuss	weaving	farbvariante	klarheit
	silence	cognition	sparks	weltanschauung	authentizität	forswear	nichtbeachtung	orientierung
sans	dream	journey	interlinked	fokus	klarheit	curst	platzierung	einfach
que	poetry	love	elegance	felicità	schöngeist	remedy	durcheinander	temperatur
	fire	why	playtest	liebe	geschichte	true	fernwirkung	raumgefühl
g	haltung	once more	interpretation	berüchtigt	faszination	behalf	landstrich	spannung
gestaltung	richtung	stories	magic wand	zuckerguss	qualität	purple	pinsel	suche
ine	raum	sense	chuckle	voranschreiten	stil	swifter	luftdruck	koinzidenz
	klar	rethink	panache	begnadet	strukturen	sorrow	kartenzeit	zeitsprung
	definiert	rituals	unexpected	wir	reduktion	marmor	blickwinkel	gänsehaut
ed	reform	heritage	cacophony	genießen	abstraktion	schiefer	gezeiten	schlaflosigkei
ation	wandel	hope	complementary	dehnen	abgrenzung	granit	fingerspitze	konzentration
sition	chance	desire	quasi-intelligence	vollenden	vision	travertin	labor	offenheit
	utopie	passion	swarm	fein	hintergedanke	quartz	sackgasse	anarchie
sions	möglich	relevance	sweatshop	nah	transformation	alabastro	flugfeld	kontext
g	spiel	distinctive	cross-platform	gut	ästhetik	basalt	schachtel	klarheit
	feld	sexy	outtake	wert	dunkel	liparit	ausschnitt	schärfe
	versuch	anarchie	concocting	gerade	struktur	amethyst	unruhe	intervention
	weiter	kawaii	neoanalog	arg	amorph	agate	auswahl	wachsamkeit
	scheitern	brachial	formatting	haltung	stabil	kalkstein	apfelernte	unbeirrbarkeit
ure	krawisuall	ballistic	in-between	mensch	formalität	träumerei	schaum	beirrbarkeit
	betablocker	bumsfidel	linearität	konsequenz	laterne	sowohl-als-auch	parallel	tiefe
	abwrackpremier	bollocks	schichtung	rau	apsis	zwischenraum	unscheinbar	natur
pe	tausendsassatum	pushy	blockrand	volupté	flügel	ambivalenz	doppelt	gott
	authentizität	process	belichtung	cyan	enfilade	ironie	atemberaubend	glatt

can design be an obsession?

obsession, in this case being obsessed with design, is a basic requirement for any designer. if you don't find yourself wanting to design everything in your life then you're in the wrong job. if you're not interested in the form, the construction, of your car or your bike, then you're seriously miscast. if you don't read anything, don't appreciate the physical attributes of paper, don't care about the fabric and cut of a coat, neglect the pens on your desk, and consider your waste-paper basket a soulless non-entity – then how can you expect to design something yourself that works, looks good and conjures a response in its user?

**what's the bigger challenge:
coming up with an idea or selling it?**

coming up with ideas is a myth. "higher powers command: paint the upper right corner black!" (sigmar polke). there is no idea. there is only the process, that – following objective, rational, aesthetic considerations – brings a solution to light. what we might refer to as an "idea" is the outcome of steady ongoing work, emerging from a dialogue between client and supplier.

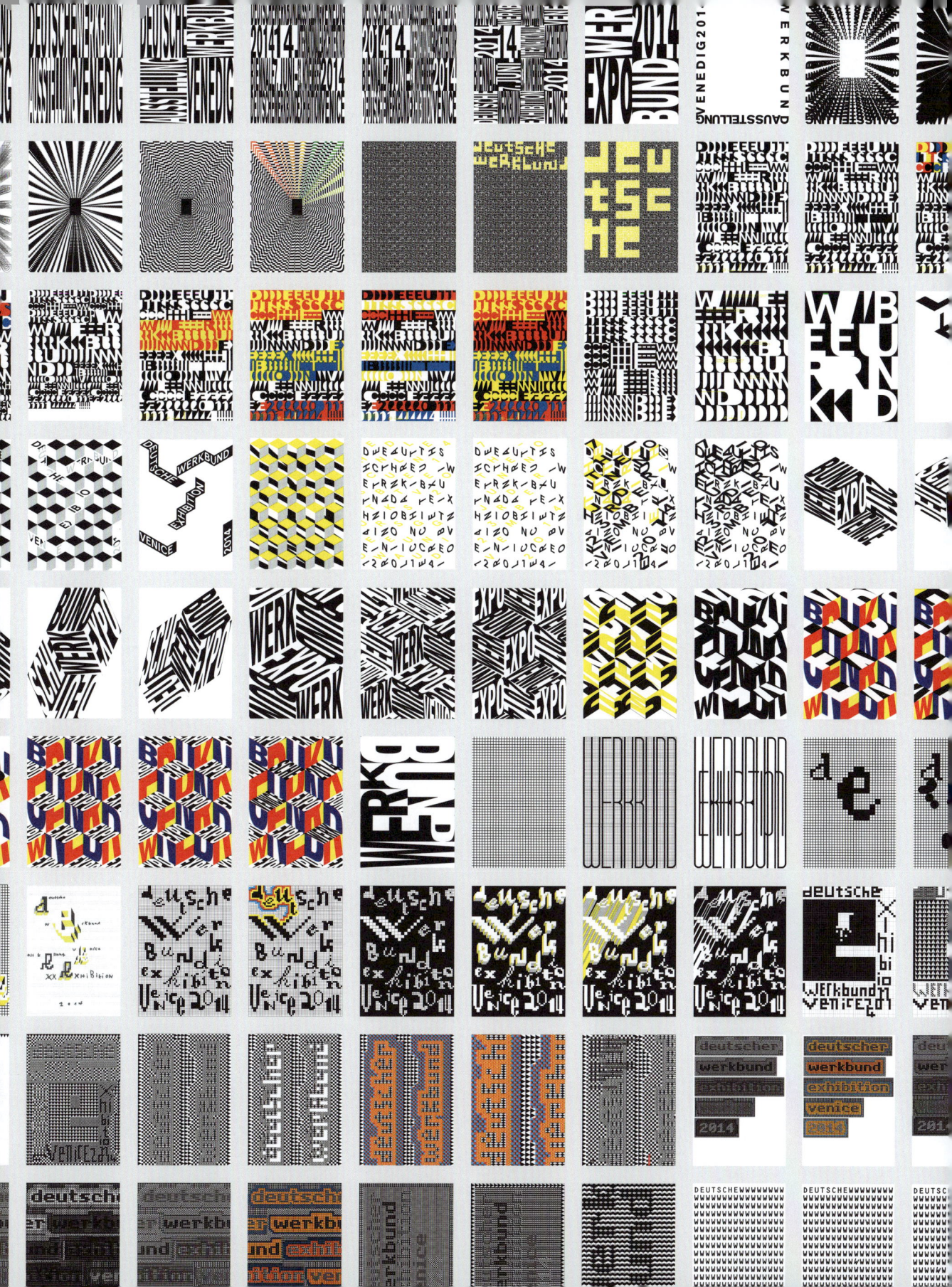

typographical perfume

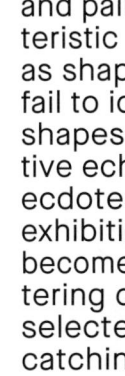

the place is characterised by a combination of odour, light, colour and lettering: bright colourful type, cast metal letters, names engraved in plaster, messages and paintings sprayed on surfaces capture the characteristic visual scent of a city. you don't perceive them as shapes but as information. you read the signs but fail to identify their messages. in the interplay of their shapes and forms they are tiny time-capsules, narrative echoes of the era in which they were created. anecdotes relating to a building and its location. in the exhibition "alphabet innsbruck" these hidden stories become visible. the advertising logos and historical lettering discovered on a walk through innsbruck were selected in line with idiosyncratic criteria: the eye-catching and the inconspicuous; the commonplace and the eccentric; the vulgar and the subtle. together they make up a typographical web in which the written culture of a place is captured. the writing or individual letters were photographed and reproduced digitally with the greatest possible accuracy. some of the letters were damaged; others could only be photographed from extreme angles. others again were three-dimensional and had to be reinterpreted in two dimensions for the exhibition. the accompanying texts about the lettering were composed by georg salden; the historical cameos of innsbruck are by gretl köfler. their contributions are the base notes of this typographical perfume and endow "alphabet innsbruck" with a very personal touch.

alphabet innsbruck
typographic installation, exhibition catalogue
2009

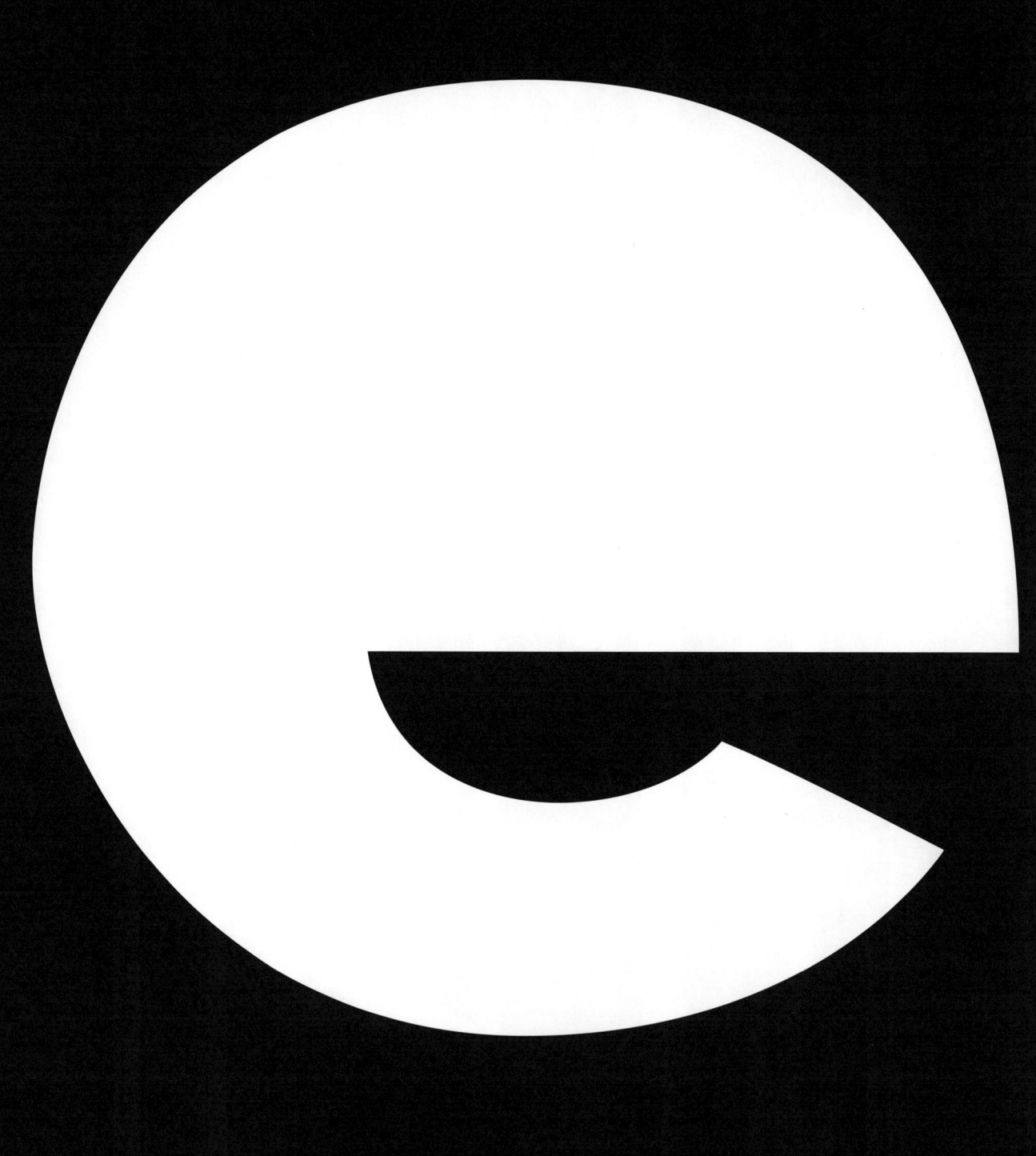

beauty's transience
on adrian frutiger's alphabet métro font

it's a terrible shame when good design is replaced by bad design. paul rand's ups logo was mutilated in the updated "3d" version; otl aicher's logo for german broadcaster zdf was disfigured by switching the z for a phonetically problematic 2. the same thing happened with the signage system for the paris métro, for which adrian frutiger designed a brilliantly clear upper-case alphabet system that's no longer in use.

frutiger's métro font is an ideal upper-case typeface for wayfinding systems, and so we approached the paris transport authority (ratp: the régie autonome des transports parisiens), to ask if it might possibly be available to use. the response was negative. the records, they said, were supposedly in a basement somewhere, but nobody knew for sure. when we asked adrian frutiger himself if we might use his métro font, as it was now no longer in use by the eponymous institution, we received a prompt and friendly reply by post. it contained, on the one hand, the answer we'd hoped for: yes, we could use his font. it also suggested that we might copy from his own records as the basis for our designs. a second enquiry sent to ratp — this time in our best french — subsequently yielded a digital version, too, which can be seen on the following page.

our delight at being personally licensed to use frutiger's typeface is dimmed only by the realisation of beauty's transience. we were able to save the métro from sinking into oblivion this time. but who knows how long for?

adrian frutiger
alphabet métro, 1973

GARE DU NORD
PONT NEUF
LE PELETIER
OURCQ
SAINT-LAZARE
OBERKAMPF
CHÂTEAU D'EAU
OPÉRA
CHÂTELET
MAIRIE D'IVRY
BELLEVILLE

leopoldstraße 11

X

schlossergasse 1

heiliggeiststraße 3: sein selbstgebauter »fetzenflieger« mit einem 130-ps-porsche-carrera-motor die sensation des rennfahrers und konstrukteurs otto mathé (1907–1995) bei berg- und sandbahnrennen in den 1950er-jahren. der gefürchtete konkurrent lenkte nur mit dem linken arm, der rechte seit einem unfall bei einem motorradrennen in graz gelähmt.

OTTO MATHÉ

back to the future (part I, II, III)

the new wordmark illustrates the connection between tradition and modernity. the logotype is an evolution in which the familiar remains and the new is added. typographic adjustments yield a visualisation of the company's distinctive strengths: this pioneering automaker looks back on a 100-year-old tradition, a tradition that is alive and well thanks to numerous technical advances. the basis of the wordmark is the house typeface, corporate antiqua bold, from the corporate ase font family developed by kurt weidemann. the antiqua typeface has a traditional look. the company's modern, technical dimension is visualised by removing some of the traditional-looking serifs; at the same time the font's distinctive formal characteristics uphold the familiar brand image. incisive modifications to the letters create a typographically progressive image, producing a wordmark that is unique and distinctive, with the whole readily identifiable by its parts. the formal language is calm, confident, unpretentious. the absence of any bells and whistles documents a self-confidence that can afford to dispense with design gimmicks.

daimler
visual identity, not realised
stuttgart, 2007

DAIM

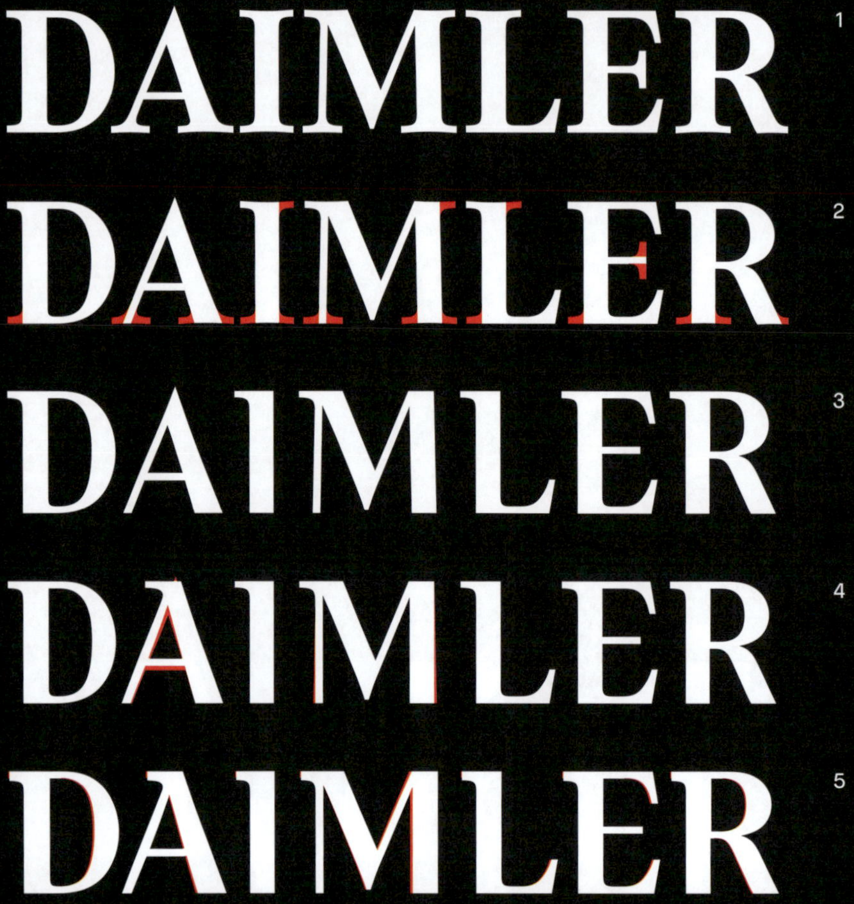

DAIMLER 1

DAIMLER 2

DAIMLER 3

DAIMLER 4

DAIMLER 5

in the version for the competition the wordmark is initially set in the house font corporate a bold (1). in the second stage some of the serifs are removed (2); after this (3) the serif brackets are straightened. now the large uppercase A stands out in visual terms, it looks too narrow and the pointed tip disturbs the overall effect. this letter is widened and softened by adding a serif that integrates the character more effectively within the overall form of the wordmark. the m's diagonals are straightened, too (4). now the logo's individual forms appear too narrow, and so the letters are widened by three percent, and the serifs are shortened and thickened (5).

magnified view of the competition entry (5). the first design of the wordmark is closer to the serif font in the letters l, e and r: here the connection with tradition is more pronounced. in the revised version (p. 46) the serifs on these letters are removed and all the characters are widened: the lettering has a self-assured, contemporary look.

in the revision phase following the competition presentation various changes were made to give the wordmark a less antiquated appearance. starting from the final pre-revision version, firstly the serifs were removed from the e and the l. this made the horizontal bars look too thin, so they were slightly thickened (1). now the lettering looked too thin in relation to its height, so the letters were cut open and enlarged with infill (2). three variants were derived from this procedure: one with wedge-shaped serifs (3), one with small, bracketed serifs (4) and the final version without serifs (5).

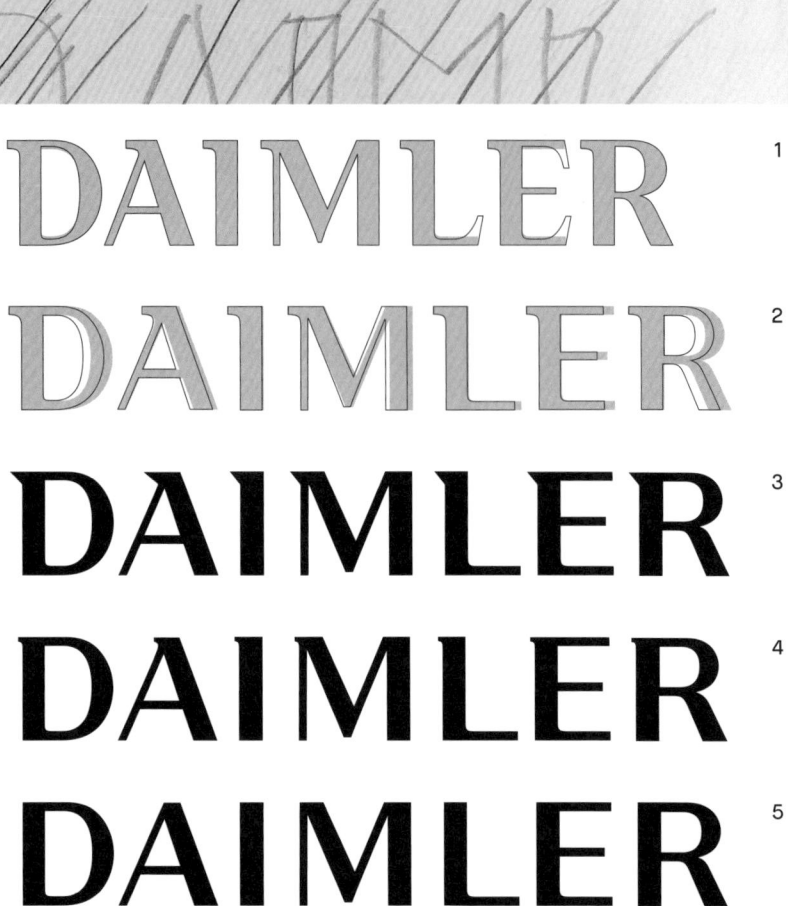

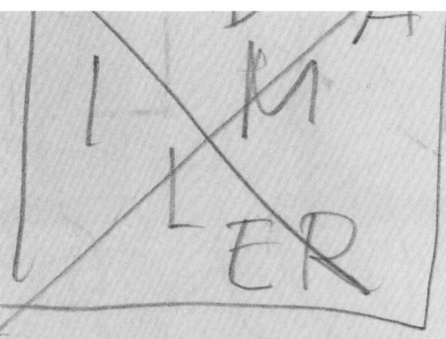

competitions

design competitions are a path to new projects. you can either win and gain recognition, or lose honourably to worthy opponents. both options are acceptable – as long as the award process is properly run.

okay. to ensure a fair process, you need fair remuneration and an independent jury made up of experts in the field. best-case scenario: a jury of external designers who safeguard the objectivity and professionalism of the process, remaining detached from the desires or expectations of the client. ideally, designers rather than clients or potential users should make up a majority on the jury, so that the submissions are actually judged on their design merits. unfortunately this is seldom the case. and if at least one of these two criteria isn't met, potential participants should carefully weigh whether or not they really want to take part in such a competition.

competitions have brought us many of our projects. in addition to our good work and a bit of good luck, the favourable outcome was always down to strong jury members who were interested in – and also willing to advocate for – the best results. the jury must have leadership and sway, and be guided by the conviction that the best entry should win – regardless of whether the participating firm is large enough or experienced enough to execute the idea.

majority decisions, on the other hand, often require compromises, which in turn result in a decision that requires the lowest level of risk on the part of the decision-makers. often this is a design that no one will find provocative or in any way moving. this is highly regrettable, and usually an unsatisfactory state of affairs for the designer. but every form is also an expression of the company's inner values, and a good logo is always in part an indication of a company's commitment to bold action. in his book "paul rand"*, steven heller shows the rejected proposal for the revamping of ford's plum-shaped logo[1].

the white script on the blue background is more disciplined; the undefined plum-like form has given way to a specific geometric figure that still recalls the old logo, yet self-confidently goes its own way. perhaps the lack of boldness within the management who rejected this design contributed to the fact that, decades later, the once-great ford brand has become just one of many weak voices within a larger chorus of brands.

a common yet deplorable practice in competitions is requiring special references. to be allowed to register for a competition, would-be participants have to show that they have carried out similar projects within the last three years and that the employees who will be working on the project have the relevant experience. this results in a monoculture in which young or unexperienced (at least in the area in question) firms are excluded from the running and are not given a chance even though they certainly could have done the job. which means that anyone who once designed a signage system is allowed to submit proposals

[1]

for signage systems — and no one else. this is absurd! norman foster would never have been allowed to submit a design for a swimming pool just because his firm (maybe) has never built such a thing. a further deplorable feature of such processes is the requirement that the fee be specified. although sometimes participants are told in advance how many percentage points are awarded based on price, they usually have no right to see how the points they received were actually awarded. sad to say, such non-transparent processes result in publically subsidized design mediocrity. when awards go to the cheapest design rather than the most attractive one, it serves as an indictment of our wealthy society and makes no economic sense, since good design is long-lived.

sometimes other factors play a determining role in the jury's decision, however. if the jury is not made up of strong individuals, for example, then neither good form, a fitting concept or technical feasibility will win the day. in such cases, any subservient individual with a halfway decent submission can prevail over a good graphic designer with a strong design and equally strong opinions. or else the in-house agency wins the race. this may be hard and unfair, but it is an occupational hazard of being a designer.

the competition held by the german bundestag (see p. 212), on the other hand, is an outstanding example of a very well organised public tender process. the jury members were well versed in the field, and the head of the organisation — the president of the bundestag — served as a jury member and was present for all important decisions and available for urgent meetings at short notice, which was very fortunate. many competitions offer a much less positive experience because the decision-makers are not present at the table. they usually blame their busy schedules, but when you call for tenders and then don't take the time to be part of the process, it says a lot about how much the project is valued.

the lesson is clear: good design solutions are possible when both sides have the courage of their convictions. good designers and good clients find each other — and so do bad designers and bad clients. either way is fine.

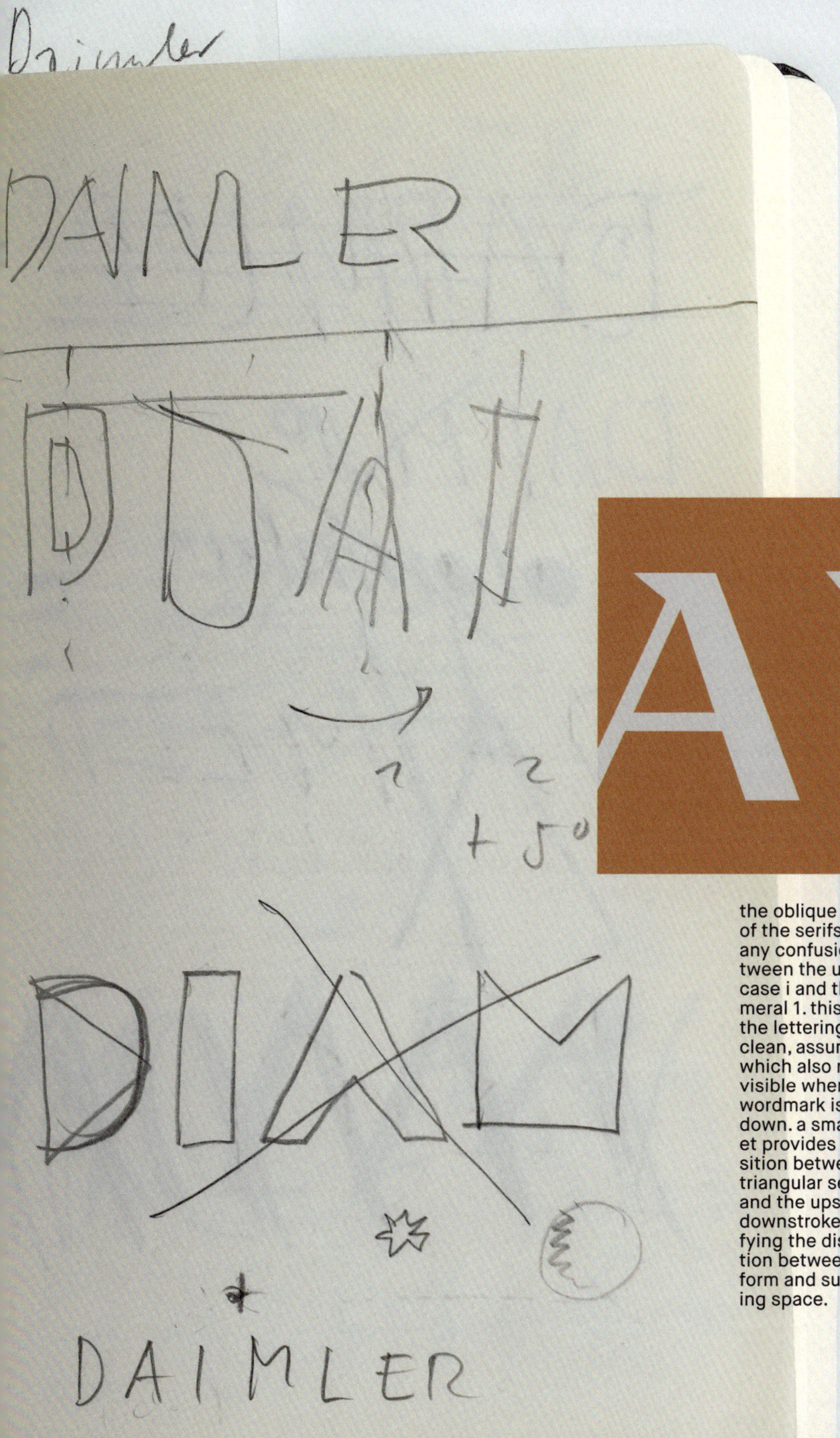

the oblique angle of the serifs avoids any confusion between the uppercase i and the numeral 1. this gives the lettering a cool, clean, assured look, which also remains visible when the wordmark is scaled down. a small bracket provides a transition between the triangular serifs and the upstrokes/downstrokes, clarifying the distinction between letter form and surrounding space.

red-brown and silver state unequivocally: i am premium. this rare and unique colour combination stands for daimler's peerless selling proposition as the producer of magnificent cars. in four-colour printing the red-brown colour shade is easily reproduced and is paired with a cool grey in place of the silver.

death by design

the typesetting may be not quite right but the subject is familiar. wrong is alright here because it's telling us what's not allowed: the typeface, almost obliterated by poster-like shapes – like so many cloths covering corpses – tells us posters can kill. bold statement comes to sticky end: it was the poster what done it! the poster tells students in the design department that putting up posters is prohibited, with immediate effect, due to fire safety regulations.

the awkward, grammatically incorrect wording – "the end by print" – is deliberate, referencing as it does a book that's well known to all graphic designers while figuratively pointing out that print products can lead to fatalities.

the end by print
poster
düsseldorf, 2012

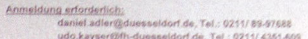

THE EN DBY PRRI NT

ALMARCEGUI
AEL BEUTLER
KARLA BLACK
RTA FISCHER
ASTER GATES
E METTE HOL
ON HUTCHINS
ABLONOWSKI
S KARSTIESS
LICJA KWADE
MARIE LUND
CAR TUAZON

DI–SO 11–17 UHR
S LANGE HAUS ESTERS
91–97 47800 KREFELD
STMUSEENKREFELD.DE

Interna

hin und wieder aber dennoch
(now and then but nonetheless)

the morgenstelle student cafeteria is a plain, functional 1960s building. following its renovation, the owners and users wanted a new interior design to create a friendly atmosphere for the space and the people in it. given the mind-numbingly short time frame – just a few weeks available, for design and execution – we picked up an idea we'd always intended to realise, "one day". now large-scale illuminated words accompany the staff and students of tübingen university – not while they're studying, but while they're eating: suspended from the ceiling in the cafeteria where the food is served, the words and their possible meanings add an element of interest and diversion to the time spent in this functional space. they are a playful adaptation of words by the philosopher hannes böhringer selected specifically for this location. light sequences of different colours create an ever-changing atmosphere, bringing the whole space to life. words, colours, image and time constantly re-define the sensory experience, so that the cafeteria's functionality fades into the background. to counter the effect of the bare end wall and the physically restricted space, the blank wall was painted with an image, made up of large and small squares in varying shades of grey, that gets people thinking. the model here was a painting by cézanne – one in which the objects depicted can be identified in more or less concrete form.

morgenstelle cafeteria, tübingen university
spatial design
2009

HIN UND WIEDER ABER DENNOCH

so that each word can be suspended as a whole, from just a few points, rather than hanging each letter individually, the letters are pushed together until they touch each other and every word forms an intrinsically stable unit. this structural particularity prompted the choice of a serif font – at such extremely close spacing readability of a sanserif would be severely impaired (with the word "hin", for example). this makes the words into sculptures, no longer subject to the rules of typography.

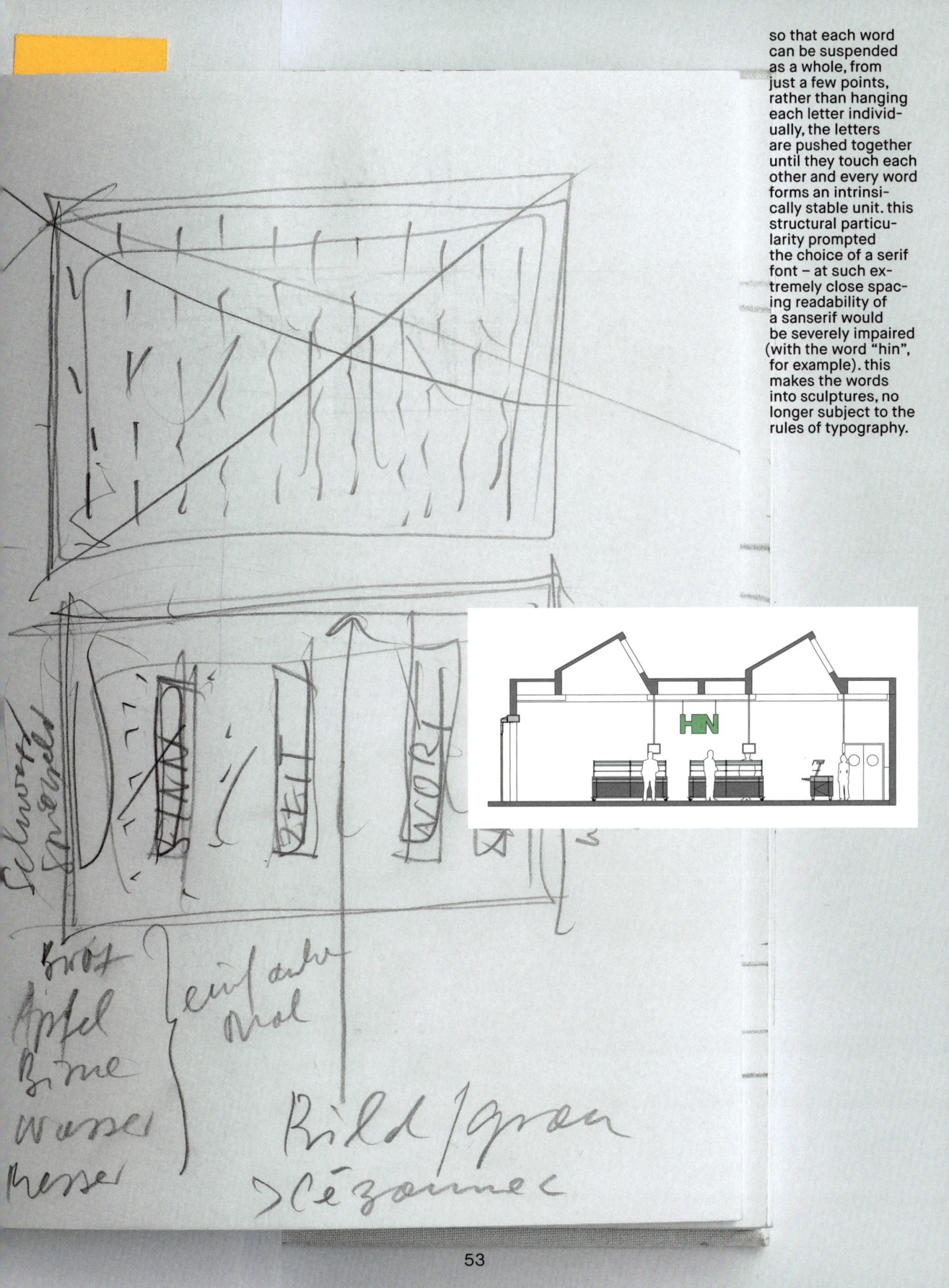

**a term for the lesikon
"the negotiation margin"**

keeping a margin for negotiation is a really good thing. there are always several possible design solutions for a formal problem. the client needs to be able to identify with the design. if they don't, then they're right, even if the work is good. and if the design was bad you're lucky: you get the chance to come up with something better. be sure to keep this margin open.

is design culture?

as soon as we stop eating meat raw and, when we catch a rabbit, cook it on a stick over a fire, this is scene one of an act of culture. it's a process we can constantly civilise and refine – to the point where we find ourselves wanting beautiful cutlery. that's culture. the next step is that we design a menu card. doing something beautifully – doing it well – is culture: something in which the designer's profession plays a key role. there isn't a day in our lives when we don't encounter type. our timepieces have faces with numbers on them; doorbell nameplates and house numbers use typefaces; street signs, the screens on our computers and mobiles are unthinkable without typefaces – typefaces that have been designed. we read newspapers, ride the subway and read digital ads. everywhere we encounter type: we're embedded in this culture.

art resonates

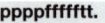

welcome to a new dimension in cultural perception: "zeigen" means "show" and karin sander is out to show art. but not in the conventional way: she's aiming to access the visual sphere via the sense of hearing, creating unique images in the observer's mind. sander asked over 500 artists from berlin to describe an art work or provide sounds and audio documents for the exhibition. with the "zeigen" audio tour, she transforms hearing into an artistic experience.

in collaboration with the artist karin sander, a folder with four screen-printed sheets was published for the "zeigen" exhibition at the temporäre kunsthalle berlin venue, each showing a graphic rendering of contributions to the exhibition.

"zeigen. an audio tour of berlin by karin sander."
visual identity
2009

aaaaaaahhhhh, ... – rrrrrrroooooooaaaarr – fffffppppphhht stkrzchrzstckrc. zzzzztk, – - zeigen. eine audiotour durch berlin von karin sander. 05.12.09–10.01.10

Josephine Meckseper

the catalogue, with its graphic design and sound transcriptions, is itself a direct interpretation of the transient medium of sound. unlike conventional exhibition documentation, which believes in weight and durability, this publication is highly fragile and ephemeral: its 600+ pages contain nothing but the artists' names, printed on extremely thin paper. the pages are transparent, like the sounds that can be heard in the exhibition. the fragile form captures the character of sound. the body of the book has no protective binding: even flicking through it once leaves traces behind. the rustling of the paper supports the radical concept, which documents only the artists, not the exhibits. this is a reinterpretation of the concept of the exhibition catalogue as a medium in its own right.

the laws of art

art writes its own laws. familiar everyday things are removed from reality. in the wordmark for the gallery for contemporary art the letters are removed as well. abandoning themselves to the rhythm of a siren song, they have sailed away from their standard spacing. through the apparently random blacking of the counters – the white spaces in the letters – the wordmark with its irregular spacing seems somehow syncopated. plain information is transformed into contemporary art.

invitations must be so attractive that the recipient wants to hang them on the wall. to keep the artists happy, too, their works are shown uncut with a constant margin on the a5 sheet. the outcome is a series of images, homogenous but by no means standardized.

parrotta contemporary art
visual identity
stuttgart, berlin, since 2006

PARROTTA
CONTEMPORARY ART
AUGUSTENSTRASSE 87–89
70197 STUTTGART
T +49.711.69 94 79 10
F +49.711.69 94 79 20
MAIL@PARROTTA.DE
WWW.PARROTTA.DE

DI – FR 11 – 18 UHR
SA 11 – 16 UHR

PARROTTA CONTEMPORARY ART
STUTTGART BERLIN

BENJAMIN BADOCK »NEWSROOM«
GREGOR GAIDA »WANING SUN«
LISA MÜHLEISEN »HELLO ILLUSION«

STUTTGART, 6. JUNI – 2. AUGUST 2014
ERÖFFNUNG 5. JUNI 2014, 17 – 21 UHR

LINIE WEST
5. JUNI 2014, 17 – 21 UHR
GEMEINSAME ERÖFFNUNG MIT DEN GALERIEN
KLAUS GERRIT FRIESE UND REINHARD HAUFF
SOWIE DEM KÜNSTLERHAUS

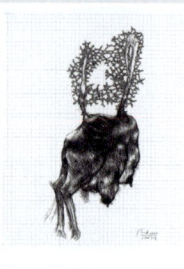

PARROTTA CONTEMPORARY ART STUTTGART BERLIN

PARROTTA
CONTEMPORARY ART GALLERY
AUGUSTENSTRASSE 87–89
70197 STUTTGART
T +49.711.69 94 79 10
F +49.711.69 94 79 20
SANDRO.PARROTTA@PARROTTA.DE
WWW.PARROTTA.DE

PROJECT SPACE
BRUNNENSTRASSE 178–179
10119 BERLIN
T +49.30.27 59 55 19
F +49.30.27 59 55 29

SANDRO PARROTTA

in one of your interviews you describe "visual translation for the complex identity" as a purifying process, like zen meditation. can you clarify this a bit? in what sense? sometimes i don't understand the things i have written myself in the past … in fact, visualizing an identity is a process that involves irrational elements. thinking about the suitability of a logo is not measurable. you come up with a design and you have to rate it. is the flavour of the brand the right one? is the typeface appropriate? is the colour discreet? who can judge that? it's more about getting a "feeling" of brand and distinction. it is like seeing tones and reading colours.

there is no capital letter usage on your website. i assume this is on purpose, right? why do you not use capital letters? PFFFFFFFT! I LOVE THE SMALL ONES! AND THE BIG ONES! in the late seventies i used to write love letters with a typewriter, using only the right forefinger to type — the left one was for shifting to upper case. to boost my performance, i started to use the left forefinger for typing too and dropped out the capital letters. many years later i came into contact with ulm and otl aicher and the notion of using only lower case letters. COOL! i did the right thing unintentionally. FUNNY! IT LOOKS MUCH BETTER!

what do your students learn from you?

composure
craft
crying

     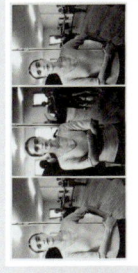

     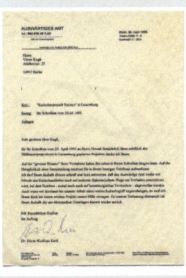

bonjour and arrivederci

a multilingual hubbub, a colourful sound and a concert of colours. the visitor's mood is set – for the exhibition, for contact with countless colleagues, for new impressions and encounters. the signage system takes them by the hand and guides them to the right place so that they won't get lost in the maelstrom. and to make the walk seem shorter, it's entertaining: outside the visitors are greeted by a welcoming committee of flags, inside they are accompanied by rainbow-striped signs and big walls of colour. these provide a constant compass and companion, just in case they forget for a moment where was it they wanted to go. the combination of colours and lettering creates a distinctive identity for the venue and the trade fair company. the chord of colours is like a pattern, like colourful wallpaper that makes the uptake of information both pleasant and easy. the use of paired shades brings the architecture to life, the colour coding of the various destinations works at subliminal level. the colourful stripes inside lead visitors to their destination: pink leads to the conference centre, red to the exhibition halls, green to the exits.

the coloured signs are constructed as floating areas of colour. a base layer just a few millimetres thick covered with coloured film hangs without visible attachments on a mirror-coated metal frame. the spatial dimension of the supporting structure seems to disappear.

stuttgart trade fair centre
signage system
2007

the special thing about this system is that the content of the signs determines their length. the longer the word, the longer the sign. this makes it possible to use the maximum type size in relation to the sign surface area, ensuring that the signs are easy to read even from a great distance. this in turn helps to reduce the number of signs required.

the typographic matrix was developed in line with aesthetic considerations: a sign is made up of four stripes of equal height with two different shades of colour. together, the four stripes form a colour chord – starting with the darker shade at the top and ending with the lighter tone at the bottom of the sign – that seems to echo onward endlessly. to provide a tranquil background against which to read the type, nuances of colour were selected that avoid any excessive contrast between the two shades. and to ensure that the stripes remain in the background, the x-line, cap line and base line of the lettering are not allowed to coincide with the edges of the stripes. as a result, the stripes "cut through" the letters in such a way that no small fragments of letters are left. this leads to a typographic system that determines the format of the signs and their different sizes. avenir is a typeface based on geometric forms but drawn by hand. it was designed by adrian frutiger in 1988. its name refers to its model: paul renner's futura of 1928. the rounded, pearl-shaped font works in counterpoint to the stark, rectangular stripes. an "upright" typeface, such as frutiger, helvetica or univers, would have bonded with the stripes. but the stripes are designed to form a pattern that slips readily under the lettering, like a carpet.

what would you change in order to significantly increase the proportion of designers who produce reasonable work?

1)
do away with tenured teaching positions

2)
cut back the multitude of
educational institutions in germany,
i.e. close universities

3)
universities to be assessed and ranked by
independent specialists with an impeccable
reputation for excellence in the sector

4)
financial rewards for good universities
(excellence initiative)

5)
train fewer students

6)
do away with bachelor's/master's degrees

how can we train design students without imposing overly-prescriptive rules?

prepare
prevent
predispose
present
pre-empt
predefine
preside
precede

two straight lines are drawn through the alphabet in such a way that they don't come too close to the edges of the letters. the distance between the two lines defines a unit that can be multiplied upwards and downwards. three of these units determine the height of a coloured stripe. placing two lines of lettering on these modules in line with the principle described above gives us the line spacing. the distance between the lettering and the top edge of the sign follows automatically. the distance from the left-hand edge of the sign is the same as from the top edge.

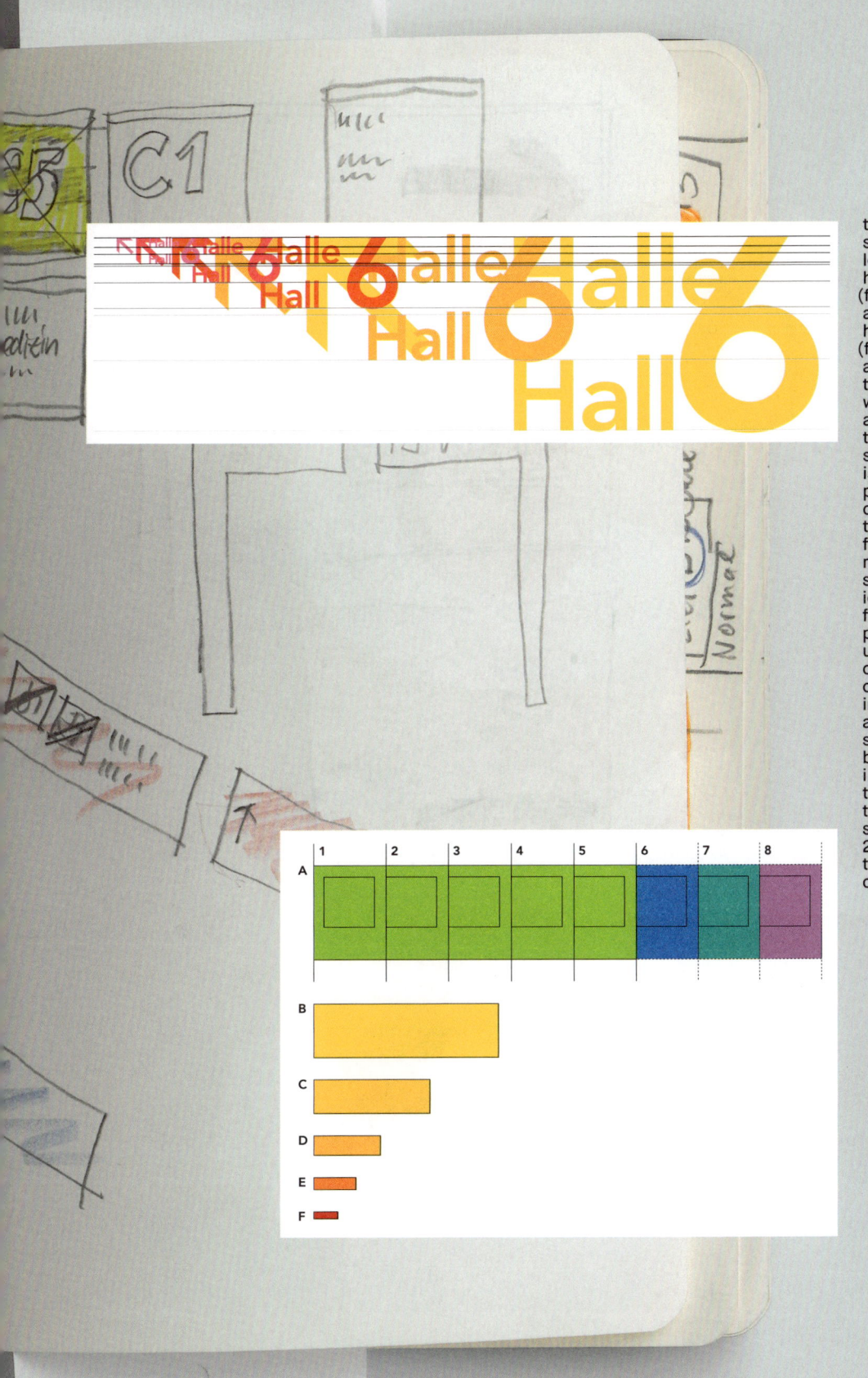

the smallest font size is 200 pt, which leads to a sign height of 260 mm (format f). to arrive at the next sign height on the scale (format e) we apply a factor of 1.75, the same factor by which the size of the arrow is calculated. the size of the next sign up (format d) is reached by multiplying the height of format f by 2.417. this factor results from the desire to make the large font size in the f series identical to the small font size in format d. positioning the modules side by side could lead theoretically to a sign of infinite length. the actual length of the signs is governed by their content, i.e. the length of the words. in practice, this means the shortest sign is 202 mm wide, while the longest works out at 16,359 mm.

in some places the typographic system that also governs the format of the signs comes into conflict with the geometry of the architecture. in these cases the lettering is applied directly to the architecture. this means that the formats are dictated by the architectural context: translucent film is used on glass, while colours, arrows and letters are painted directly onto the walls.

the size of the pictograms and the height of the capital letters in the large font (as in the figure 6 in the picture) are twice the height of the capital letters in the small font plus the line spacing. the smallest unit of a sign is a module defined by the size of a pictogram. the spacing between modules is the same as the distance from the top and bottom edge. the arrow in the module is kept small so that a larger white space is created, making for better legibility and clearer segregation of information and direction. the size of the arrow is 1.75 times that of the small font size. the tip of the arrow is always on the edge of the matrix towards which it points. arrows pointing to the right are located at the right-hand edge of the sign.

blue flag-like signs concern the traffic, green ones are for pedestrians, while yellow ones indicate the entrances to the trade fair, congress centre and main hall. their size is determined by the people who will read them: bus and truck drivers, pedestrians and car drivers read the information from different angles and distances.

what do designers do?

"i'm a communication designer." "huh? are you connected with telecommunication?" "no, i'm a graphic designer." "ah! you work in an advertising company." "erm, no — we are the schilderfritzen."

what makes a good designer?

design – to put it crudely – is a pinball machine. the ball rolls through a labyrinth where it's nudged this way and that, eventually – at some stage – falling into the right hole. you mustn't try to force it into a particular place. you need to be able to listen and coax the intrinsic form out of its core context

the hall doors also function as signs. when they are open the signs can still be read from all directions – even if a truck is parked in front of them – because the information appears on both sides of each door leaf.

inside the halls, visitors are provided with information in a structured way. the hall designation is shown on the largest sign format and at the highest level, while the way-finding and infrastructure signs use the next size down and are hung at a lower level. signs with no information on the back are given a mirror finish so that they blend in with their surroundings.

BUONGIORNO
HELLO
BUENOS DÍAS
BONJOUR
GOEIENDAG
GOD DAG
DOBRÝ DEN
JÓ NAPOT

the words "area" and "level" appear in eight different languages. it's a hospitable gesture to visitors from other countries. at the same time these words help visitors remember locations and find their way around. they may read the czech word "oblast" for area or "úroveň" for level without understanding them. yet as they find their way around they remember the strange word and it helps them locate their parking space again. the doors of the car park greet visitors with "bonjour" while their reverse side says "au revoir". the language gives the place character in an unexpected way and helps visitors identify the area they've parked in. hasta la vista! vaarwel! arrivederci!

ARRIVEDERCI
GOODBYE
HASTA LA VISTA
AU REVOIR
VAARWEL
ADJÖ
NA SHLEDANOU
A VISZONTLÁTÁSRA

the big box

the 1952 mercedes 300 sl racing car marked mercedes-benz's post-war return to motor racing. the few surviving examples – five or six of them out of the original eleven – today change hands for sums measured in millions, if indeed they ever change hands at all. the 300 sl (w 194) was one of the most successful contenders in 1952 and laid the foundations for the success of the mercedes-benz brand in the years that followed. this car has iconic status. daimler ag invited submissions for a competition for the design of – well, actually the briefing left almost everything open – a kind of mega book box set (or whatever) that the few proud owners of a w 194 and the many owners of the road-going 300 sl (w 198) could purchase as a rare object of desire. this delightful challenge automatically led towards marcel duchamp and his "boîte-en-valise" (box in a suitcase) so that here, too, a variety of items are gathered together in a black linen-covered box, items that bring to life this cult car that only few people can possess.

the box contains – by way of eye-witness relics – original fabric samples obtained from specialist restorers, facsimiles of 60-year-old newspaper clippings from the archives, a usb stick and – reflecting the audio media of the day – a vinyl single with the glorious roar of a w 194 in full flight. along with various other period documents, all the numbers assigned to the cars were reproduced in the appropriate font and original colours.

**mercedes-benz w 194
historical documentation, not realised
stuttgart, 2012**

56

to add to the perceived value of this limited edition, four artists were asked to contribute artworks for the box related to the w 194. harald f. müller produced a mysterious technoid edited photo of the atavistic construction of the vehicle; eva-maria schön created a poetic (re)vision of the gullwing doors; thomas ruff reworked two old photographs of the 300 sl to forge a fantastic technicolour portrait; and karin sander contributed a typographic audio image of the w 194. but not even the original design drawings that we included as photocopies, the existence of which came as a surprise to mercedes-benz, were enough to win the day. the client opted for a totally conventional documentation in the shape of a book. in the words of marcel duchamps: "sélavy".

eurythmics

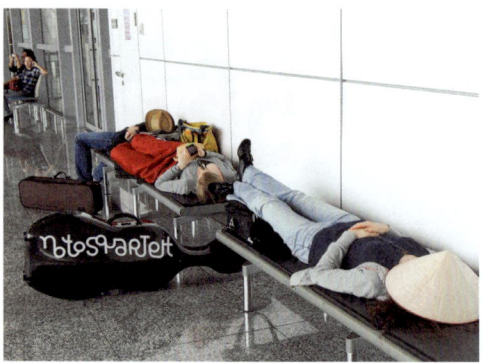

circles, semicircles and demisemicircles are a play on musical note values – and their up-and-down movement "plays" the quartet's name, in a legato style. the logo's rhythmic movements visualise the various sounds that come together to form a harmonious whole as the quartet plays. finely-tuned shades of grey for the logo and the sender's details communicate that sounds aren't plain black or white but need interpretation – accurate differentiation, precise playing, careful listening.

notos quartett
visual identity
berlin, 2012

blåsarkvartett

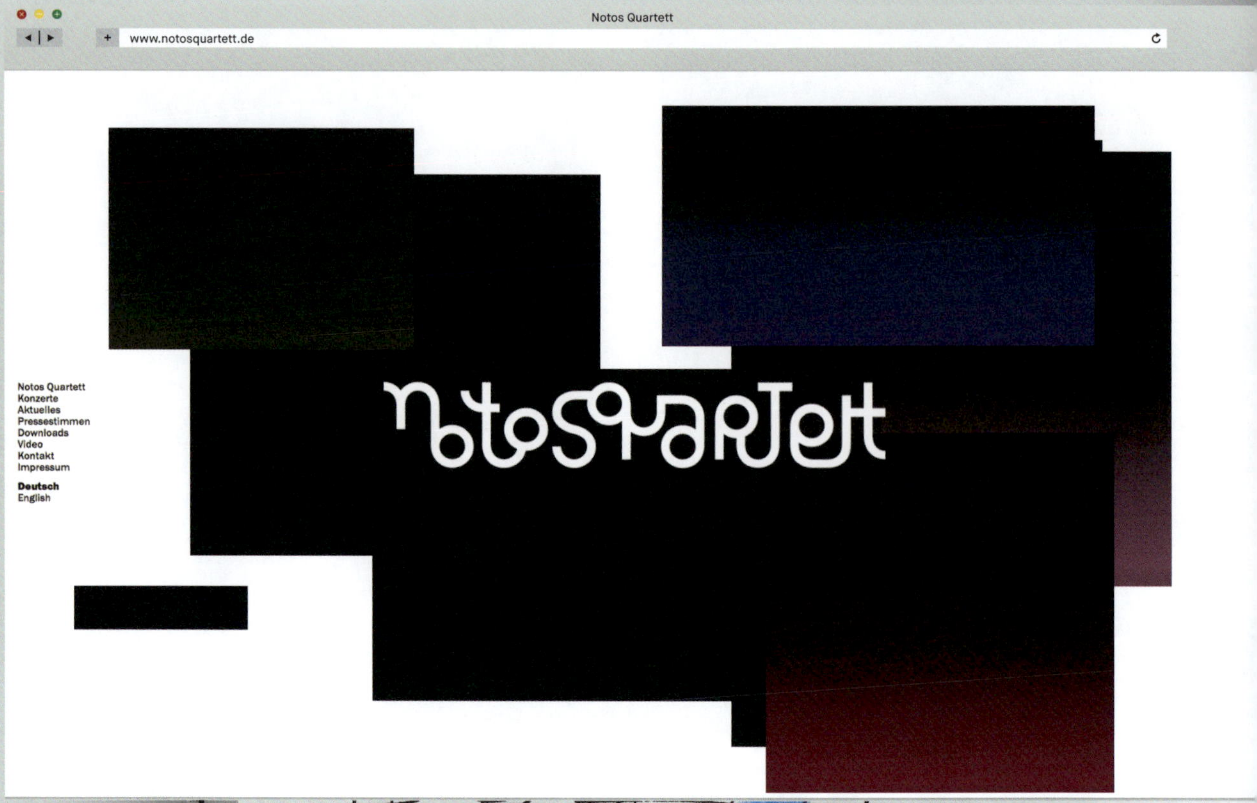

www.notosquartett.de

Notos Quartett
Konzerte
Aktuelles
Pressestimmen
Downloads
Video
Kontakt
Impressum

Deutsch
English

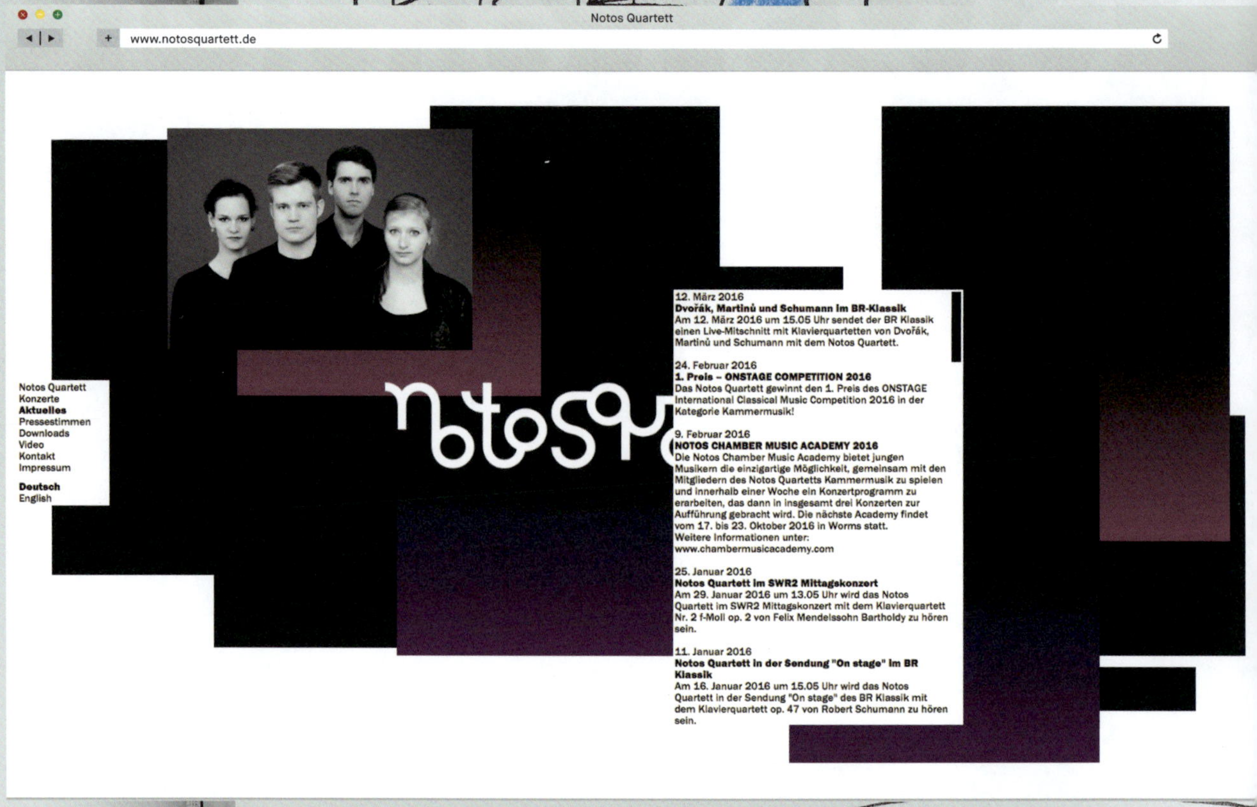

notosquartett

---

www.notosquartett.de

Notos Quartett
Konzerte
Aktuelles
Pressestimmen
Downloads
Video
Kontakt
Impressum

Deutsch
English

12. März 2016
Dvořák, Martinů und Schumann im BR-Klassik
Am 12. März 2016 um 15.05 Uhr sendet der BR Klassik einen Live-Mitschnitt mit Klavierquartetten von Dvořák, Martinů und Schumann mit dem Notos Quartett.

24. Februar 2016
1. Preis – ONSTAGE COMPETITION 2016
Das Notos Quartett gewinnt den 1. Preis des ONSTAGE International Classical Music Competition 2016 in der Kategorie Kammermusik!

9. Februar 2016
NOTOS CHAMBER MUSIC ACADEMY 2016
Die Notos Chamber Music Academy bietet jungen Musikern die einzigartige Möglichkeit, gemeinsam mit den Mitgliedern des Notos Quartetts Kammermusik zu spielen und innerhalb einer Woche ein Konzertprogramm zu erarbeiten, das dann in insgesamt drei Konzerten zur Aufführung gebracht wird. Die nächste Academy findet vom 17. bis 23. Oktober 2016 in Worms statt.
Weitere Informationen unter:
www.chambermusicacademy.com

25. Januar 2016
Notos Quartett im SWR2 Mittagskonzert
Am 29. Januar 2016 um 13.05 Uhr wird das Notos Quartett im SWR2 Mittagskonzert mit dem Klavierquartett Nr. 2 f-Moll op. 2 von Felix Mendelssohn Bartholdy zu hören sein.

11. Januar 2016
Notos Quartett in der Sendung "On stage" im BR Klassik
Am 16. Januar 2016 um 15.05 Uhr wird das Notos Quartett in der Sendung "On stage" des BR Klassik mit dem Klavierquartett op. 47 von Robert Schumann zu hören sein.

black spaces shift with every click, drifting apart, together and over one another like ice floes, as if following some invisible musical score. forming erratic images and abstract structures, they generate colour tones like a vibrating string. and like the music of the quartet that sounds different from one day to the next, the colours and shapes are bound only to the here and now, forever changing.

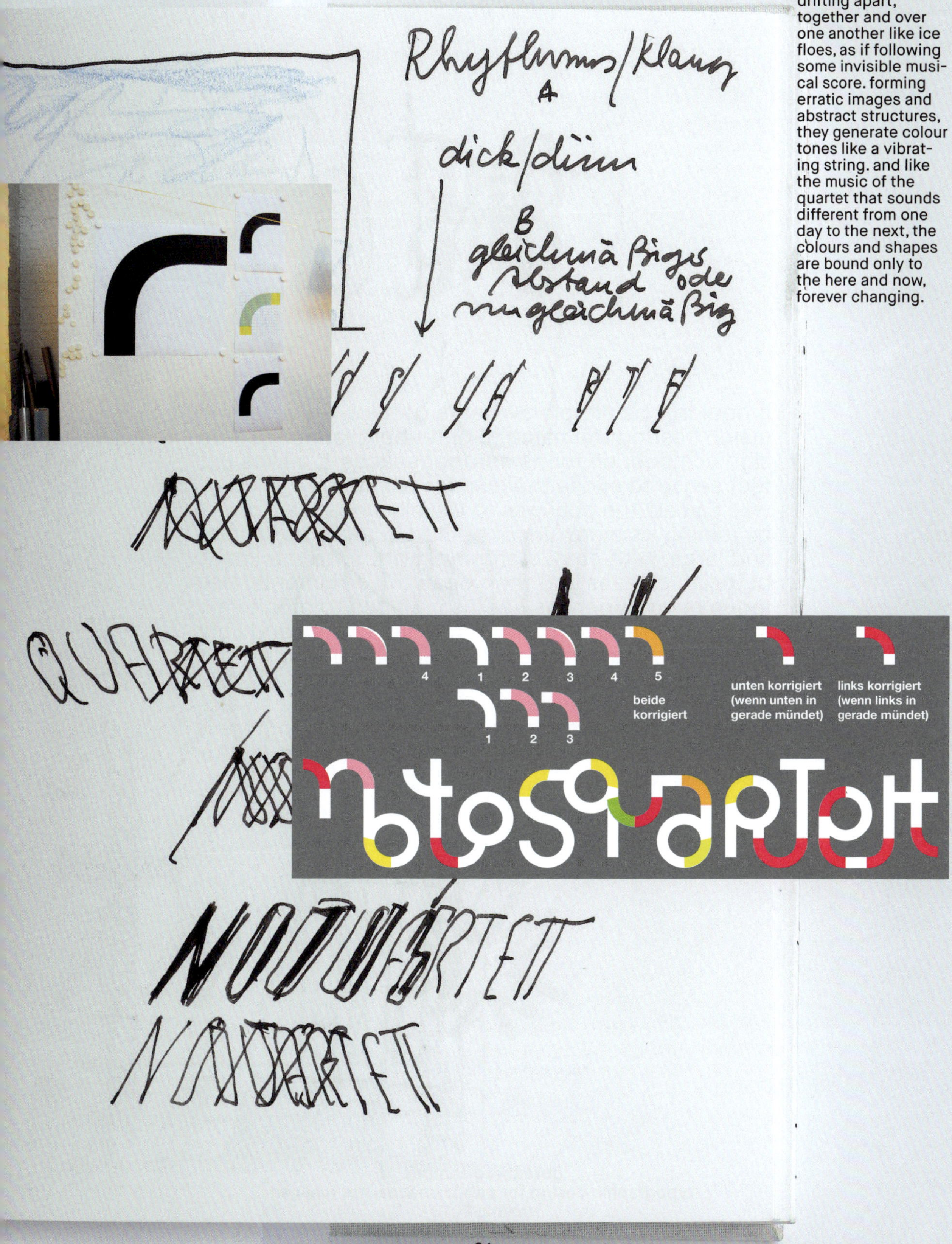

Rhythmus/Klang
A
dick/dünn

B
gleichmäßiges
Abstand oder
ungleichmäßig

my type of place

it couldn't be simpler. when a german university in mainz bearing the name of gutenberg launches a design competition for its outdoor spaces, it makes perfect sense to evoke the man for whom the institution was named. the goal was to visually unite the campus by joining its many unconnected spaces, both small and large, with an overarching motif. with the image of italian piazzas and their beautiful ornamental paving in mind, type was set into shapes to give every space its own distinct look. the use of dark and light paving stones is not only a contemporary interpretation of typesetting for the grid-and-pixel age, but also provides a classic, attractive and durable surface for the public spaces. at first glance the typographic images cannot be read as such; instead, they subtly trace the identity of the place.

gutenberg campus
typographic design for public spaces, not realised
mainz, 2010

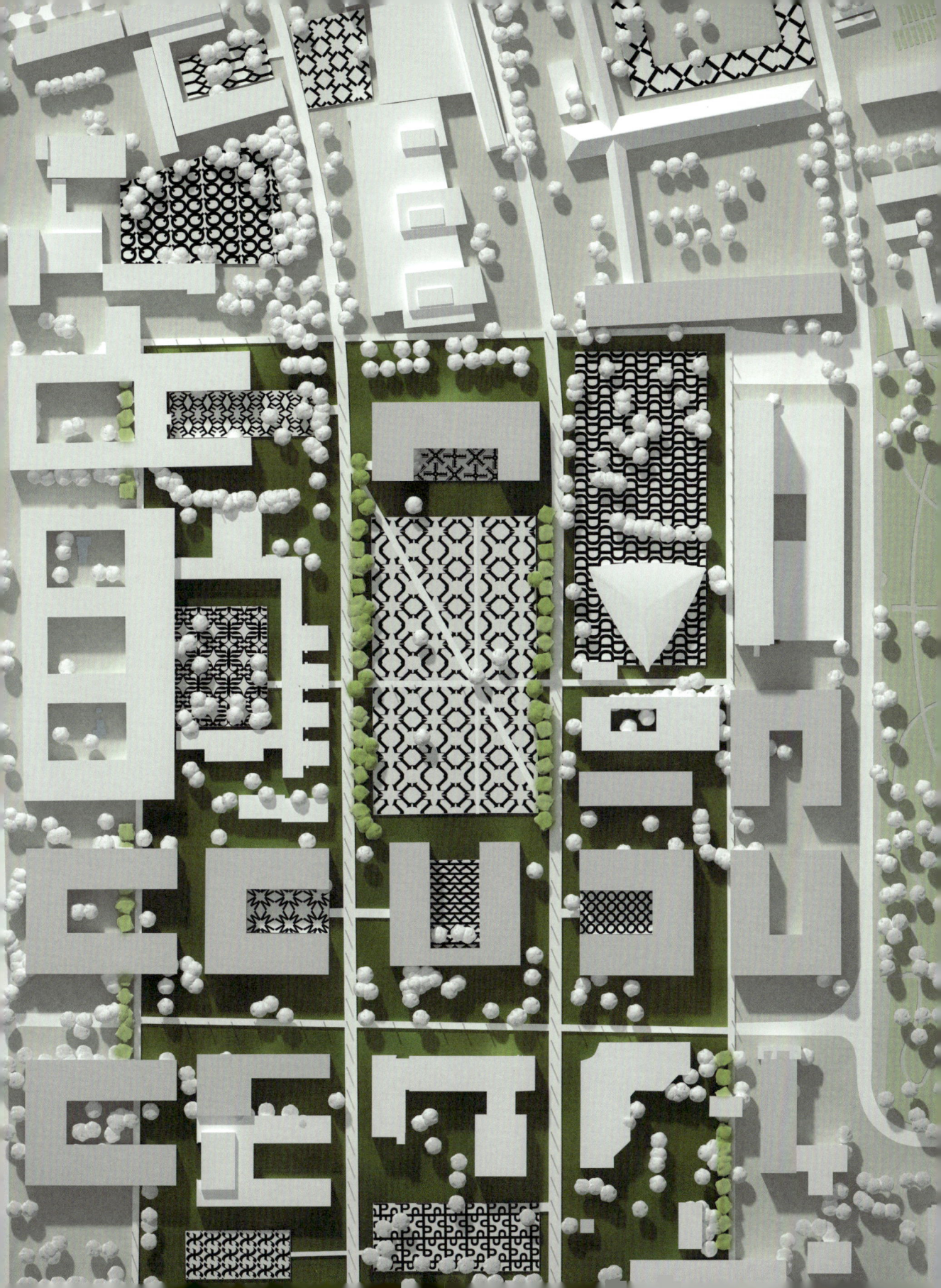

white cold plastic is used to form the patterns on the asphalt surfaces. this low-cost, low-tech process is varied accordingly for granite or paving-stone surfaces. in the case of granite surfaces, the slabs are cut along the pattern and the white graphics are formed by replacing the dark stone with light granite. if this process proves too expensive, the pattern can also be painted on the untreated stone. in the case of paving stones, the pattern is formed by exchanging dark stones for light without disturbing the laying pattern of the pavement.

what can we do without?

certain english phases — 'kick-off meeting', 'warm-up', 'high attraction' — have become embarrassingly common german expressions, completely lacking in modesty and precision. i take a positive view of the ongoing evolution of the german language, and that includes adopting words from other languages. but these words should be chosen carefully and should never serve to cover up a lack of imagination on the part of those who use them. the way i use language is generally reflected in the way i act. precise, careful and coherent usage goes hand in hand with design that is natural and appropriate, unique and personal.

ness-essity is the mother of invention
(a typographic game)

the shyness of small type
the coolness of big type
the bitchiness of acid yellow
the lightness of matte white
the endlessness it takes to answer all the hows and whys
the fleetingness of an idea of what was where when how
the casualness of gigantic fees rolling in
the carefulness with detail
the carefreeness of heads of design
the seriousness of design, gone awol
the bumpiness of saying sustainability
the subtleness of that adjective, sustainable
the obnoxiousness of the avantgarde
the ambiguousness of avantgarde
the humourlessness of the design world
the speechlessness of the design world
the tediousness of the helvetica aesthetic
the superciliousness of the helvetica haters
the prissiness of gill
the everlastingness of akzidenz-grotesk
the permeableness of accomplished typesetting
the forcefulness of solid type design
the timelessness of breaking the rules
the meaningfulness of order
the fickleness of words
the steadfastness of uncertainty

a tribute to the here and now

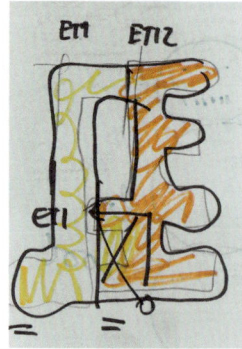

a chance to remedy our earlier mistakes is something we all often wish for later in life, in a professional context, too. the signage system designed by our office 15 years ago – and since unchanged – looked good, but in corridors where lighting levels can be subdued it was hard to read. the understated lettering in purple and black echoed the architecture, but didn't contrast strongly enough with the silver-coloured background strips. now the whole thing's been spruced up, freshly painted in fluorescent colours, and finished off with lettering in black – a sharp and effective contrast. the result is clear to see – the messages stand out in vibrant neon shades against the grey concrete walls, proclaiming: read this! here! now!

| Ebene 0 | 1 | 2 |

Elektrische und Optische Nachrichtentechnik, Ebene 2
Zi. 2.423

Nachrichtenübertragung, Ebene 2
Zi. 2.342

Kommunikationsnetze und Rechnersysteme, Ebene 1
Zi. 1.344

Halbleitertechnik, Ebene U1/0/1
Zi. 1.422

Energieübertragung und Hochspannungstechnik, Ebene U1/0
Zi. 0.444

Elektrische Energiewandlung, Ebene U1/0
Zi. 0.335

Automatisierungs- und Softwaretechnik, ETI 1
Zi. 2.115

Photovoltaik, ETI 1
Zi. 1.213

Leistungselektronik und Elektrische Antriebe, ETI 1
Stellow Zi. 1.276

Hochfrequenztechnik, ETI 1
Zi. 3.213

Theorie der Elektrotechnik, ETI 1
Zi. 3.114

Signalverarbeitung und Systemtheorie, ETI 1
Zi. 2.234

Technische Informatik (Fachbereich Informatik), ETI 1
Zi. 3.162

V47.01 bis V47.06, ETI 1

personal touch

healthcare in the true sense of the word becomes tangible through personal contact. the concentrated circular contact between an ink-dipped fingertip and a sheet of paper leaves a mark, a graphic personal signature. the fingerprint is a symbol of the doctor's personal concern with the well-being of his patients. it argues that the physician's key contribution lies in his personal dedication to the patient – and not just in applying advanced diagnostic processes or communicating a factual diagnosis. consequently, the logo has no need of the formal aspects that are otherwise required. it is not a graphic sign made up of specially designed elements, but a human record. its message to patients is that here, at this surgery, they will be treated as individuals and benefit from personal care and attention.

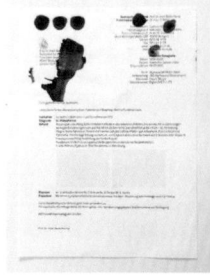

drawing is the language of the designer: the notion of including something "personal" was translated during a discussion of "the appropriate form" quite literally and spontaneously into a hand- or rather finger-drawn image.

gastroenterology and oncology at st. anna's clinic
visual identity
stuttgart, 2010

Gastroenterologie und Tumormedizin an St. Anna
Prof. Dr. med. Bodo Klump
Innere Medizin, Gastroenterologie
Dr. med. Oliver Nehls
Innere Medizin, Gastroenterologie,
Hämatologie, Onkologie

Die beigefügten Unterlagen erhalten Sie
- gemäß telefonischer Absprache
- auf Ihren Wunsch
- mit Dank zurück
- zum Verbleib

Die beigefügten Unterlagen erhalten Sie
- Anruf
- Kenntnisnahme

Gastroenterologie und Tumormedizin an St. Anna
Dr. med. Oliver Nehls
Dr. med. Pia Clemens

Praxis
Untersuchungen
Häufige Fragen
Links
Kontakt

Leitbild
Sprechzeiten
So finden Sie uns
Ärzte
Team
Räumlichkeiten

Die Praxis
Die Praxis Gastroenterologie und gastrointestinale Tumorerkrankungen an St. Anna wird 2010 in Räumen der St. Anna Klinik in Stuttgart Bad Cannstatt von Professor Dr. med. Bodo Klump, Internist und Gastroenterologe, in einer Praxisgemeinschaft mit den chirurgischen Kollegen Dr. med. D. Wolken und Dr. med. H. Stoeltzing gegründet. Im Juli 2010 ist Herr Dr. med. O. Nehls, Internist, Gastroenterologe und Hämato-Onkologe, als Partner eingetreten und aus „Gastroenterologie und gastrointestinale Tumorerkrankungen an St. Anna" wird „Gastroenterologie und Tumormedizin an St. Anna". Zum 1. April 2012 ist Frau Dr. med. P. Clemens, Internistin und Gastroenterologin, als Partnerin eingetreten. Sie hat den Praxisanteil von Prof. Klump übernommen.

Die St. Anna-Klinik befindet sich zentral in Bad Cannstatt, einer traditionsreichen Stadt und dem grössten Stadtteil Stuttgarts.
Die Geburtshilfe und Frauenheilkunde, die Viszeralchirurgie, Anästhesie / Narkosemedizin und operative Augenheilkunde sind hier im Belegarzt-Modell als stationäre Einheiten vertreten und werden durch Praxen auf dem Gebiet der Kinderheilkunde, Chirurgie und Gynäkologie ergänzt.
Klinik und Praxis sind mit öffentlichen Verkehrsmitteln gut erreichbar, bei Anfahrt mit dem Auto stehen ein Parkdeck und ein Parkhaus zur Verfügung.

Auf ca. 400 Quadratmetern wurde eine ehemalige Krankenstation im 3. Obergeschoss in eine grosszügige Praxis verwandelt, die eine Endoskopie-Einheit, eine Tagesklinik für Tumorpatienten sowie chirurgische und proktologische Behandlungsräume beherbergt. Die Praxis ist über einen Aufzug erreichbar.
Die Raumplanung und Bauleitung erfolgte durch Herrn Peter Wetzel, Wetzel Architekten, das Innendesign wurde von Frau Stefanie Bürg (Projektleitung) und Frau Professor Diane Ziegler, ZieglerBürg Büro für Gestaltung, entwickelt.
Die Endoskopie-Einheit wird von der Fa. Olympus, Japan, betreut, die Ausstattung der Ultraschall-Einheit erfolgte von der Fa. GE, U.S.A. mit einem Logic-System.

Die Praxisgemeinschaft von Internisten und Chirurgen sowie die Einbettung der Praxis in die St. Anna-Klinik fördern die interdisziplinäre Betreuung sowie eine optimale Abstimmung von ambulanter und stationärer Medizin - wobei die Wahlmöglichkeit des Patienten und seines Hausarztes im Hinblick auf den betreuenden Facharzt und die zuständige Einrichtung vollständig erhalten bleibt.

Gastroenterologie und Tumormedizin an St. Anna
Dr. med. Oliver Nehls
Dr. med. Pia Clemens

zurück   weiter

what means and strategies can we apply
to revolutionise design?

words: oxblood-red
lines: sulphur-yellow
numbers: inky-black
surfaces: bone-white
ideas: pale-lilac
dreams: emerald-green

drawing by hand

the hand guides the pencil. it feels how the line changes with the pressure applied on the paper. it feels the paper's resistance, senses if it is rough or smooth. it notes that the pencil responds, like a musical instrument, as you alter angle and speed. it understands: drawing isn't a casual, unreflective action. it's a controlled process, full of attention and intention. the eye sees the line, sends a signal to the hand. a closed loop forms, building awareness: now the hand knows if the line is straight, heavy or light. drawing by hand is an unmediated, manual craft. it heightens the practitioner's feeling for form, develops their powers of discrimination. drawing is a beautiful activity, a precise language for the designer.

deductions

our tax consultants reduce our tax bill. we reduced the letters in their name.

**reuter & kucher tax consultants
visual identity
stuttgart, 2004**

r   t r&k ch r

junk font/small caps

in his USURA CANTOS, ezra pound castigates usury, the charging of interest, as the root of all the world's evil. with admirable foresight, we might think, nearly 100 years later, surveying recent years in which such bizarrely named phenomena as CALL and PUT OPTIONS, CREDIT DEFAULT SWAPS and JUNK BONDS were being sold off by the millisecond. ultimately it wasn't just FUTURES that were being traded here but the future itself that was at stake, prompting this typographer to design SMALL CAPS for the art magazine vorn's current issue, which is dedicated to the topic of MORALITY. and the moral of this story is: BUY SELL PUT XYZ ASAP SWAP MAYBE OMG.

"vorn" magazine
typographic contribution
berlin, 2014

30

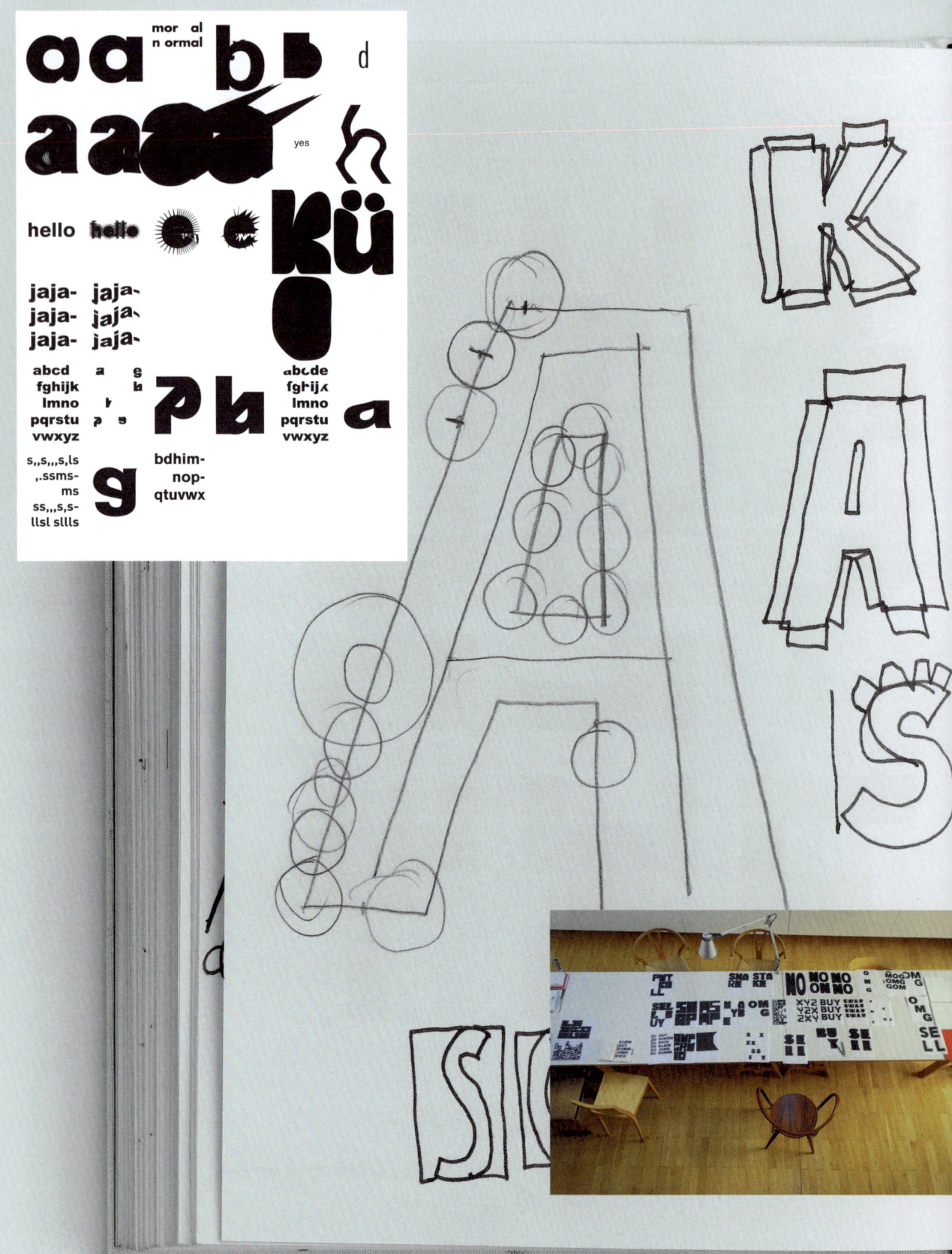

black

deep, vertical black: light disappears, there's nothing for the eye to rest on. the ray of light wanders aimlessly, with no end in sight. the space between the black wall and the viewer expands, making the room bigger. the black printed surface tilts at an angle. light, falling on it diagonally, reveals a structure, as if under a microscope. the paper fibres form a coarse texture, like fine grains of sand. this is light and shade, and the mixture of the light elevations and the dark valleys produces a new tone, a dark grey. the next tone after this is a lake, a horizontal surface that's a deep mirror, moonlight shimmering on the velvety structure. colour becomes liquid. it floats. the matte darkness brightens, the depths sound a silvery note.

**the most important design developments
of the last five years**

badass fonts

WERT
SATZ
WIEDER-
SPRECHEN
NO
YES

ASAP
FYI
YO
ASAP

CHILL MAL
EY,
ALTER

LG
MFG

CALL ME
SAY YES
MAYBE
SUPERNORMAL

INNERE KRAFT
ERKENNTNIS
(GENERATION)
PFLICHTGEFÜHL
ANSTAND

OMG
LESS IS LESS
STRUKTUR
ARBEIT

junk font/small caps · gestaltung: büro uebele visuelle kommunikation, yanik hauschild (projektleitung), andreas uebele

27

sign here

an icon, derived from the greek for image (eikṓn), is just that: an image that is also a sign or symbol, designating something beyond itself. here the iconic image is a character – also designating its own larger system of typological signs – that points to an app you can use to generate (iconic) artistic images ... without knowing the first thing about semiotics.

**karin sander app
icon design
berlin, 2014**

→ Dateien

jeder recht?

skywriting

the notion of writing on the ceiling, thrown jokingly into the conversation, was the fruit of the principle of permitting maximum openness at the draft stage (i.e. while talking with one another). the "idea" was originally conceived as a provocative statement, because where were we supposed to put the signage when all the other spaces – the floors and walls – were already taken?

a sky of black letters and numbers, interspersed with red clouds. words like stars show the way, guiding the traveller. the ceiling is the firmament, scattered with words, the concrete walls are bare. as people look ahead of them, they naturally locate the repeated information that guides them through the building – the text is big enough to grasp instantly, so there's no danger of anyone losing their footing. the space adapts to the user. the pure austerity of the floor and walls reaches a brilliant culmination in this starry sky, with its pattern of images the eye can read: cassiopeia, ursa minor, pollux, andromeda.

university of applied sciences osnabrück
signage system
2004

where do you find inspiration for your design work?

design is a process, something that happens. it is an evaluative deep-scrutiny of the assignment, a desire to get to grips with the subject, a drafting and redrafting of design possibilities. generating different forms and variants allows the designer to make judgements. considering these variants objectively, dispassionately, frees the designer from his or her personal preferences, from "design ideas" or – even worse – "creative inspiration". there are no right or wrong solutions. the "right" one is just one possibility among many. creative inspiration is an inevitable consequence of the working process. every designer has different intentions and preferences. these reflect his or her inclinations in terms of music, fashion and furniture, books or pay tv, and determine the form. the form is like a container, receiving whatever we want: feeble or daring, cheap or beautiful. it's putting it into the form that counts. the outcome of this input is inspiration.

can writing support the design process?

a good idea sounds good and reads well

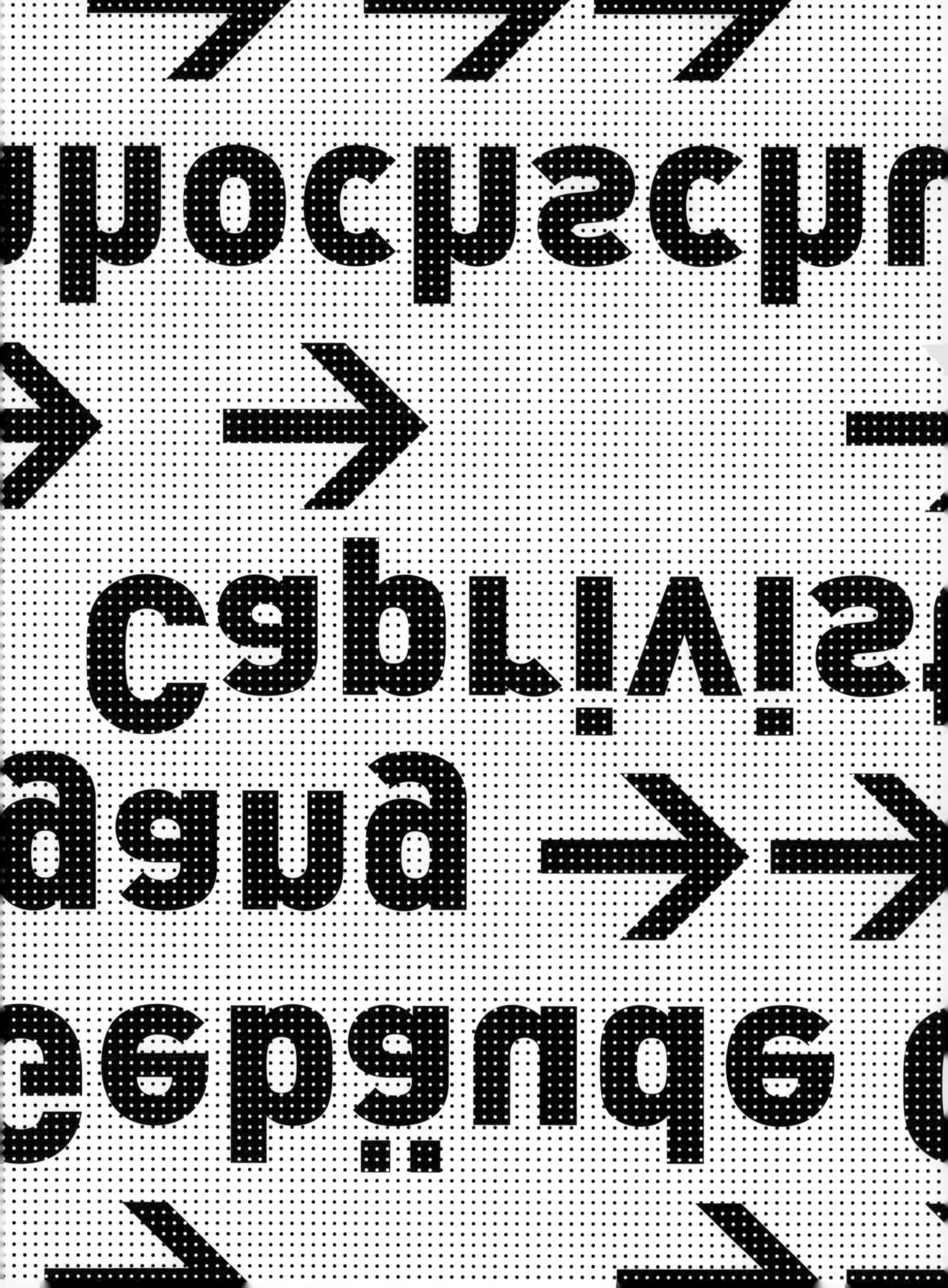

signature tune

the logo traces the proprietor's handwriting. his good name becomes a seal of quality. his personal signature comes to stand for a mindset, a mission. the clear alignment of the corporate information mirrors the engineering services rendered in multiple locations around the world. the company's courteous approach serves to guarantee its clients outstanding performance. the signature is an image that inspires trust in the brand and lends an anonymous engineering practice a human face.

werner sobek
visual identity
stuttgart, 2007

WERNER SOBEK.

werner sobek

werner sobek

werner sobek

werner sobek

werner sobek

werner sobek

werner sobek

werner sobek

are trends the visualisation of contemporary aesthetic sensibility?

the other way round perhaps, or: yes, that too

**a term for the lesikon
"fixed"**

a design that's closed and set in stone is not open to interpretation. it's a bad design. fixed design is mono-dimensional and bound up in rigid theory, determined solely by the designer's viewpoint. non-fixed, lighter design is universal, timeless and lends itself to any number of perspectives. it's like a game: outcome unknown.

Wherever the structure of a building becomes visible, Werner Sobek aims to integrate this structure perfectly within the overall architectural intention. This requires the engineer to have a deep understanding of the architectural intention – and the architect to have an understanding of the possibilities and limitations of the supporting structure. It requires cross-disciplinary skills and interdisciplinary ability.

Achieving harmony between function, materials, form, and design of all building components is one of the greatest goals of architecture. This is possible only if the boundaries between architect and engineer are dissolved. Werner Sobek develops structures built according to constructive logic, design quality, lightness, and transparency. But the studio not only develops such structures, it also adapts them to fit harmoniously into the overall context. For Werner Sobek, the designing of a structure involves a reduction to the quintessential, at all times testing the limits of what is physically and technically feasible. Minimized structures with very wide spans and an extremely high degree of design quality are the result of this approach.

Überall dort, wo die tragenden Teile eines Gebäudes hervortreten, wo die Konstruktion eines Gebäudes sichtbar ist, kommt es auf die perfekte Einpassung des Tragwerks in den Gesamtkontext, auf die Abstimmung von Konstruktion und architektonischer Intention an. Dies erfordert ein tief greifendes Verständnis des Ingenieurs für die architektonische Intention und ein Verständnis des Architekten für Möglichkeiten und Grenzen der tragenden Konstruktion. Es erfordert eine die Disziplinen übergreifende Qualifikation und interdisziplinäres Können.

Die Übereinstimmung zwischen Funktion, Materialität, Form und konstruktiver Ausbildung von Bauteil und Bauwerk ist eines der großen Ziele der Architektur. Möglich wird sie nur durch die Auflösung der Grenzen zwischen Architekt und Ingenieur. Werner Sobek entwickelt gebaute Strukturen nach konstruktiver Logik, Gestaltqualität, Leichtigkeit und Transparenz und passt diese harmonisch in den Gesamtkontext ein. Das Entwerfen einer Tragstruktur bedeutet hier eine Reduktion auf das Notwendigste, ein Arbeiten an den Grenzen des physikalisch und technisch Machbaren. Minimierte Strukturen mit großen Spannweiten und höchster Gestaltqualität sind das Ergebnis dieses Ansatzes.

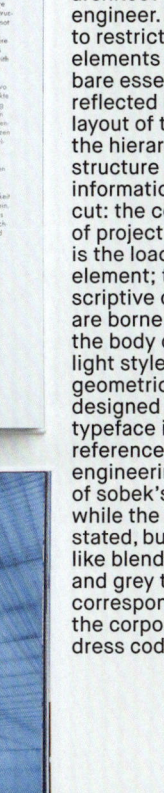

werner sobek's work stands for a melting of the boundary between architect and engineer. his claim to restrict structural elements to the bare essentials is reflected in the layout of the book. the hierarchical structure of the information is clear cut: the column of project data is the load-bearing element; the descriptive contents are borne along by the body copy. the light style of the geometrically designed future typeface is another reference to the engineering side of sobek's skills, while the understated, business-like blend of black and grey type corresponds to the corporate dress code.

The extension of the Cologne-Bonn airport at Terminals 2 and M does not exhibit anything like the dimensional scales of the airport in Bangkok. However, both terminals demonstrate in an impressive manner how close cooperation between architects and engineers can lead to filigree and extremely transparent structures of the highest structural quality. The completely glazed facade of Terminal 2 runs over a length of 800 m around the entire building. The almost dematerialized facade is split into sections, with a length of approx. 40 to 70 m, and a height of between 10 and 20 m. What is special about the facade is its point-anchored insulated glazing that places extremely high demands on the support construction with regard to deformation behavior.

Die Erweiterung des Flughafens Köln-Bonn um die Terminals 2 und M weist bei Weitem nicht die Dimensionen des Flughafens in Bangkok auf. Beide Terminals demonstrieren aber in eindrücklicher Weise, wie eine enge Zusammenarbeit zwischen Architekten und Ingenieuren zu filigranen und äußerst transparenten Strukturen höchster Gestaltungsqualität führen kann. Die vollkommen verglaste Fassade des Terminals 2 verläuft über eine Länge von 800 m um das gesamte Gebäude. Die nahezu entmaterialisierte Fassade ist in Abschnitte mit einer Länge von ca. 40 bis 70 m aufgeteilt und zwischen 10 und 20 m hoch. Ihre Besonderheit besteht in der punktgehaltenen Isolierverglasung, die hinsichtlich des Verformungsverhaltens extrem hohe Anforderungen an die Tragkonstruktion stellt.

order from chaos

tight budgets don't necessarily mean poor design. here, the extremely small bankroll led to the unconventional yet thrifty solution of painting the information directly onto various parts of the building. these graphical wall coverings also solved the problem of how to deal with architectural challenges like unusually narrow structural elements, unattractive insulated façades and wavy washboard surfaces.

innsbruck. a characterless exhibition centre has been given a new identity: old-style cacophony has been overlaid with a new and harmonious vibe. a beautiful new hall has been added to the old buildings, and the former chaotic muddle of juxtaposed language, architecture and routes through the complex is at once echoed and resolved in a signage system that draws on the forms, colours and formats of flag design. national flags – intrinsic to the exhibition centre's business – form the basis of the graphic design. they have been divested of their heraldic elements – the shields and animals, the swords, sabres and stars – and of their national colour schemes, and allocated a single colour shade along with text. the individual text-patterns are assigned to particular halls where they fulfil a wayfinding function. when the text-patterns are lined up together in the orientation overviews, the individual patterns become part of a different, larger system. the result is a systematic chaos, an orderly disorder, that responds to the venue's intrinsic disorderly qualities. the brightly coloured strips make a bold statement, standing out against the non-uniformity of the setting. in the neatly dimensioned and relatively monochrome new building they add contrast and variation, providing a rhythmic element that naturally expands to cover whole walls in particular locations – such as staircases, a restaurant and the underground car park.

innsbruck exhibition center
signage system
2012

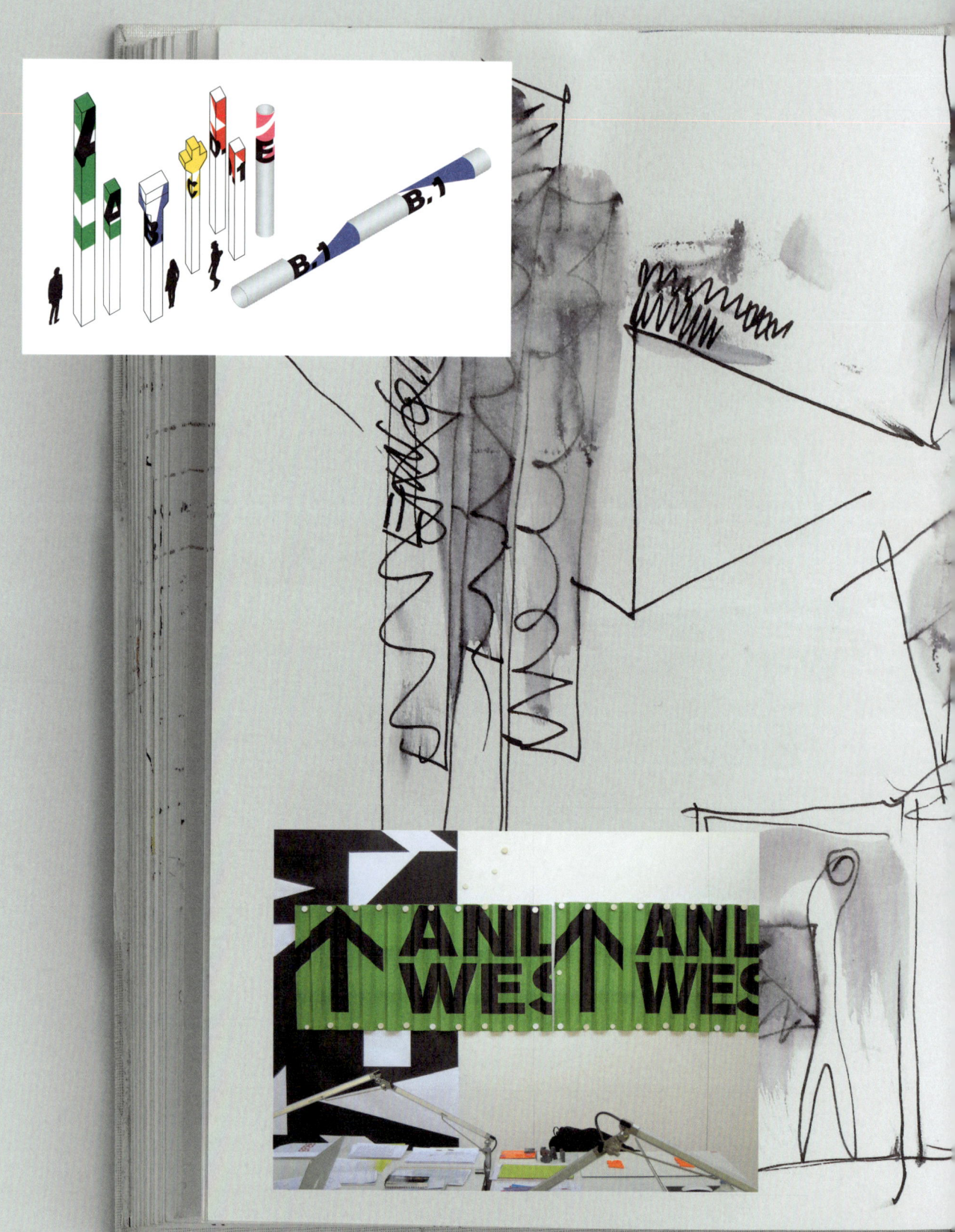

Innsbruck

Messeforum011
A1A2A3.

blue

a heavenly blue, so innocent and pure, radiating cleanliness, as if freshly washed: a likeable, appealing colour. everyone loves it. is it too beautiful? what would it be like to have a corridor wall painted this colour? why not? you can get little, fast cars in this colour; you can also get tights, scarves, caps. a cable on your desk in this colour is friendlier than a grey one. so is blue the ultimate amenable colour? one that's to everyone's taste? yes, it probably is, and can this simple, undefined blue help the fact that it is just what it is – without even a shimmer of green, without so much as a hint of red? is it a bad thing that it reminds us of a summer evening, just before the light begins to fade?

how important is accessibility in your projects?

accessibility means applying a completely different mindset to a design. you have to try to reconcile the creation of an attractive system with the creation an accessible system, because accessibility places significant limitations on design. this is not to say that both are not possible. however, accessibility considerations have significant ramifications for the design process. we are in the business of developing systems that are on the cutting edge of both design and technology, that take many different requirements and variables into account. and we need to strike a balance between all these functional parameters — of which accessibility is one.

as the son of a disabled person and someone who is therefore intimately familiar with how things are experienced by the "other" side, let me raise a question based on a highly controversial assertion, namely that, from a design perspective, accessible systems have their weaknesses: in order to make a system serviceable for a very small minority, are we justified in making it ugly, and therefore unserviceable — in the aesthetic sense — for the majority?

while this point of view is obviously questionable, i would also like to note that, for questionable political and economic reasons, a very high level of accessibility is called for, even though the actual benefits derived are small. the result is an overengineered system that is both expensive and ugly.

one special feature of the system is the two dots of the umlauts. so they won't be cut off by the full-bleed printing style, they lie directly on top of the letters – creating distinctive silhouettes.

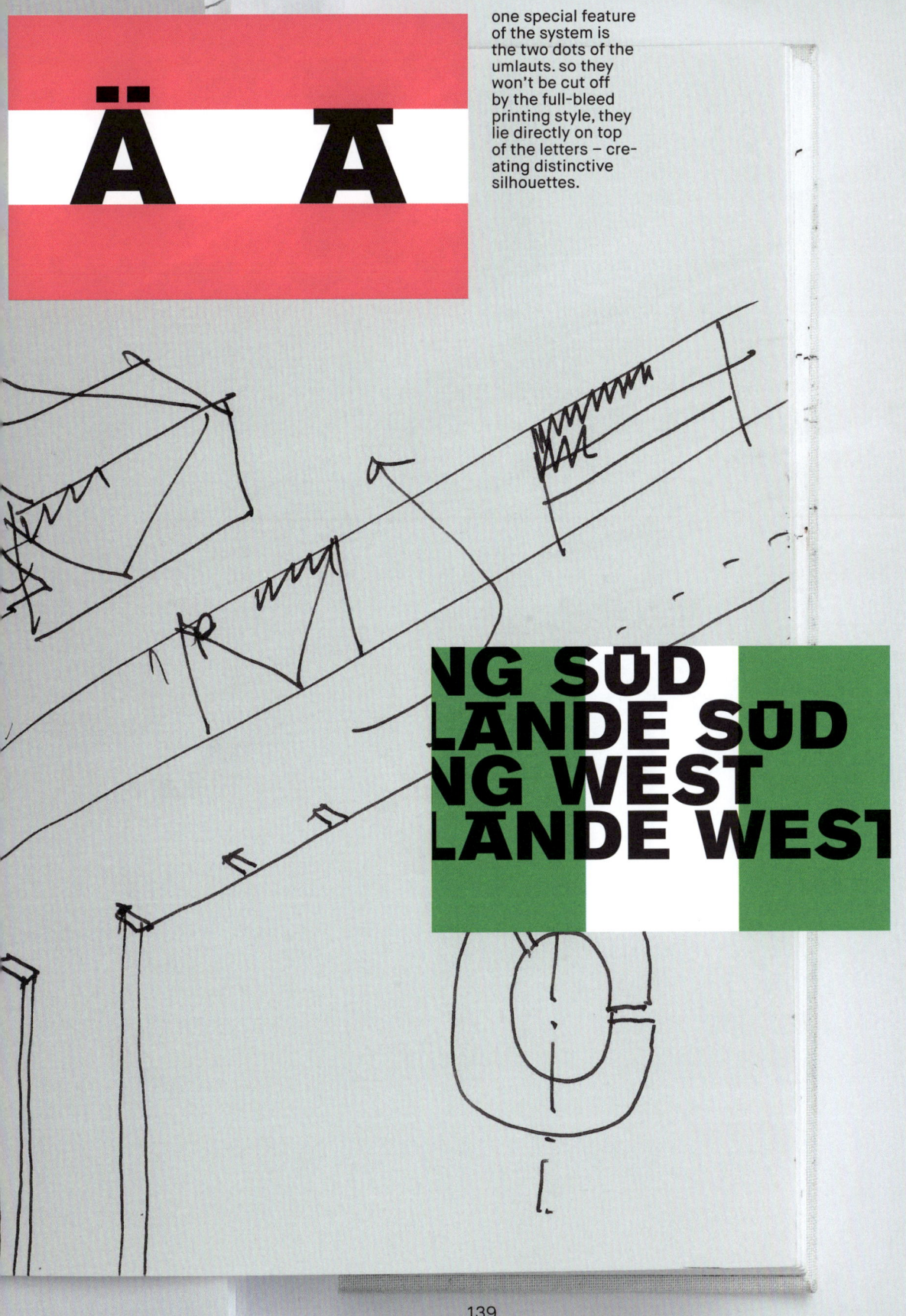

views on pictograms

obviously you are renowned for your work on wayfinding projects. can you recall how much/what type of research you undertook for these projects?
we don't do any specific research. mainly we consider how to solve the very special problem of a job. every signage project has such different circumstances, that an overall "law" wouldn't be suitable. our "research" process is based on thinking, talking, listening and rethinking. we really talk a lot. we talk with every person who is – or might be – involved in the project. for us, research means developing many variations of a problem and discussing them in the office, with the users and the clients. it goes without saying that we read all the literature about signage and we try to get all specific information about the legal, cultural, historical and technical aspects of the project, as well as budget, spirit and location.

charles trueheart highlights in sign language the dilemma where cultural and religious associations threaten to undermine global intelligibility in pictograms. trueheart raises the point that 'neither do all people eat with a knife and a fork, the supposedly universal symbol for restaurant'. in relation to this, to what extent do you think pictograms can be biased towards western culture?**
yes, they have been designed from a eurocentric or western angle. but the pictograms and the designers are not at fault. if you are a designer from the western hemisphere, when you are designing a new alphabet, you first design the latin glyphs. later, if your typeface is successful, the greek and coptic versions, the tamil and indian letters, and then maybe the arabic version and so on. considering how long we've been using visual languages, designing pictograms is a very young discipline.

in 2007 vienna city council launched a campaign that showed images of women as well as men on public information signs. for instance, in their town hall the signs for nappy-changing facilities were redesigned. the old version, which showed a mother and child, was replaced by a new image of a man changing his baby. sonja wehsely, the vienna city councillor for women's affairs, states: "we are used to seeing pictograms of men for everything, and only pictograms of women when it has to do with children. that's not reality." with this in mind, do you think pictograms discriminate against gender?
the gender dicussion often misses the point. in words (in the german language) only the male version is used for the plural. is this discriminating against women? many people say: "yes". for me, it is very obvious that you can't design language.

mixing male and female pictograms is possible and it could be a funny contribution to this debate with a serious context. at the moment, we are designing our own pictograms, it's a kind of homage to gerd arntz (see p. 332ff) and we use a female and a male person for handicapped. all our pictograms show a wide range of gender, hairstyle, skin colour, accessories and clothing to communicate the cultural diversity of people.

and yes, the woman escaping from a fire in the emergency pictogram[1] could be a good way to approach this debate, though i don't like her boots or her hairstyle.

in the context of international graphic symbols, joel arnstein argues that 'graphic symbols have created a language of their own'. symbols such as hazard notices and washing instructions have a 'universal meaning' and usage. what is your opinion on pictograms being described as a universal language?
pictograms are a universal language, because they allow us, without knowledge of a particular language, to communicate with everybody. but this universal language has to be adapted or rather translated into the very specific cultural idiosyncrasies of the particular country or region. we designed the signage system for the makkah clock tower exhibition and the specific problem was to distinguish men and women by their clothing[2].

the pictogram system designed by otl aicher for the 1972 olympic games in munich formed the role model and basis for the designs that appear on pages 142 and 376f. www.piktogramm.de

2

fractal typography

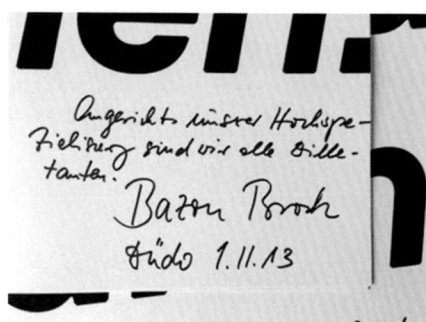

the title of his lecture: "creating problems makes perfect. the humanist must criticise the truth. errors are excuses for laymen." was so enormous that we split it into three manageable pieces. now, each poster by itself is totally unreadable and we have a nice typographic ruin that fosters the spirit of the lecture by making people think.

bazon brock speaks
event poster
düsseldorf, 2013

Poster 1 (top):
> e schaffe[n]
> [Mei]ster. Die
> [kriti]sieren,
> [mach]t. Irrtüm[er]
> für

Poster 2 (middle):
> [Irrtümer]n, macht
> [die] Wahrheit
> [...] hat der
> [Meist]er sind
> Laien.

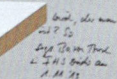

Poster 3 (right):
> Probleme
> den Meis[ter]
> zu kritis[ieren]
> Humanist[ische]
> Ausreden

Vortrag von Bazon Brock am 1. November 2013 um 18.00 Uhr im Raum N 1.40 der Fachhochschule Düsseldorf im Fachbereich Design.

FH D FB 2

giving the place a face

this is a campus that's short on homogeneity and entirely lacking in cosmopolitan ambiance: faceless buildings stand unevenly spaced amidst neglected green spaces, generating the kind of impression normally associated with a military barracks, not a university campus. the wayfinding system is a response to this situation: it uses large formats to make sure it gets noticed and can hold its own in this not-to-scale environment. and it introduces bright and cheerful colours to distract the attention from the inhospitable surroundings. also, the big colourful formats bring art to the streets and, almost incidentally but nonetheless reliably, provide clear orientation. on another level the system communicates with the campus community – visitors, employees, teaching staff and students: some of the large-scale signs tell the 'citizens' of this small 'town' stories about würzburg and its history, about the campus and what's special about the university, and by doing so create a distinctive sense of identity and identification. other panels introduce an ever-changing line-up of deans, staff and students, giving the campus its own unique character: an anonymous place takes on a face of its own.

**würzburg university
signage system, not realised
2010**

"the first step is learning to trust your gut"

when did you decide to go into graphic design?
graphic design was something i'd always done on the side. but since i had a degree in architecture and had worked for a good architect, initially i also went into business as an architect. but i wasn't having fun and i could tell things weren't taking off. i didn't really think i could work as a professional graphic designer, but a friend talked me into giving it a go.

how did things kick off? did you opt to be self-employed from the start?
things got off to a fairly prosaic start. i threw away all my business cards that said "andreas uebele, architect" and had some new ones printed that said uebele visual communication". i was out a lot in the evenings and handed a card to whoever would take one. i ended up being invited to a big ad agency in stuttgart. the group honcho liked my work and asked about my hourly rate. i thought about it for a minute. at the time, 45 deutschmarks would have been outstanding. but my gut was telling me that i really didn't want this job, that it would be selling my soul. the advertising language and all the posturing at the agency got on my last nerve. so i brazenly asked for four times as much – 180 deutschmarks. i was blushing inside and thinking, ok, that's my ticket out of here. he looked around at the team and said, "that's a pretty hefty price, but your work is good. let's do it."

you hit the jackpot!
that's what i thought, too. at the time my rent was 470 deutschmarks, which meant i'd only have had to work for three hours to pay it! but my gut kept saying that this wasn't really what i wanted to do. i backed out, and of course the agency was not happy, but i've never regretted the decision. so next i grabbed a phone book and started calling all the architects, asking if they needed some corporate design, a book, anything. i started with a, and by friday afternoon i'd got to f. f urgently needed a signage system, and the rest is history.

so it's important to say no?
yes, it's very, very important. taking a stance and saying no.

is it a stance you've been able to maintain? or have there been jobs where you thought, "okay, i need this one"?
no, i've always been able to hold out. otherwise i'd be rich! running an office isn't always easy, financially speaking. but if i give a good employee a job that isn't challenging, that's not good for job satisfaction, and then i start burning through employees.

are you happy with how things are going right now, or are there some specific goals you'd still like to meet?
i've never chased specific goals in my life. a lot of people want to be rich and famous – me, too! but the question is, how important is that to you? what are you willing to do? how much do you contort yourself to get there? i'm happy to put the pressure on myself, because otherwise i wouldn't be able to do what i like to do – creating beautiful things – and i also couldn't allow myself this luxury. by which i don't just mean material things, but also the freedom to shape my own life to the greatest possible extent and the freedom to say no sometimes. i'm only interested in achieving success or fame through the quality of our work, and i wouldn't want to let that take a back seat to anything.

can long-term trends lead to new design rules?

a trend is a machine that spits in your face if you make yourself its servant. a trend is a designer's declaration of bankruptcy, a cheap temptation.

handmade

for their clients, these architects design buildings that are individual, 'handmade' creations. and so from their graphic designer they get an individual, handmade house typeface – a typeface so distinctive that they don't need any additional image or wordmark. the typeface used to set the company's name and address was hand-drawn specially for the client. it communicates the unique personal element that design instils in the planning process. this literally unique alphabet captures – and releases – the essence of individuality through the flow of its hand-drawn lines, the transparency of the ink, the irregularities that naturally arise in the handmade. to conserve the uniqueness of the handwritten through the transition to the technical process of printing and minimise the appearance of identical letter forms in the type, seven complete settings of the typeface were drawn. this passion for typographic detail honours the high standards that the architects themselves insist on in their work.

aaaaaaa
bbbbbbb
ccccccc
ddddddd
eeeeeee
fffffff
ggggggg
hhhhhhh
iiiiiii
jjjjjjj
kkkkkkk
lllllll
mmmmmmm
nnnnnnn
ooooooo
ppppppp
qqqqqqq
rrrrrrr
sssssss
ttttttt
uuuuuuu
vvvvvvv
wwwwwww
xxxxxxx
yyyyyyy
zzzzzzz

bächlemeid
visual identity
constance, 2015

bächlemeid

büro meyer
stadt- und landschaftsplanung
königstraße 129
70180 stuttgart

30 04 2014
informationsmaterial zum
bauentwurf »grünanlage
hubertus«

sehr geehrte damen und herren,

die senkrechte linie und fläche, welche wir niemals körperlich, sondern bloß mit auge und fantasie ersteigen, machen einen ernsteren, gewißermaßen mehr idealen eindruck. die vertikale, geradlinigt begrenzte wand wirkt sehr verschieden, je nachdem die höhe oder breite mehr vorherrscht. ein übergewicht der höhe über die breite hat den ausdruck des stolzes; dieser geht bei zunehmender höhe in kühnheit über. der eindruck des emporstrebens, welcher mit allen sehr schlanken verhältnissen verbunden ist, beruht nicht bloß auf erinnerung des entstehens der formen durch allmäliges aufbauen und einem unwillkürlichen vergleich mit dem natürlichen wachstum sondern auch namentlich auf der stellung unseres auges. denn während wir das zu unseren füßen ausgebreitete fast ohne bewegung der augen weiterhin übersehen, und auch uns gegenüber in horizontalem sinne eine große breite ohne mühe beherrschen, so ist dagegen das hinaufblicken an einem uns etwas nahe stehenden sehr hohen gegenstand mit einer bedeutenden bewegung der augen, des kopfes, ja des leibes verbunden.

mit freundlichen grüßen

martin bächle

---

bächlemeid architekten stadtplaner bda • zollernstraße 4
78462 konstanz • telefon 07531 95 50 15 • fax 07531 95 50 14
www.baechlemeid.de • info@baechlemeid.de

abcde
fghijk
lmnop
qrstu
vwxyz

twenty friends

"permanent marker with bullet tip. smudge-proof and water-resistant. permanent, low-odour, quick-drying ink. colours: 001–020. for writing, colouring, labelling on virtually all materials. width of stroke: approx. 1.5–3 mm. replaceable tips. colours 001–010 refillable."***
for all the manufacturer's passionless prose, this product is a source of daily delight to me. my friends, twenty in number – packed side by side in their designated pen-holder – are squeaky, addictive markers, with which, while busily sniffling the solvent fumes, you can produce a fat line on any background you care to name. you can also smudge the colours together, like watercolours, which doesn't look so good but is unavoidable – and therefore best admired and labelled "beautiful!" – when using one colour directly alongside another. or you can stand the markers in a pot on your desk, like flowers in a vase, because after all they too will dry up eventually. unaltered in their form since time immemorial, in equal parts distinctive and unpretentious – making them, refreshingly, the exact opposite of a german designer luminaire – but at the same time as instantly recognisable as a signal toothpaste tube. you can draw anything with them, including – for example – a beautiful, classical public square.

two hundred enemies

my enemies are the squares, streets and tumbling, crumbling stairways of my home city — down-at-heel documents of uncaringness, narrowmindedness and stupidity. all of them cut a sad figure, bearing witness to the administration's obtuseness — for example in not recognising the value of stuttgart's topography as an asset to be cherished and maintained. how quick and easy and above all — listen up, pen-pushers! — how relatively cheap it would be to make the streets, squares and "stäffela" (unique historic stairways) that criss-cross the stuttgart valley basin, interlacing its steep-sloping sides, more beautiful. all you'd need to do is tidy up a bit: do some resurfacing, level out the streets, plant the right trees. just look to italy to see how it's done. in short: get rid of all those proliferating kerbs, the german designer luminaires, the designed-by-committee vandal-proof benches — and everything's sorted. and beautiful! and for the benefit of efficiency-obsessed bureaucrats and aesthetically indifferent mayors: you can call the whole thing local character — so marketable — and write in big letters on your flip-chart, with your edding 3000: profit! revenue stream! public space — once a nightmare, now a dream.

(redits

bächlemeid
büro projekte
==wettbewerbe== aktuell
bad saulgau →
kreuzkirche bregenz
→ gemeindehaus
aach → hwf freiburg

---

bächlemeid | 2008 familienzentrum tuningen
www.baechlemeid.de/projekte/familienzentrum-tuningen

familienzen trum tunin gen

familienzentrum tuningen
2008 1.rang mehrfachbeauftragung
2008 fertigstellung

das grundstück wird von der unmittelbaren nähe zum kindergarten und zur grund- und hauptschule, sowie der platzsituation zwischen den öffentlichen gebäuden und baumstrukturen geprägt.
das volumen des neuen bauwerks wird parallel zum bestehenden kindergarten als leichter, frei geformter baukörper entwickelt.
es entsteht ein kompaktes gebäude, welches nicht als rechteck, sondern als kubus mit leicht verschwenkten wandelementen und freier form sichtbar wird.

bächlemeid
büro
projekte
wettbewerbe
aktuell

caractère typographique sur mesure

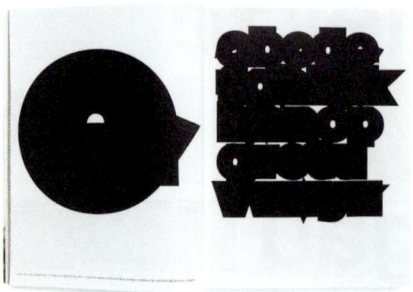

the sole specification of our client – the free-thinking art magazine "vorn" – was that we should respect no rules as we played with type. so we treated the alphabet like a fabric and asked ourselves what vivienne westwood, geoffrey beene or rei kawakubo would make of the letters. an art directrice experimented with the material, much as a fashion designer would. she produced a range of patterns, each leading to the creation of a different item of clothing. the eight garments made of the akzidenz-grotesk typeface reveal what a rich and variable means of expression type is. from seductive lace dress to elegant evening attire or austere uniform, they can all be tailored from this simple fabric. type is just as versatile as fashion: it can surprise and disguise, entice and improvise.

"vorn" magazine, edited by photographer joachim baldauf, is a genuine luxury project, giving carte blanche to its contributors from the worlds of literature, art, fashion, photography and design. without any intrusive advertising they're free to explore fashion, in the best sense of the word: contemporary trends, the avant-garde ("vorn" translates as ahead, or in front), experimentation, a belief in the challenging, the uncomfortable. it's an approach valued by – among others – claudia schiffer, who appears on the cover.

"vorn" magazine
typographic contribution
berlin, 2010

ABCDEF
GHIJKL
MNOPQR
STUVWXY
Z

language and dialect

although the formal characteristics of hgb grau basis allude to geometrically constructed typefaces, it runs narrower because its round shapes – such as a, e and o – are close to elliptical. as a result the letters create a warmer impression, as though they had been written by hand, and convey a straightforward and nonpretentious image. the large x-height and open counters of this font make it easy to read even when it is scaled down, making it well suited for use as body copy. the name hgb grau basis stands for its position as an oasis of calm between the extremes of the other eleven fonts.

the brief was developing a new corporate design for the academy of visual arts (hgb) leipzig, a place where new fonts have been developed for centuries. so instead of designing a logo or wordmark, a new typeface was created to draw on and continue this tradition. hgb grau basis is a basic sanserif geometric linear antiqua typeface that was specially developed for hgb leipzig. to meet the many-faceted demands of a modern corporate design, the idea was to design a diverse font family that can be used to express a polyphonic yet visually unified language. ten quintessential typefaces were chosen to represent the cultural legacy of hgb leipzig. a number of especially distinctive or attractive glyphs were then selected from these alphabets. these characters were re-interpreted in the hgb grau basis graphic style and added to the hgb grau basis character set. thus ten new fonts were created – with the historic forms adapted to the basis font in accordance with not only the norms of typeface design, but the rules of aesthetics as well. for example, to preserve the distinctiveness and beauty of the letters, an interesting j was not necessarily forced to conform to the similarly-shaped i. by mixing all the special forms of the ten typefaces, an eleventh was created: hgb grau leipziger allerlei, destined for overarching applications.

academy of visual arts (hgb) leipzig
visual identity, not realised
2015

Körper

Schwung

Duktus

Meister

Tradition

Kraft

depending on the glyph set or source material, between ten and 42 characters each were taken from older or more recent hgb typefaces and added to hgb grau basis. this resulted in ten different fonts with distinctive characteristics. their names refer to their creator or original name. the proportion of few or many "new" glyphs creates ten diverse typefaces featuring striking details which leave a strong, memorable visual impression. all fonts come in six weights – thin, light, regular, medium, semi-bold and bold.

HGB GRAU NEUDEUTSCH
HGB GRAU DELITSCH ANTIQUA
HGB GRAU BELWE ANTIQUA
HGB GRAU ELEMENTAR DEUTSCH
HGB GRAU SCHLEMIHL
HGB GRAU SHAKESPEARE MEDIÄVAL
HGB GRAU FREUNDSCHAFTS ANTIQUA
HGB GRAU SPATELSCHRIFT
HGB GRAU STENTOR
HGB GRAU FLEISCHMANN
HGB GRAU BASIS
HGB GRAU LEIPZIGER ALLERLEI

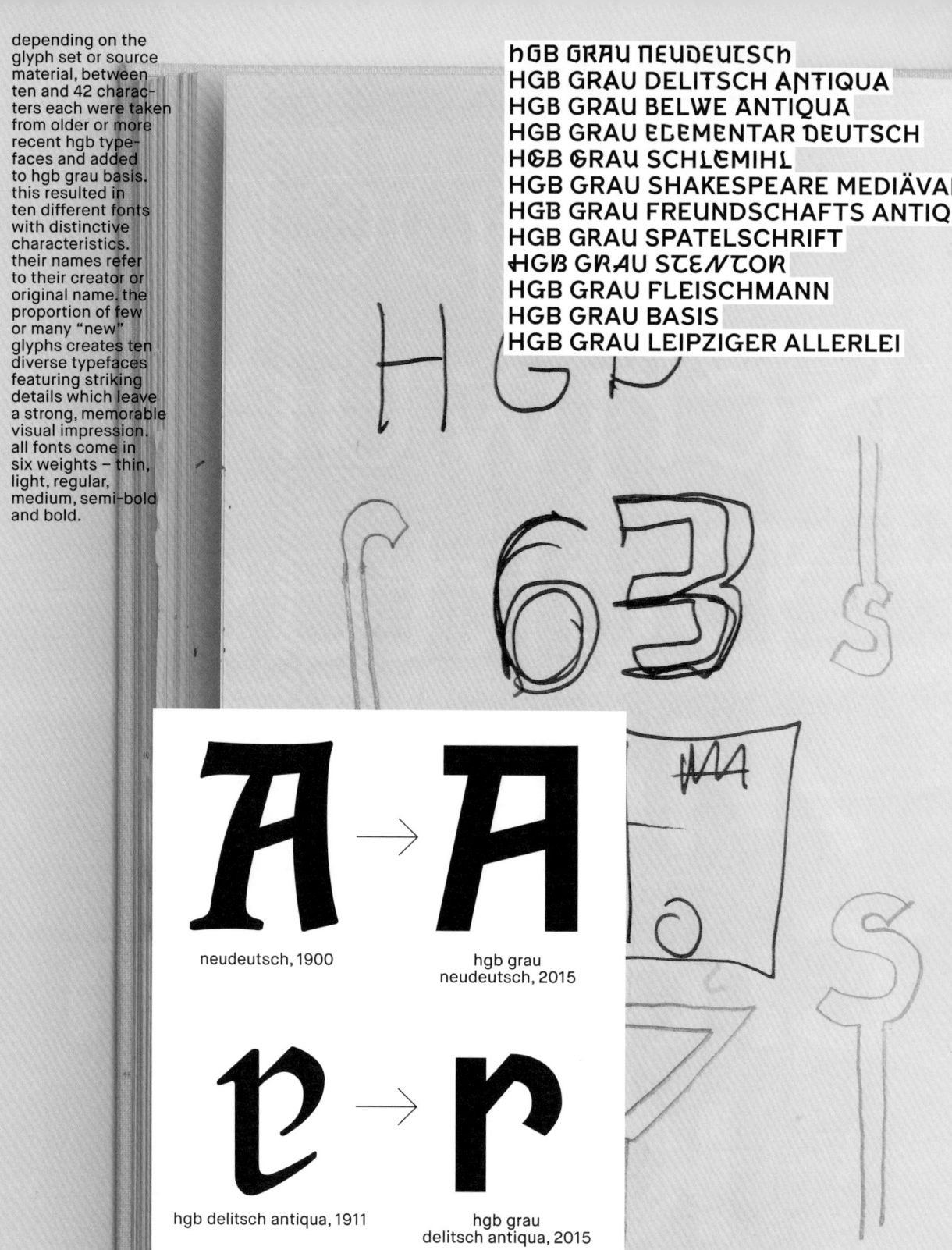

neudeutsch, 1900 → hgb grau neudeutsch, 2015

hgb delitsch antiqua, 1911 → hgb grau delitsch antiqua, 2015

**karin sander
kitchen pieces**

xxxix

hans hansen

the institution's brand consists of a letter logo and a wordmark. the hgb letter logo presents the name of the academy. six versions are available to be used in turn and in equal measure by all parts of the organisation – a precise graphic analogy reflecting the pluralistic image of hgb leipzig.

AAAAAaaaaaaaaBBBBBBBBBB
BBBbbbbbbbCCCCCCCCcccccD
DDDDDDDdddddddEEEEEEEEeee
eeeeeFFFFFFFFfffffffffffGGG
GGGGGGGGGGGGGGGGGGGgg
ggagggHhHHHHHHHHHHHhhh
hhlliiiJJJJJJJJjjjjjKKKKKKKKkk
kkkkLLLLLLLlllMMMMMMMMM
MMmmmmmmmNNNNNnnnnnn
OOooPPPPPPpppppQQQQQQQ
QqqqqRRRRRRRRrrrrrrrrrSSSS
SssssssTTTTTTTtttttttttttUUUU
UUUuuuuuuuVVVVvvvvWWWWW
VwwwwwwwXXXXXxxYYYYYYYyy
yyyyyZZZZZzzzzzÄÄÄÄÄäää
ääÉÉÉÉÉÉÉÉééééééééééÖÖööÜ
ÜÜÜÜÜÜüüüüüüü!"#%&&'()*+,-./
=?@_|§«»¶×-—'',""„•...‹›/€€←↑
↓↙↗↘↖↪↩-□ß0011122223344
55666777889⁹9

Karin Sander
Hans-Thoma-Preis 2011
Ausstellung 14. August–
18. September 2011, Hans-
Thoma-Kunstmuseum,
Rathausstraße 18, 79872
Bernau im Schwarzwald.
Mittwoch–Freitag 10.30–
12.00 Uhr, 14.00–17.00 Uhr,
Samstag, Sonntag und
Feiertag 11.30–17.00 Uhr.
Katalog zur Ausstellung:
Staatliche Kunsthalle
Baden-Baden und Kunst-
museum St. Gallen. www.
hans-thoma-museum.de

printed matter

a poster. a text. a prize. an exhibition. no content but a closing date. no underlying concept. no idea. just tidy typesetting. but suddenly there it was: a finished announcement. until someone jostled it, sending shock waves along the lines. then someone else tumbled and jumbled the poster.

**karin sander, hans thoma prize 2011
exhibition poster
bernau**

the typographic canopy

text becomes textile, the characters knitted into a light fabric which roofs the square. as if sustained by levitation, a tapestry of dancing sunlight and letters cloaks the area; a transparent web of interwoven strips of text forms a typographic canopy. characters wait to be discovered, their shadows tracing the course of the sun across the ground. they are there for the deciphering – words, whole sentences. this canopy of type is set in futura, which was developed by paul renner in 1927. the name of the font says it all. renner's 1932 polemic in defence of modernism, "cultural bolshevism?", could not be printed in germany. he himself was imprisoned by the nazis in 1933 and fled to switzerland shortly thereafter. his typeface was part of a larger movement towards modernism in the arts. it represented a typographical revolution and remains an attractive, contemporary font to this day – a fitting choice for this project.

the typographic canopy uses a text by the philosopher hannes böhringer to communicate the idea of unity and freedom. the design is a text collage with quotations from eichendorff, epictetus, hobbes, hopkins, joplin, kant, lincoln, rilke, rousseau, schiller and thucydides. of course the words unity and freedom form an important part of this collage, emphasised by their larger size. the two superimposed layers of text on the top and bottom sides minimise the immediacy of the text and create a dance of light and shadow.

**monument to freedom and unity
typographic canopy, not realised
berlin, 2010**

what's the difference between art and design (going forward)?

art = nasty
design = nice

case study

the case in point is an open and shut case: look inside, it will show you the solution. the case contains — encases — its own solution. the solution is a perfect fit for the case in hand. the trap for any designer — the worst-case scenario — is style, the insouciant gesture, the unthinking imposition of a form that doesn't fit the case. study me, says the case, inviting the designer to look and think. guided by the structure of the case, the answer flows into it as into a mould, then sets into a case-sensitive design.

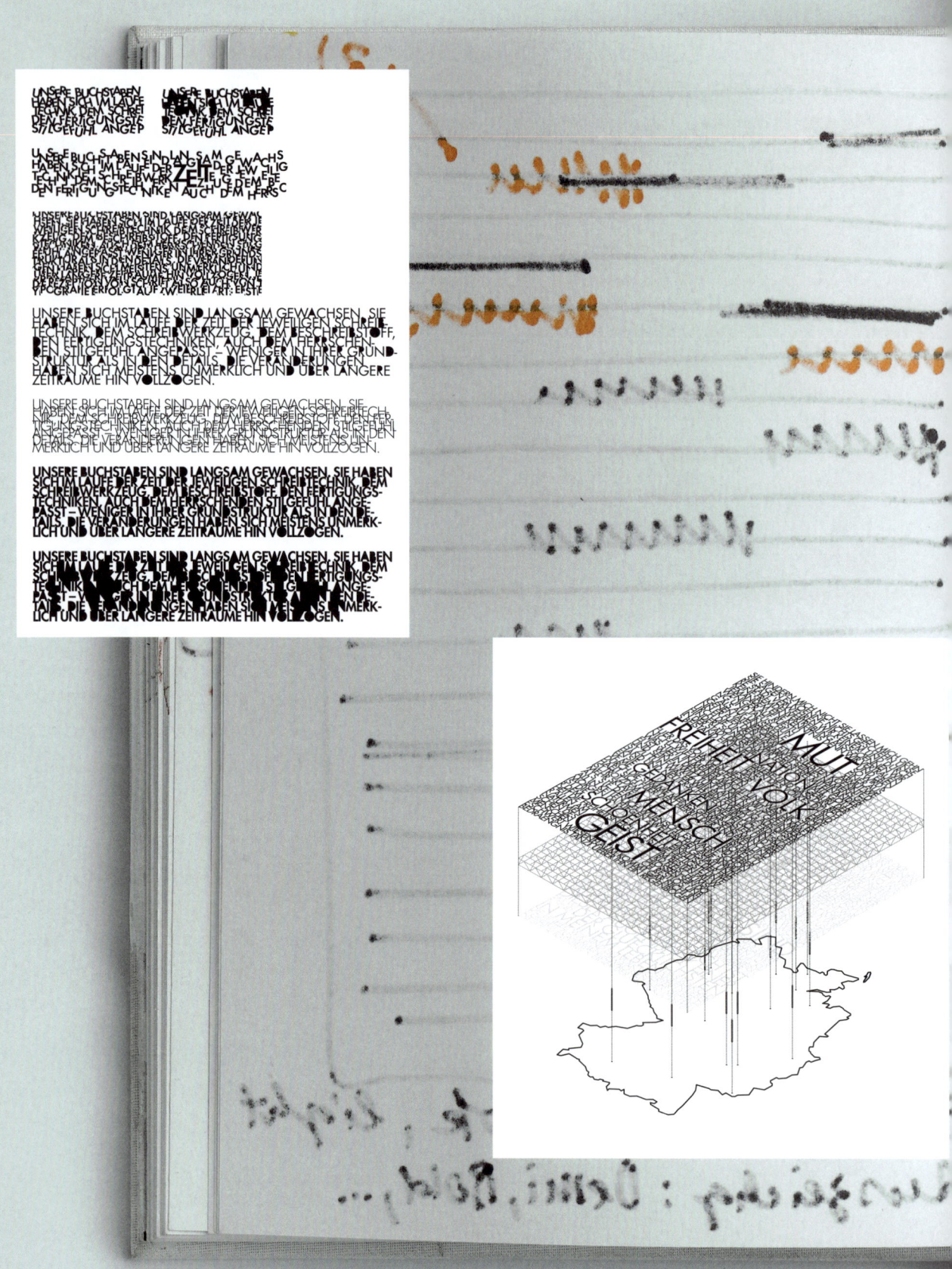

NSERE BUCHSTABEN SIND
AM GEWACHSEN SIE HABE
IM LAUFE DER ZEIT DE
TIGEN SCHREIBTECHNIK
CHREIBWERKZEUG DEM BE
BSTOFF DEN FERTIGUNGS
KEN AUCH DEM HERRSCHE
ILGEFÜHL ANGEPASST
IN IH
IN DE
ERUNGE
UNMER
E ZEIT

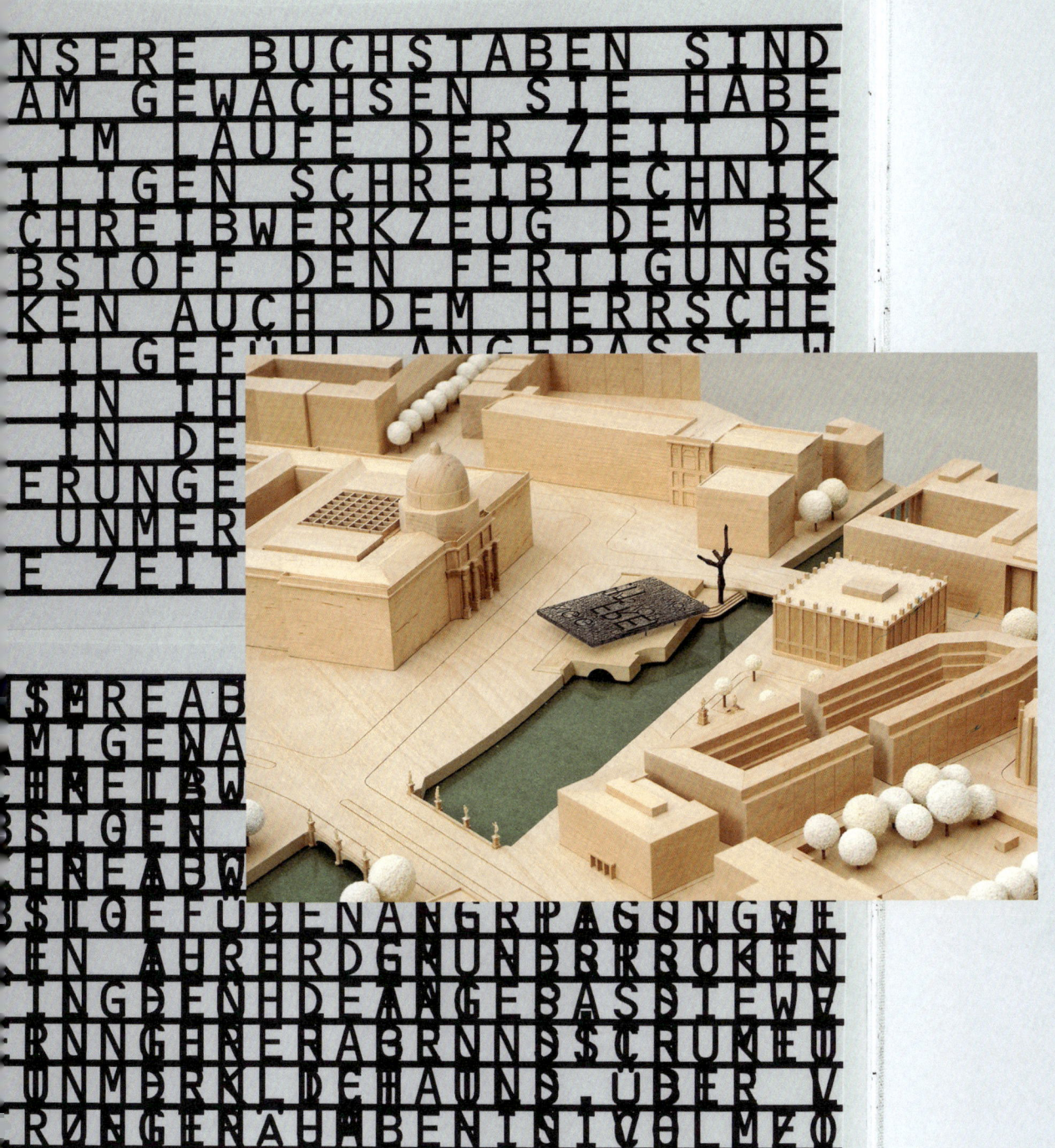

eggs for you

"selling someone an x for a u" is the german for pulling the wool over someone's eyes. the two letters themselves can't help it – typefaces can't distinguish between fact and fiction, between story and history. but the truth is: there is no truth. because like typefaces, history is refashioned by time. and today's story could well be tomorrow's history.

**x/u
exhibition poster
düsseldorf, 2009**

merhaba, bonjour, hello

the colourful melange of brightly coloured characters can be used to construct a visual language – a pattern that reflects the diversity of the region, the participating institutions and the countries of origin of its residents.

the welcome center is an institution organised by the city of stuttgart and the prosperous surrounding region. it aims to welcome new residents who want to work in the city or area by showing them the ropes of their new home. the symbol, a letter logo, symbolises coming together, forging networks and interconnectedness. the diagonally overlapping bars paint a positive picture of integration and internationalism. the diversity of nations, identities and cultures is graphically integrated in a single shape, communicating that every new resident is welcome here. four coloured stripes form a memorable and distinctive w that is universally understandable. the colours invoke state and regional identity and can be varied according to use – just the colours of the region on the regional website; the colours of the city's coat of arms on the municipal page. similarly, the colours of the various host towns or cities can be integrated when the logo is used at information events in other parts of the region.

welcome center stuttgart
visual identity, spatial design
2014

what's your view of order in society?

it would be a good thing

what's your view of order in design?

putting things in order

the way things are arranged — or the way parts of a whole are positioned vis-à-vis one another — speaks volumes about the person doing the ordering. how one part relates to another — neatly or not — says something about the individual who took the parts and piled them on top of each other, laid them side by side, or muddled them up. ordering is the possibility of creating relationships between the parts. they're no longer just hanging around randomly, disconnected: they all have their place. this act of ordering calls for the will to act and the ability to think incisively. it is easier to leave the parts as they are. but it's far better, more beautiful, to create order, to forge relationships and structures. when it works it's like a game and things fall into place almost by themselves.

the distribution of the colour fields was optimised with the aid of a program specially developed for this purpose.

a ward welcome

a visit to hospital is usually associated with less-than-positive feelings – unless, of course, it's for some minor ailment or to greet a new-born baby. in all other cases the touch of warmth and sympathy provided by a signage system that presents its factual information in a welcoming way offers a little comfort in an otherwise cool and clinical space. an array of attractive geometrical coloured patterns guide visitors to their destination and lighten the mood of this sterile setting. each of the numerous locations – over 70 of them spread across the hospital – has its own special combination of pattern and colour to set it apart. a signage system that relied entirely on colours or shapes wouldn't have worked. and with so much information to communicate, a conventional list would have been too confusing. it's only through the characteristic combination of colour and pattern that this large number of destinations can be clearly designated. the offices and duty rooms of the individual wards as well as the ward reception areas are identified by large areas of characteristically coloured, patterned wallpaper, with identical designs on the counters and doors. this visual coding gives these areas their own distinct identity, so that they form familiar landmarks in an otherwise featureless environment. the splashes of colour these surfaces provide make a welcome contrast to the cooler and more technical hospital backdrop. the 20 different ornaments are all based on a common isometric vector. 11 different pairs of colours can be used to form 220 patterns to act as destination codes. 70 such combinations that are easy to distinguish from one another were selected for the signage system.

offenbach hospital
signage system
2010

together with zieglerbürg büro für gestaltung we designed a highly versatile profile that can be modified fast and easily. sharp-edged extruded aluminium profiles are fitted seamlessly to an extruded aluminium substructure and fixed in place with a plastic clip. the info panels are laminated with digitally printed film. the open side of the profile is closed with a plastic clip. there are no inconvenient end profiles at the edges so that any number of info panels can be used, added or removed as necessary.

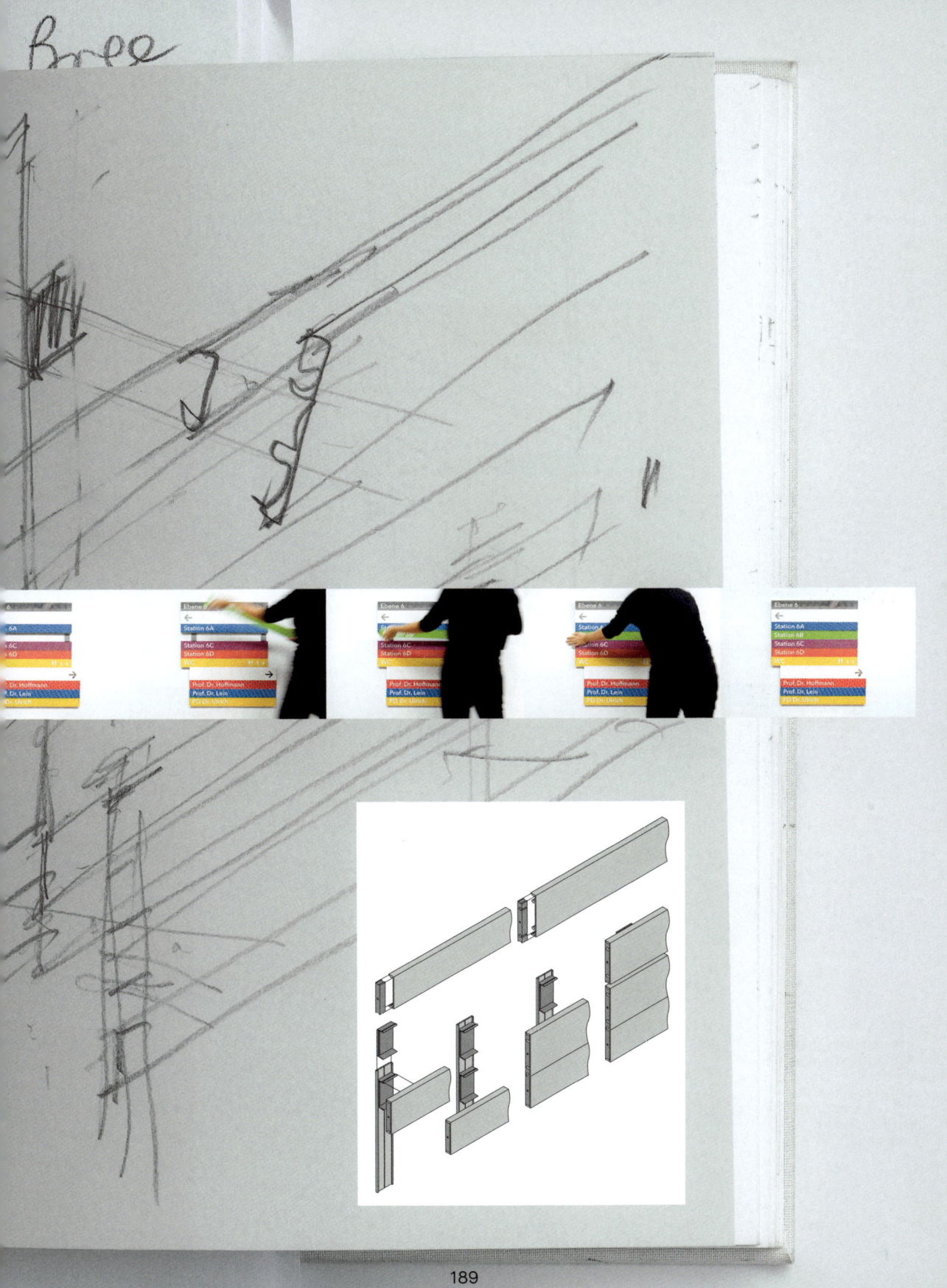

the self-explanatory signage is backed up by auxiliary boards, offset to illustrate the relative positions of the various locations.

you often seem to "break the rules" in your work, whether by using type in unconventional ways or ignoring clients' edicts. is rule-breaking a part of your ethos or mission, or does it just seem to happen?

breaking rules is important in design. nothing new will happen if you accept all the rules. but we don't break rules because we think it's funny or exciting. it just happens. when you are working seriously on design, the process leads you to a certain form. the solution is always embedded in the matter (affair/case/object). if we are convinced that the briefing is wrong, we break the rules by designing something unexpected. sometimes we are lucky; sometimes we lose.

a soft shade of magenta blends gradually into orange, fades away, dissolving, and finally morphs into a new colour chord, a composition of yellow and red, capturing one moment in a cycle: frozen in time, we see a transition — from old to new — from cool to warm — from stillness to movement. if we shift our perspective or viewing angle this colour suddenly becomes an image: a horizon, lit up with a promise of sunrise. it's the allure of the uncertain, the possibility of something that we long for.

Café Medicus
Information
Kindernotaufnahme
Notaufnahme
WC

→

Aufnahmestation
Helmut-Nier-Saal 1
Helmut-Nier-Saal 2
Kinderärztlicher Notdienst
Kiosk
Labor
Nuklearmedizin
Radio Brinkmann
Radiologie
Prof. Dr. Rilinger MBA
Strahlentherapie
Tommy Hall

the system is underpinned by an information sheet handed out at reception. this shows all the locations and their colour-coding. for those not familiar with the language or unable to read, reception staff mark the destination on the sheet. then each visitor can identify "their" colour and pattern that will guide and accompany them through the hospital complex. the destinations are clearly and logically named, avoiding any technical or in-house jargon. the system, which is easy for everyone to grasp at a glance, makes a small but important contribution to a sense of well-being in a potentially critical or unpleasant situation.

the wall in the foyer is 137 metres long and dotted with whirls made out of high-gloss aluminium strips or "profiles"– one for each of the hospital's centres of competence – illustrating how the various departments are networked.

capriciously seductive

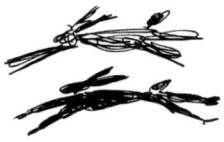

julia münzing's masterpieces mine the decorative dimension of technology. a master goldsmith, she combines german precision with french savoir-vivre to produce – et voilà! – such distinctive treasures as a ring crafted from heat shrink tubing and a cultured pearl. this franco-german creative entente is also communicated through the brand name custom-forged for the client: schmuque, a fusion of technique and elegance based on the boutique font and endowing the eminently german word 'schmuck' – jewellery – with a french-style conclusion. this artificial construct in itself, arguably, captures something of the jewellery's innate appeal: isn't it precisely this capricious, irrational quality that seduces, adorns and delights us? mais oui! the logo is like a mobile that's been set in motion, remaining constant even as its form shifts and alters. it's like the subtle movement of a necklace, continually shifting position on the wearer's skin: jewellery's delicious and fascinating spectacle, translated into a design.

schmuque by julia münzing
visual identity
stuttgart, 2015

as the world becomes increasingly technology-driven, complex and fast-paced, how do you cope with the demands of shorter project timeframes and the pressure to create good design ever faster?

working fast is okay

really? you like it fast? well, what do you find most challenging about the work you do today, versus how you worked 10 or 20 years ago? are clients different, are their expectations different?

yes, i think working fast is good training. the more you do, the faster you have ideas. i don't see any difference in clients now from ten years ago. clients want good work, and there is no excuse for ugly or bad design. we can say no.

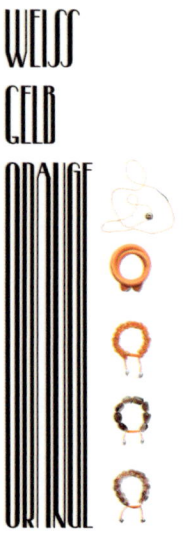

TRIP ZEPPELIN

Armband
Karneol facettiert
Zugperlen Zuchtperlen oval hellgrau
Zugband orange

AABBCDEEFFGHIJKKLMNNOPQRRSTUVVWXYZZ
0123456789

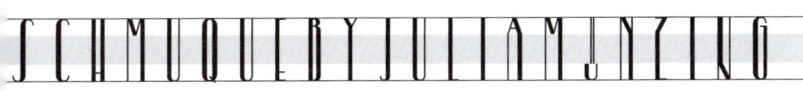
SCHMUQUE BY JULIA MJNZING

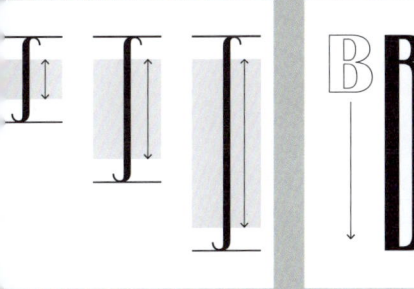
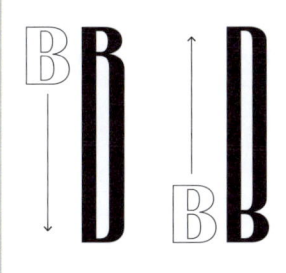

black bloc

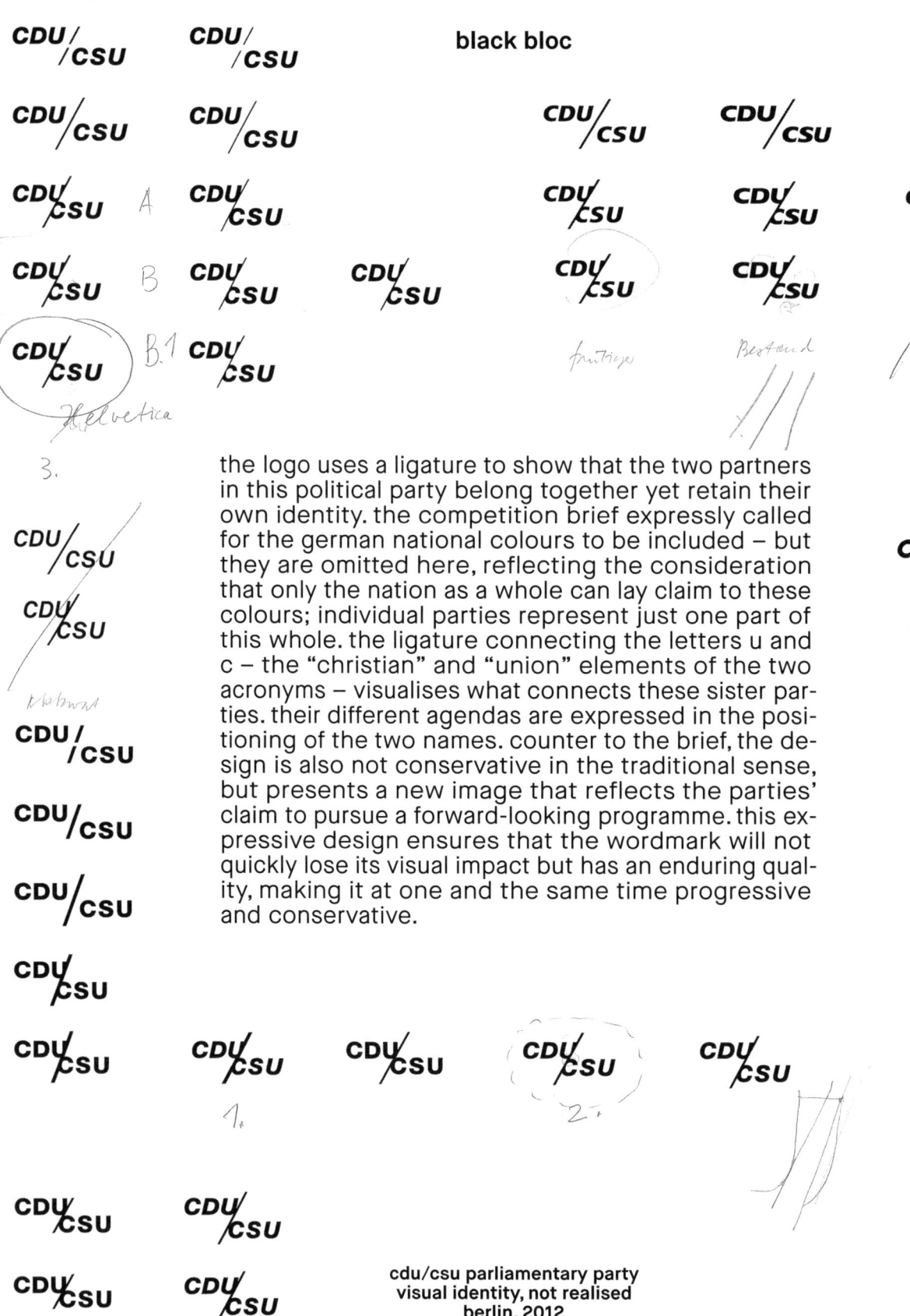

the logo uses a ligature to show that the two partners in this political party belong together yet retain their own identity. the competition brief expressly called for the german national colours to be included – but they are omitted here, reflecting the consideration that only the nation as a whole can lay claim to these colours; individual parties represent just one part of this whole. the ligature connecting the letters u and c – the "christian" and "union" elements of the two acronyms – visualises what connects these sister parties. their different agendas are expressed in the positioning of the two names. counter to the brief, the design is also not conservative in the traditional sense, but presents a new image that reflects the parties' claim to pursue a forward-looking programme. this expressive design ensures that the wordmark will not quickly lose its visual impact but has an enduring quality, making it at one and the same time progressive and conservative.

cdu/csu parliamentary party
visual identity, not realised
berlin, 2012

CDU/CSU

rhythm and blue

∆ ᗺ Ǝ H ſ ⊥ ӘΡ Ŧ ∩ ∨ ✕ ⅄ Z

a sequence of cheerful colours, a syncopated rhythm that disrupts and structures the tedious row of doors and corridors. every place becomes identifiable, in the simplest terms: for example, the lime green door with dark brown stripe is next to the bright red wall. for the residents – people who have had mental disabilities since birth – the combination of colour and form offers a way of quickly and easily finding the doors to their rooms. a helpful aid for people with cognitive impairments that makes the spaces so much more attractive for staff and visitors as well.

st. damiano, residential community for the mentally disabled
signage system
stuttgart, 2010

bright yellow

bright yellow is the colour of new beginnings. the corn-yellow seed bursts from the ripe fruit, attracting canary-yellow birds. lemon yellow is the colour of temptation: go on, pick me up and eat me. chalk yellow is hard, absinthe yellow is soft. traffic-light yellow says: be alert. light yellow is the midday sun at its highest point; honey yellow is a soft, warmly resonant tone that gladdens my heart. after the deep red of recession and the blue notes of crisis, sulphur yellow signals recovery, the green shoots of prosperity pulsing within it.

pink

in german, pink is 'rosa', which is also a name – its feminine sound like a promise; seductive without being vulgar. it is a light colour, with a brittle tenderness when mixed with cool blue. with red overtones it becomes soft. pastel pink, dusky pink, rose pink, rustling like silk, discreet but immaculate: tenderly approaching white, lending it enchantment, with a soft shimmer.

trinity

LEDERER
RAGNARSDÓTTIR
OEI

one firm, three names. from stuttgart to reykjavik via vienna and zurich. from first draft to final construction, from architecture to costume and stage design, this is anything but a conventional architectural practice. with a duly unconventional wordmark. the wordmark is a graphic take on three leading figures who stand for a specific mindset. the numerous letters and the names – short, medium and long – are moulded into a unit. the ensuing typographical problem zones are resolved pragmatically – by forging links where the opportunity arises. microtypographical features visualise the firm's attention to architectural detail.

lederer ragnarsdóttir oei
visual identity
stuttgart, 2012

just as in real life, the artificial desktop simulated by the computer is untidy. not always, of course, and not in every case, but now and again having everything partly visible can serve a purpose. as in the website for the architectural practice lederer ragnarsdóttir oei, where image and text appear to overlap. like on a real desktop, everything looks to be in an untidy heap, but there's method in the madness. people like to eyeball the architecture, so the images are in the foreground, while the text takes a back seat. but when you need the text it surfaces from under the pile of photos. it's a journey of discovery – not about tidiness, certainly, but perhaps about patterns and proportions.

from sketch to symbol

the new uniform visual identity for the german parliament is the face of democracy. its potential for expressive diversity evidences a commitment to the whole: all the different parts are related to each other. both small and large elements contribute to the overall harmony. the quality of the design expresses the attitude that well-made things are not just an objective necessity but also beautiful in themselves and a source of delight.

does the german parliament – the bundestag – need a visual symbol? a communication designer is not just responsible for the appropriate design and colours of an organisation's visual appearance; he also has to ask questions and advise the client. he must ask whether a symbol is necessary, whether it is beautiful and whether its symbolic qualities are appropriate for the client. he must ask whether the client's understandable desire for a symbol makes sense. he bears responsibility not only for the design but also for the message this design sends out. he has to understand this message from the perspective of both the sender and the recipient.

the competition for the new corporate design – to date the german parliament had lacked an overarching uniform visual identity – raised the question of whether the directly elected authority needs an identity like a brand does. did it need to be provided with a new logo, one that would then be evaluated and compared in the world of logos and emblems? the answer was simple: no, because it already had one. the existing emblem that identifies the german parliament is unique and therefore valuable. everyone knows this symbol: the federal eagle. an established, untarnished logo – and one that shouldn't be discarded without very good reason.

**german parliament
visual identity
berlin, 2009**

what drives you?

what interests us first and foremost isn't a client's size, importance or wealth, but whether they give us the freedom to do good work. our main aim is to bring beautiful things into the world. that might sound rather grand — but it's genuinely the engine, the motivation, that drives us. we just want to do good work — no matter who it's for.

how to measure the quality of a design?

is it useful?
is it coherent?
is it melodious?
it it helpful?
is it durable?
is it surprising?
is it enticing?
is it inconspicuous?
is it restrained?
is it unobtrusive?
is it entertaining?
is it amusing?
is it comprehensible?
is it humorous?
is it moving?
is it easy?
is it child's play?
is it foolproof?
is it new?
is it imaginative?
is it modest?
is it precise?
is it playful?
is it effortless?
is it powerful?
is it delicate?
is it subtle?
is it eloquent?
is it clear?
is it striking?
is it memorable?
is it meaningful?
is it beautiful?

the eagle of the federal republic of germany, top to bottom: national coat of arms; federal president's standard; small federal seal; plaster relief by ludwig gies in the former plenary chamber in bonn (drawing by büro uebele); the federal eagle by ludwig gies, which can be seen in the plenary chamber of the former parliament building in bonn, by günter behnisch, and in the plenary chamber of the reichstag building in berlin, by norman foster (drawing by studio laeis), and its redesign by büro uebele.

the bundestag's symbol – the likeable heraldic bird, familiar to generations of german citizens – has to communicate that it's the state that is speaking: dignified, but not superior or looking down from a great height, representing the people, with the corresponding authority and seriousness. the heraldic figure communicates that the german bundestag is not just any enterprise, but the state, in the very best sense. it is answerable not to the laws governing brands and the marketplace but to its citizens. this constitutional body may rightly adorn itself with the symbols of state. the bundestag eagle and the federal eagle – unequivocally german and clearly state symbols – are present in many variations on coins and flags, all referencing one another.

the three-dimensional form designed by cologne artist ludwig gies for the bundestag in 1953 uses formal abstraction to maintain a sympathetic balance between majestic detachment and expressive naturalistic depiction. every member of the administrative staff and every bundestag delegate will use this symbol on their letterhead with pride. and so there is a great deal in favour of retaining this iconographically unequivocal emblem. however, because this figure was designed for a three-dimensional application, it has some weaknesses in two-dimensional applications. which is why the heraldic bird was radically reworked while maintaining its clear connection with the famous gies eagle.

...ische Staatspräsident Peres am 27...
Seine Rede am Gedenktag für di...
...elische Verhältnis wird hier un...

...arabischen Län-
...deren Tore blie...

...nwesenden, v...
...uns damals...
...en, von u...
...ten wu...
...nd. Z...

Deutscher B...

Deutscher B...

Deutsch

Auftrag

Frau Angela Klasar
Arminstraße 27
70180 Stuttgart

Berlin, 27. September 2012

Referat Zentrale Beschaffung, ZT 2
Geschäftszeichen: 89/123 456
Bezug: Besprechung 17. August 2012
Anlagen: 2

bearbeitet von:
Franz Rück

Platz der Rer
11011 B
Tele
Fax:
franzis

Dienstgeb
Luisenstra

Belegexemplare

Sehr geehrte Frau Klasar,

Ur

Deutscher Bundestag

aben sind langsam gewachsen. Sie h
er jeweiligen Schreibtechniken,
reibstoff, den S
efühl, den Fertigungstechniken,
s angepaßt – weniger in ihrer
's. Die Veränderungen haben sich
längere Zeiträume hin vollzoge
f zweierlei Art: ers
er gesehenen Buc
s (meist

Deutscher Bundestag

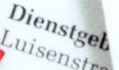

Petra Pau
Vizepräsidentin des Deutschen Bundestages
Vice President of the German Bundestag
DIE LINKE / THE LEFT

Platz der Republik 1
Telefon: +49
Mobil:

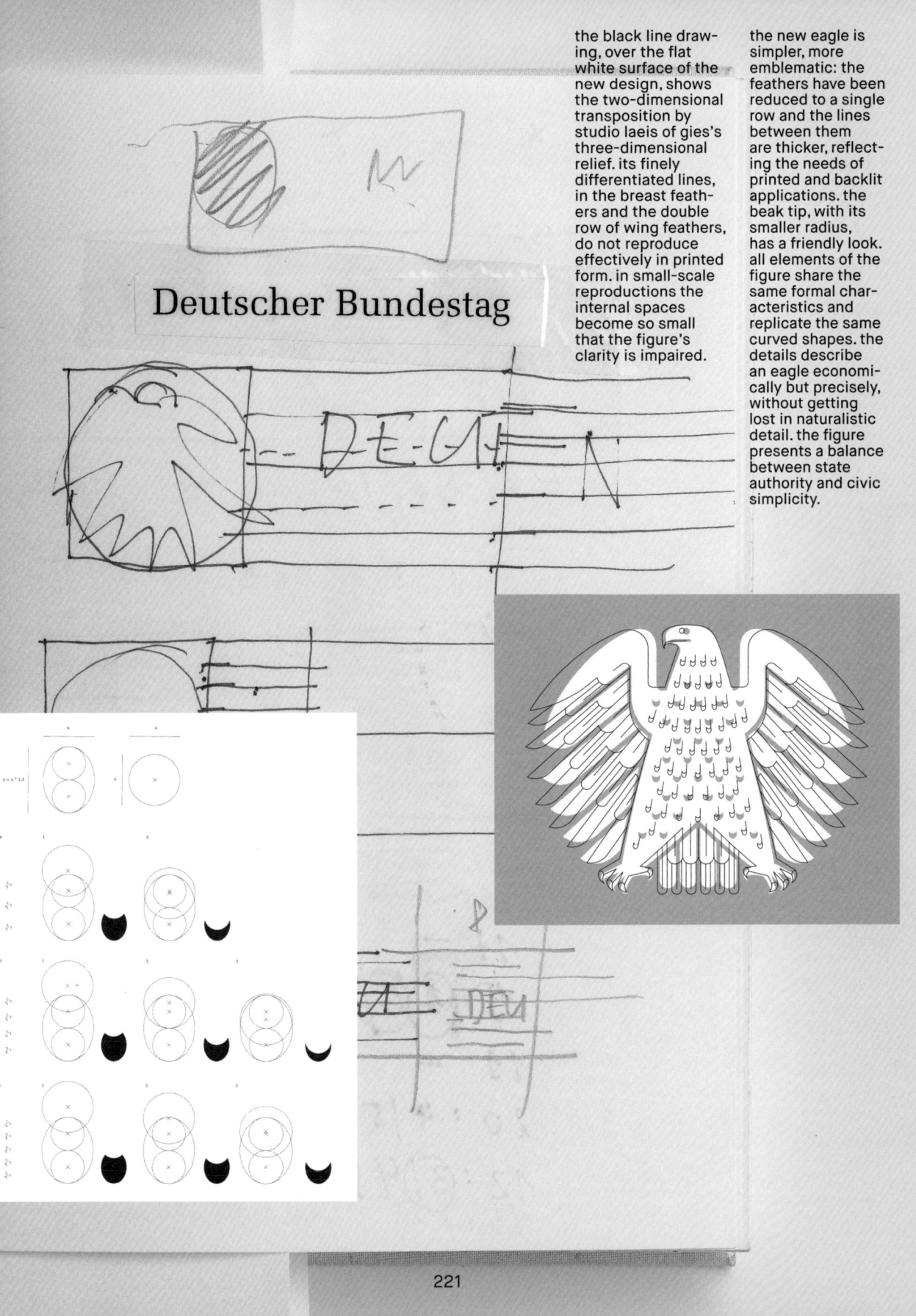

the black line drawing, over the flat white surface of the new design, shows the two-dimensional transposition by studio laeis of gies's three-dimensional relief. its finely differentiated lines, in the breast feathers and the double row of wing feathers, do not reproduce effectively in printed form. in small-scale reproductions the internal spaces become so small that the figure's clarity is impaired.

the new eagle is simpler, more emblematic: the feathers have been reduced to a single row and the lines between them are thicker, reflecting the needs of printed and backlit applications. the beak tip, with its smaller radius, has a friendly look. all elements of the figure share the same formal characteristics and replicate the same curved shapes. the details describe an eagle economically but precisely, without getting lost in naturalistic detail. the figure presents a balance between state authority and civic simplicity.

to ensure that the logo as a whole doesn't look too distant and official, the powerful visual symbol with its multiple curved shapes is paired with a fine but rigorously and clearly constructed serif typeface, which maintains a balance, in formal terms, between rounded and angular shapes and offers a visual counterweight to the eagle emblem.

**hermann zapf
melior antiqua**

melior antiqua was developed as a special typeface for the type foundry d.stempel ag in frankfurt am main and for linotype gmbh's typesetting machine factory. work on the font began in 1948. the aim was to create a new typeface that was easy to read in small sizes and also suitable for magazines and newspapers.

at the time it was designed both for manual setting, using lead type cast by the centuries-old method invented by johannes gutenberg, and for use in linotype typesetting machines. in the 1990s, melior antiqua was revamped for digital reproduction and adapted to meet present-day technical requirements. from the outset, the proportions of the lower-case letters relative to the upper-case letters were based on the golden section. the problem for the type designer was that due to the technical constraints of the typesetting machine, all the letters had to have the same width – even in the italic and bold versions. no overshoots were allowed either – in the lower-case f, for example.

these technically imposed constraints complicated the task in hand. the cap height was 20 mm. back then, all of the letters had to be drawn by hand in the original sizes. many of the trials were conducted in the challenging conditions of the post-war period, and it proved quite impossible to test the new typeface under the special conditions of the gravure process used for magazines back in the 1950s. in order to optimise the readability of small font sizes, i came up with the idea of making words look more ribbon-like, to guide the eye, by giving the curves a form midway between circle and square and drawing the round letters with an oval shape that optimally filled the inside of a square. without any mathematical intentions, this gave rise to an artistic concept that the danish mathematician piet hein referred to in 1959 as "superellipses" (described in detail in the september 1965 issue of scientific american, pp. 222–236). this design principle of melior antiqua, which emerged in 1948 for purely aesthetic reasons, was to prove very useful in later applications. in 1952 the hannoversche allgemeine zeitung became the first german daily newspaper to be printed in linotype melior. the gravure-printed tv magazine hörzu followed later, at which point it emerged that the typeface's somewhat thicker serifs were very advantageous for gravure printing. melior is general-purpose typeface, usable for all applications and free from any historical baggage – an outstanding example of industrial design in our times.

a brand shouldn't be over-used. the desire to use the symbol as often as possible is understandable, but diminishes the brand's value. because of this, for casual applications where the brand is not fulfilling a sovereign function we developed a special form which shows only the left section of the logo — what looks like one half of it. cutting the image exactly down the middle would have produced an unattractive outline, which is why it is divided slightly off-centre.

the outline of the eagle describes an approximate circle. our eyes – or rather, our brain – complete this irregular form, making it a regular one. for this reason the visual focal point of the design lies not at its mathematical centre but a little lower, at the centre of this "imagined" circle. we took this into account when combining the wordmark with the visual symbol: the lettering is aligned exactly with the mathematical centre of the eagle design, which would normally be avoided as it might appear to be too low.

so that different font sizes can be combined with the symbol in a standardised way, the image is set within a square which is divided horizontally into 48 segments. these units are multiplied to arrive at the three potential font sizes.

the competition brief asked for two designs. it was accompanied by a drawing of the relief eagle hanging in the plenary chamber of the german parliament. this drawing could be used, the brief specified, but for copyright reasons it could not be amended in any way. contravening this requirement would result in exclusion from the competition. in smaller sizes, however, the finely differentiated drawing of a three-dimensional relief produces an unclear image. so that it could work as a logo and in small print applications – on a business card, for example – we pared it back to the essentials. before the competition presentation the result of this graphic simplification was shown to a lawyer – who unequivocally contradicted our hope that this work could be described as a new creation. the changes, said the lawyer, clearly evidenced the characteristics of a redesign, as expressly prohibited in the competition brief. nonetheless we firmly believed that this was the right path to take and so we took the risk of submitting the work – which convinced the jury.

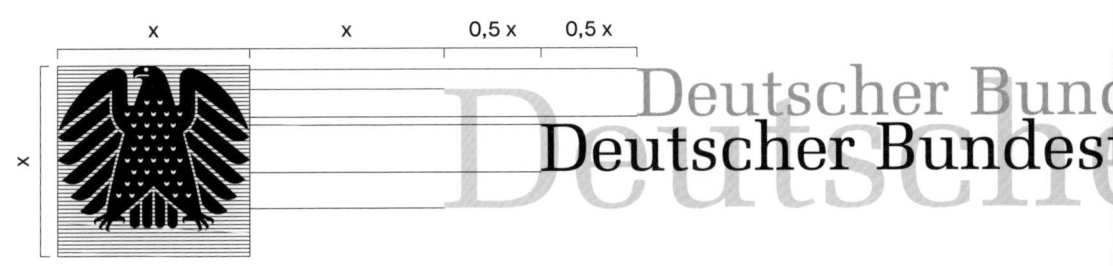

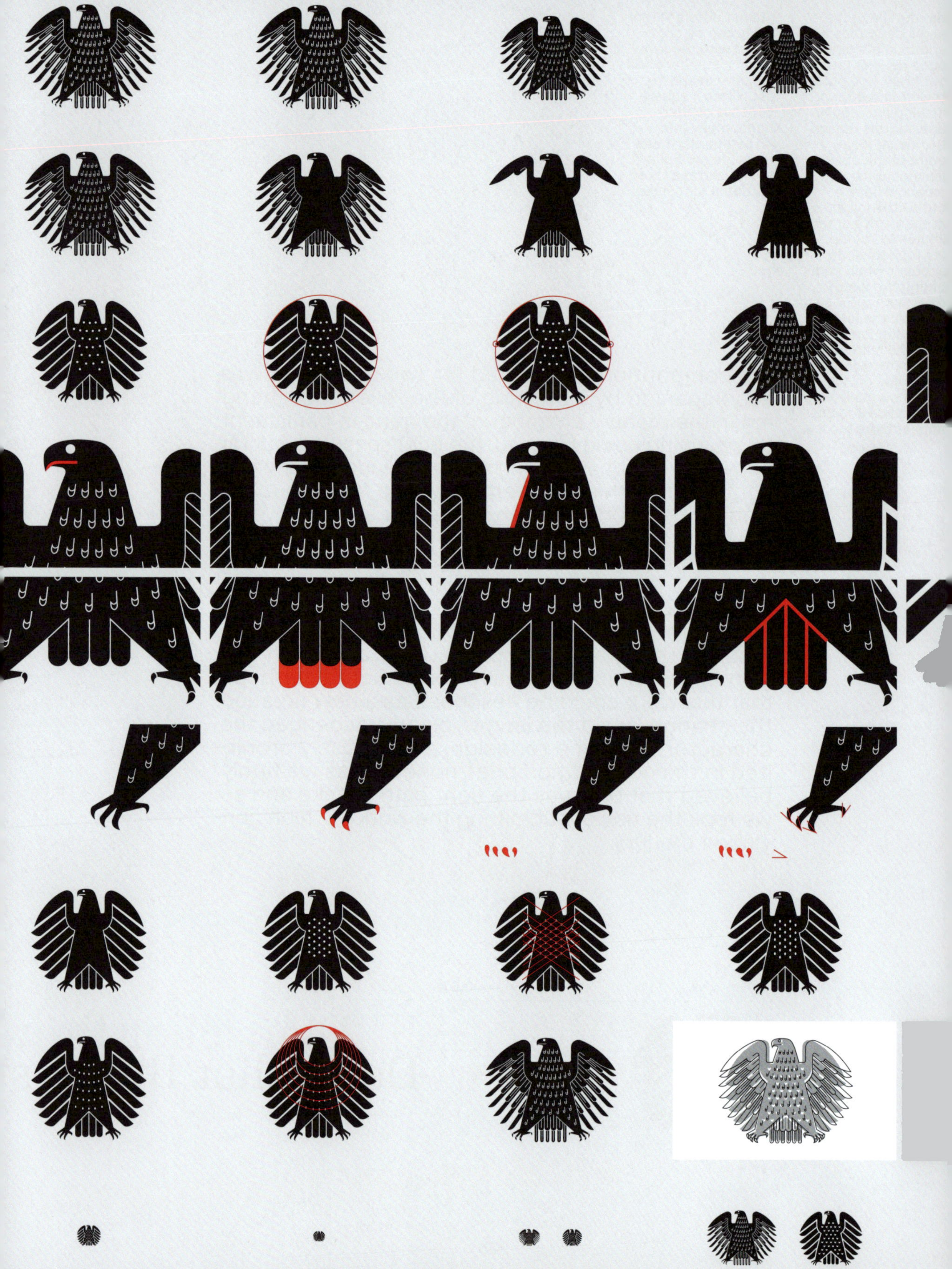

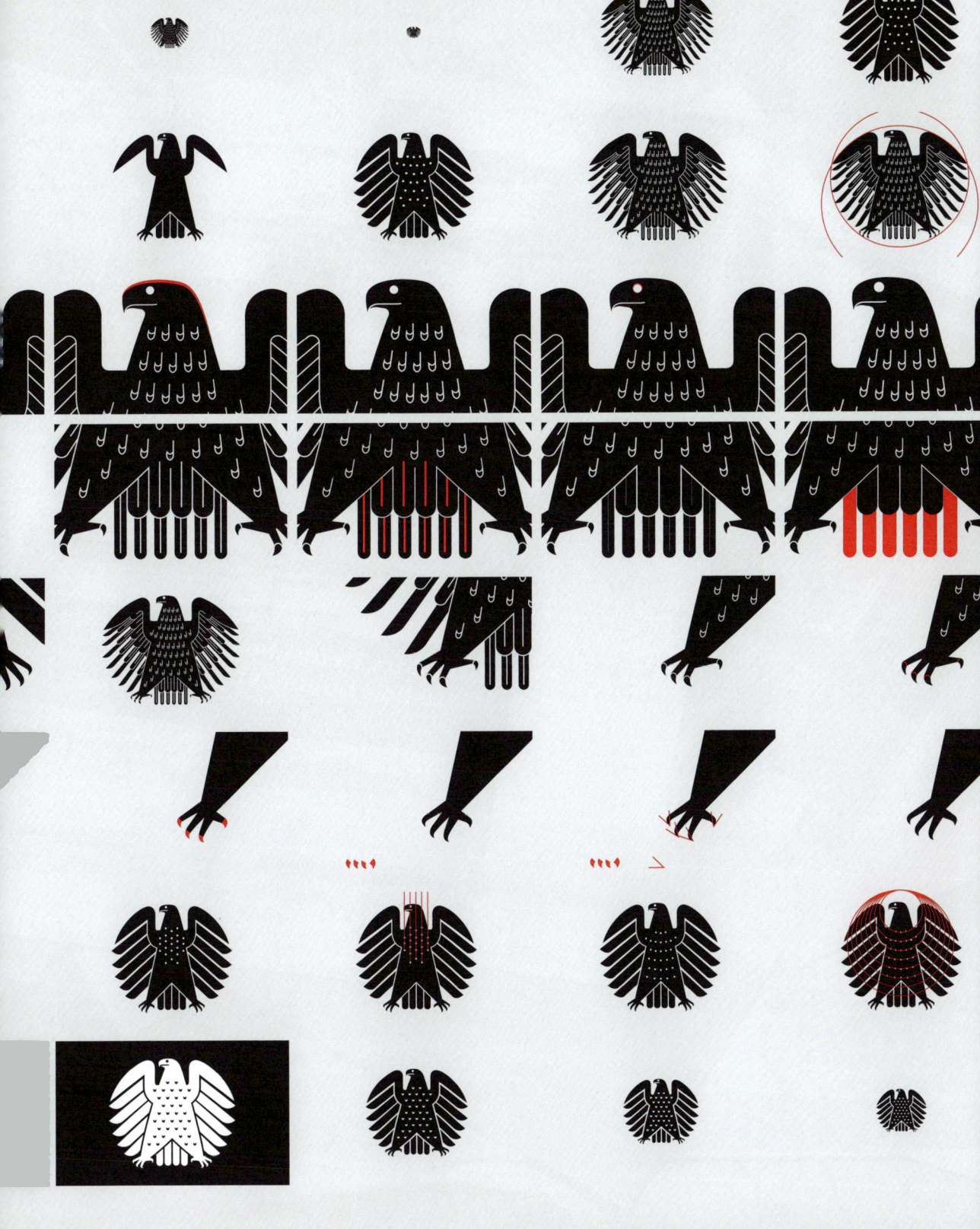

eagle, bear, stag and griffin feature as heraldic animals in the emblems of nations, federal states, districts and towns. the eagle has special status, being unequivocally assigned to one nation: the eagle is german. on a sports shirt the eagle sends a clear message that doesn't need words or national colours to get across. other countries may also have an eagle on their coat of arms, but the eagle is linked, first and foremost, with germany. in branding terms this is a key strength. just as with the stars and stripes, suggestive references are enough to establish the link with a specific nation.

the eagle has been an emblem of sovereignty since the days of the holy roman empire, its form subject to alteration over time. today it is the symbol of a nation state, one that is visible for everyone in the german parliament. the federal eagle in the plenary chamber in bonn has several interesting features. the breast feathers are arranged asymmetrically, the right shoulder is higher than the left and the lower left tail feather doesn't lie parallel to the others but twists away from them, at an angle (see p. 217). maybe these irregularities were intended to remind the delegates of their human imperfections – it's an appealing thought. the disrupted symmetry is also attractive from a design perspective.

for blind embossing and very small applications a modified design ensures good print reproduction. here the internal markings are wider, the eye is bigger and the beakline is omitted.

art, as always, does things colourfully and disregards the rules. but the visual identity guidelines include measures to accommodate even this: a banner, wrapped around the art works, must be designed and located for minimum obtrusion. the identifier, in any of the seven corporate design colours, can be placed in six different positions, always aiming to show the image to best effect.

for internet and
e-mail applications
georgia is used
(shown in white).
this typeface
was designed by
matthew carter
in 1996 specifically
for screen appli-
cations and is very
similar to melior
(in grey).

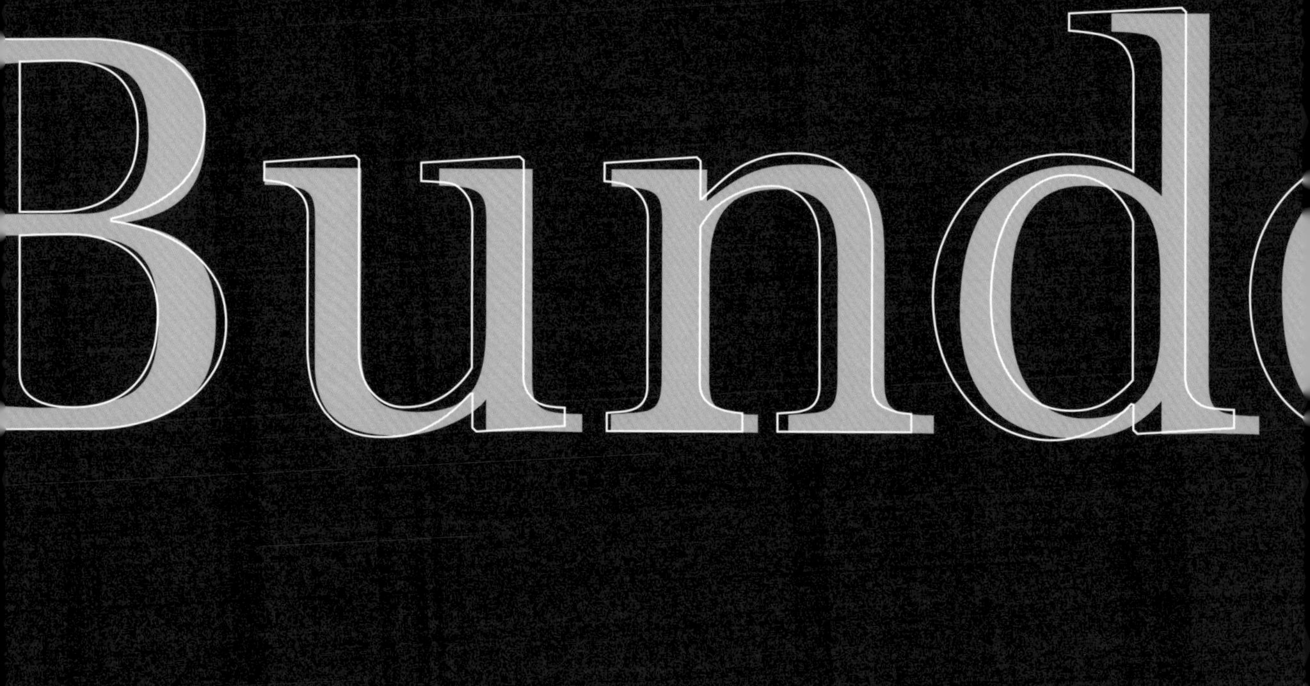

Bundo

matthew carter
verdana and georgia

when verdana and georgia were designed for microsoft in the mid-1990s the intention was to make verdana more legible on screen than previously available sanserifs, and georgia more legible than other seriffed faces. they were meant to be complementary designs, not competitors, and were (and still are) often used together, either with verdana for display and georgia for text, or vice versa. i agree with the british design critic alice rawsthorn, who suggested recently that when users were learning the web in its early days they tended to choose verdana because of the apparent simplicity of its sanserif forms. as users have become more experienced they have started to use georgia more confidently and more effectively on screen. blogs and websites set in georgia are now so common that even if it began its life on screen as an alternative to sanserif types georgia has gained acceptance by now as a general-purpose font in its own right. both georgia and verdana were designed specifically for display on screen. both were original designs, not adaptations of pre-existing printer fonts. they took into account the problems of screen resolution and the technical aspects of rendering type on computer monitors. i do not consider either verdana or georgia to be objectively the more legible. as type designers have always acknowledged, a typeface is raw material; how it is used (on paper or screen) has as much influence on its legibility as any inherent qualities. all the typographic variables – size, line length, leading, colour, background contrast and so on – can be adjusted to make a typeface work well or badly, and this is true of sanserif and seriffed designs alike.

norbert lammert

a uniform visual identity: for the distinctive individuals who make our parliament what it is, this is an idea that's anything but flattering – indeed it might even be regarded as demeaning. after all, any democracy worthy of the name isn't about uniformity but about conflicting interests, differing opinions, which come together in parliament. for this hub of political policy formation, however, for the place itself, a uniform identity is eminently desirable – indeed very important, in terms of how it is perceived.

a few years back büro uebele developed a design for the german parliament to fulfil just this purpose. at the heart of this design is the federal eagle, albeit in a revised form – a choice that's certainly in line with public perception, even if many would now ascribe a similar iconic status to the dome of the reichstag. either way the design was very successful – in my personal view and in the judgement of the specialist design community. it's compelling, contemporary and achieves high recognition levels. in short, büro uebele's work made a major contribution to the german parliament as an institution, helping to consolidate its profile with the public and the media.

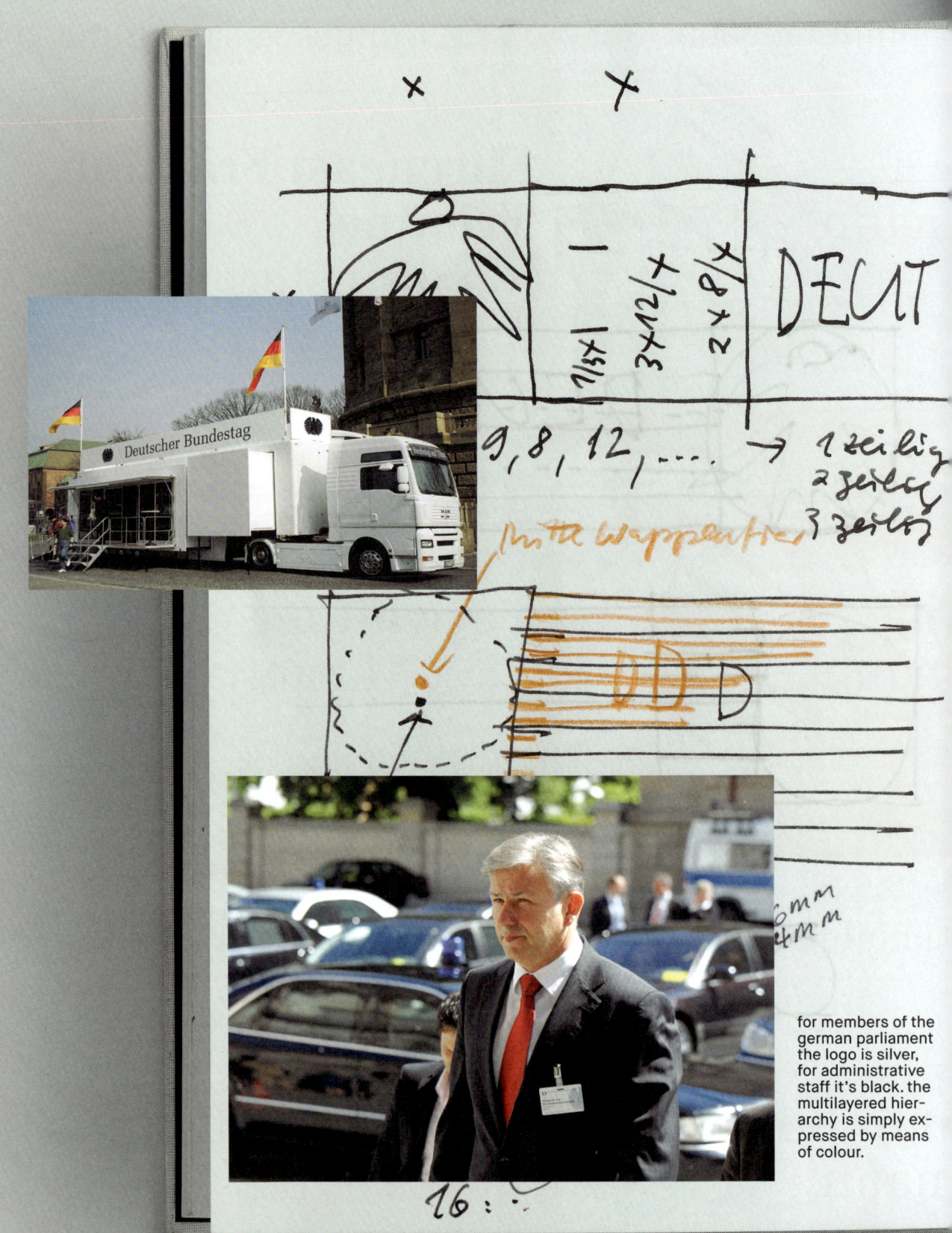

for members of the german parliament the logo is silver, for administrative staff it's black. the multilayered hierarchy is simply expressed by means of colour.

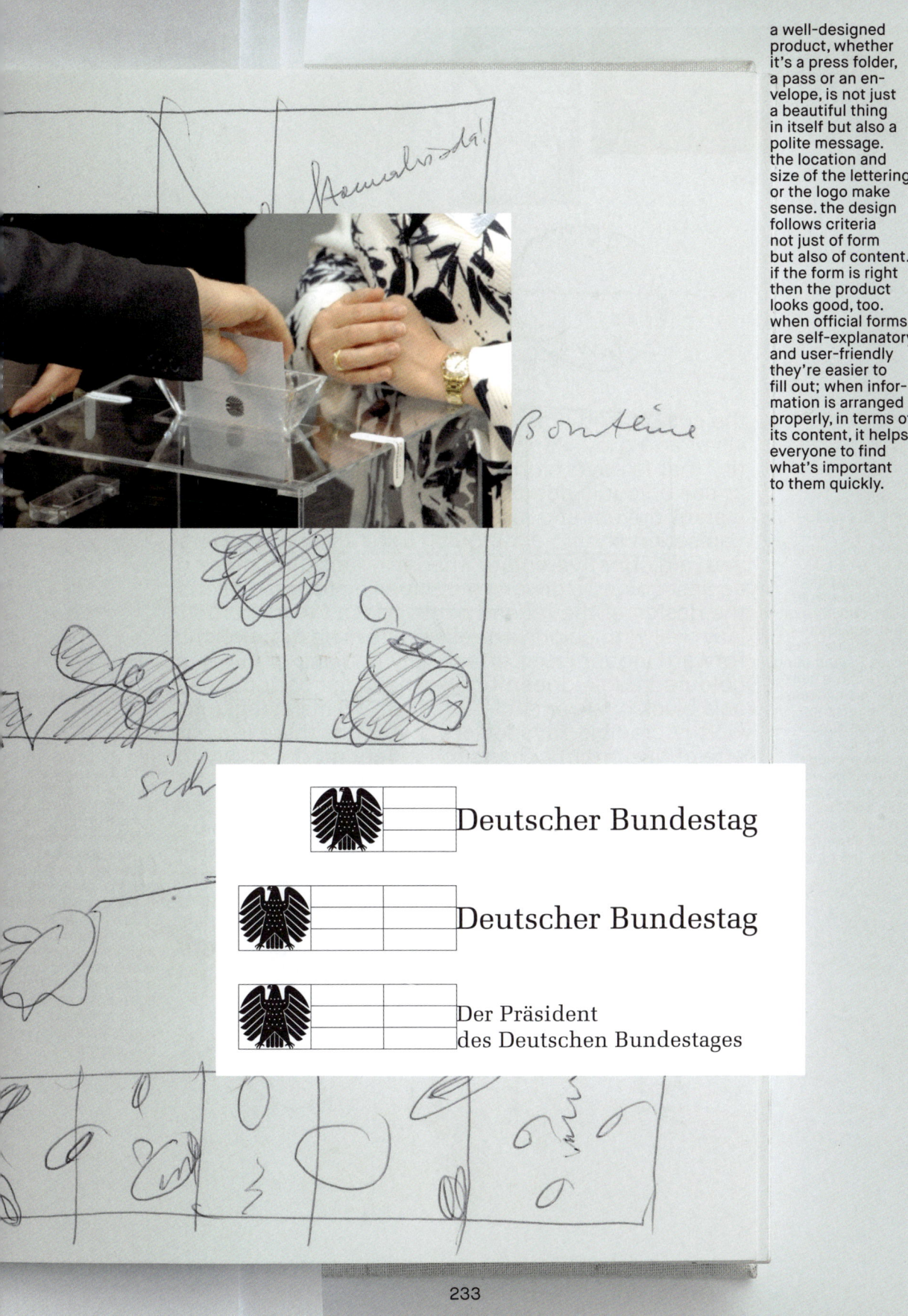

a well-designed product, whether it's a press folder, a pass or an envelope, is not just a beautiful thing in itself but also a polite message. the location and size of the lettering or the logo make sense. the design follows criteria not just of form but also of content. if the form is right then the product looks good, too. when official forms are self-explanatory and user-friendly they're easier to fill out; when information is arranged properly, in terms of its content, it helps everyone to find what's important to them quickly.

today, just a few years after the corporate design for germany's bundestag was completed, the eagle can be found all over the place. most of the uses are not permitted, or even – as in the background of stefan raab's tv studio – poorly executed, unauthorised modifications. this isn't a bad thing. in fact, on the contrary, it's a success. whether on shopping bags or posters, the eagle has become a symbol for the nation, like the stars and stripes or the tricolour. the logo has been accepted, appropriated by the people.

the colours of the new visual identity are black, white, silver and grey – appropriate for conveying an identity that is sovereign and serious. the decision not to use colour is not just about rising above the usual market-driven (and justified) concerns that every organisation should distinguish itself from the others with a distinctive colour shade. in fact the decision against colour is driven by compelling formal reasons. the design of the federal eagle doesn't work particularly well with colour, expressing its majestic, straightforward vigour most effectively in black or silver. a coloured eagle doesn't have the same seriousness as a black or silver eagle, which looks majestic, trustworthy, credible. for special applications there is a palette of five bright colours to identify products which have a different expressive value, in a way that's appropriate to the specific circumstances. press passes or invitations can be ranked using different colours and the blue jacket of the visitor reception team sends out a conspicuous, friendly signal among the bustle of tourists. according to how they are combined and emphasised, the colour and brand elements can strike a serious, ceremonious or bright and cheerful note.

when apparently insignificant things are given the same attention as important things, when a pencil and a key ring are designed with the same attention to detail as an envelope and a business card, the organisation demonstrates its understanding that all parts or elements make a contribution to the whole. a uniform design that's visible on jackets, brochures and bags expresses the management's sense of commitment towards its employees and partners.

$c_0 = 299.792.458$ m/s $m_{Sonne} = 1,9891$ **"this is ground control ..."** $h = 6,62606896 \cdot 10^{-34}$ Js   Mars um die

2012, stuttgart university campus. saturn, quaoar, orbital velocity, planck's constant: such were the underlying design parameters for a world-class institutional building. on arrival, the only way is up, heading for orbit, as indicated by the sign in the foyer. this three-dimensional lettering rotated through 90° – representing many times the mass of the interstellar dust entering the earth's atmosphere each year – seems to defy the laws of gravity. bearing the names and rooms of the people of this cosmic location, it helps to locate them in the twinkling of a star.

the collision protection concept expresses the extreme order of magnitude of space travel. a number alone cannot convey the meaning of a light year or a light minute, but it does communicate an approximate idea of the dimensions which the institution deals with every day.

baden-württemberg space center
signage system
stuttgart, 2012

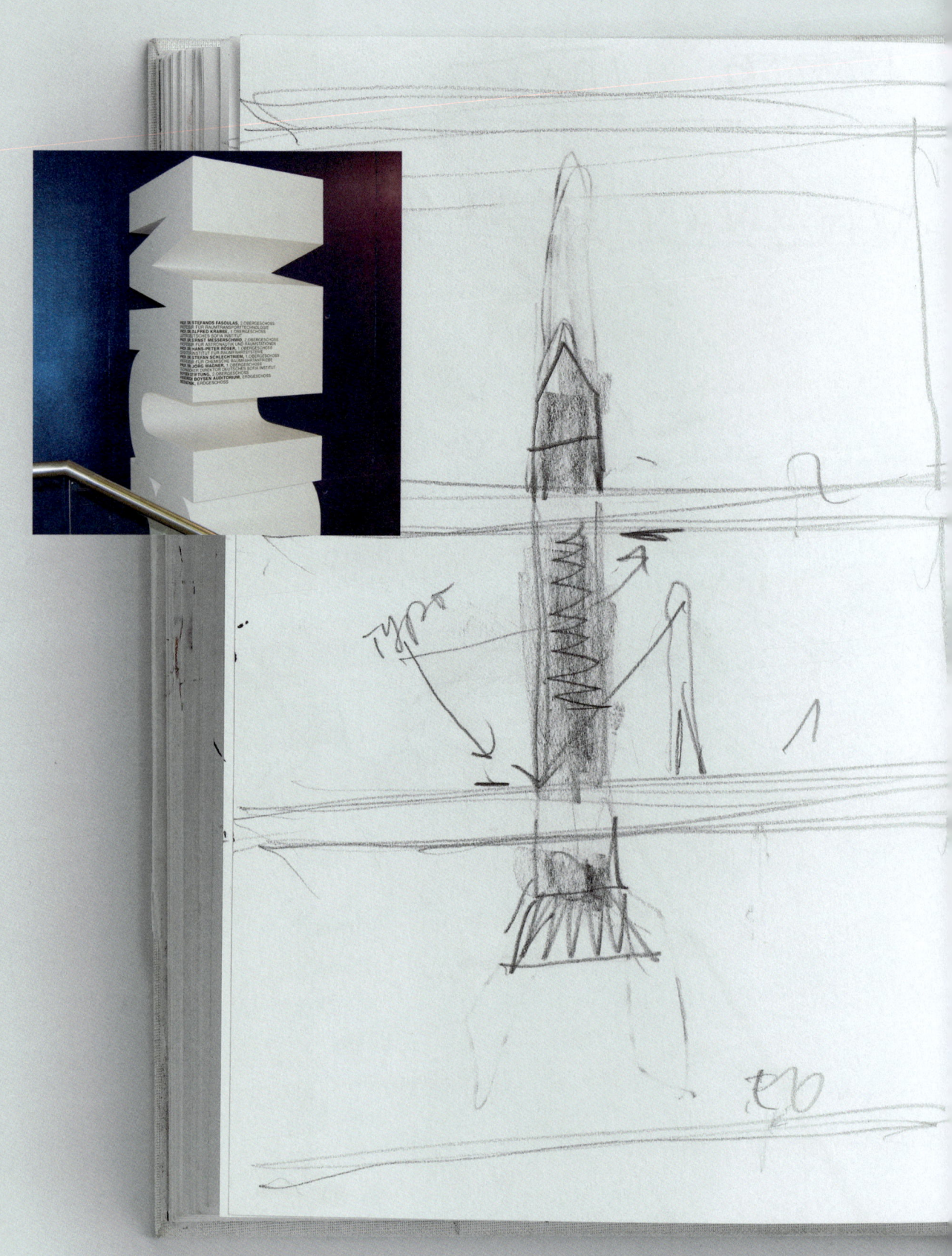

**parallels between rhetoric and design?
how do designers use words?**

design is a visual discipline — one that's not possible without thinking. talking or writing about design reflects your own work and nourishes it. language supports the design process. if a design can't be explained clearly then it isn't a good design. whereof one cannot speak, thereof one must be silent" (ludwig wittgenstein). an idea can take shape through talking: the linguistic materialisation of an assignment; words as wayfinding aids.

can using grids or following typographic rules deliver an aesthetically appealing outcome? can these rules be used to learn design? should design rules be timelessly applicable?

rools? whott rr thay phor?

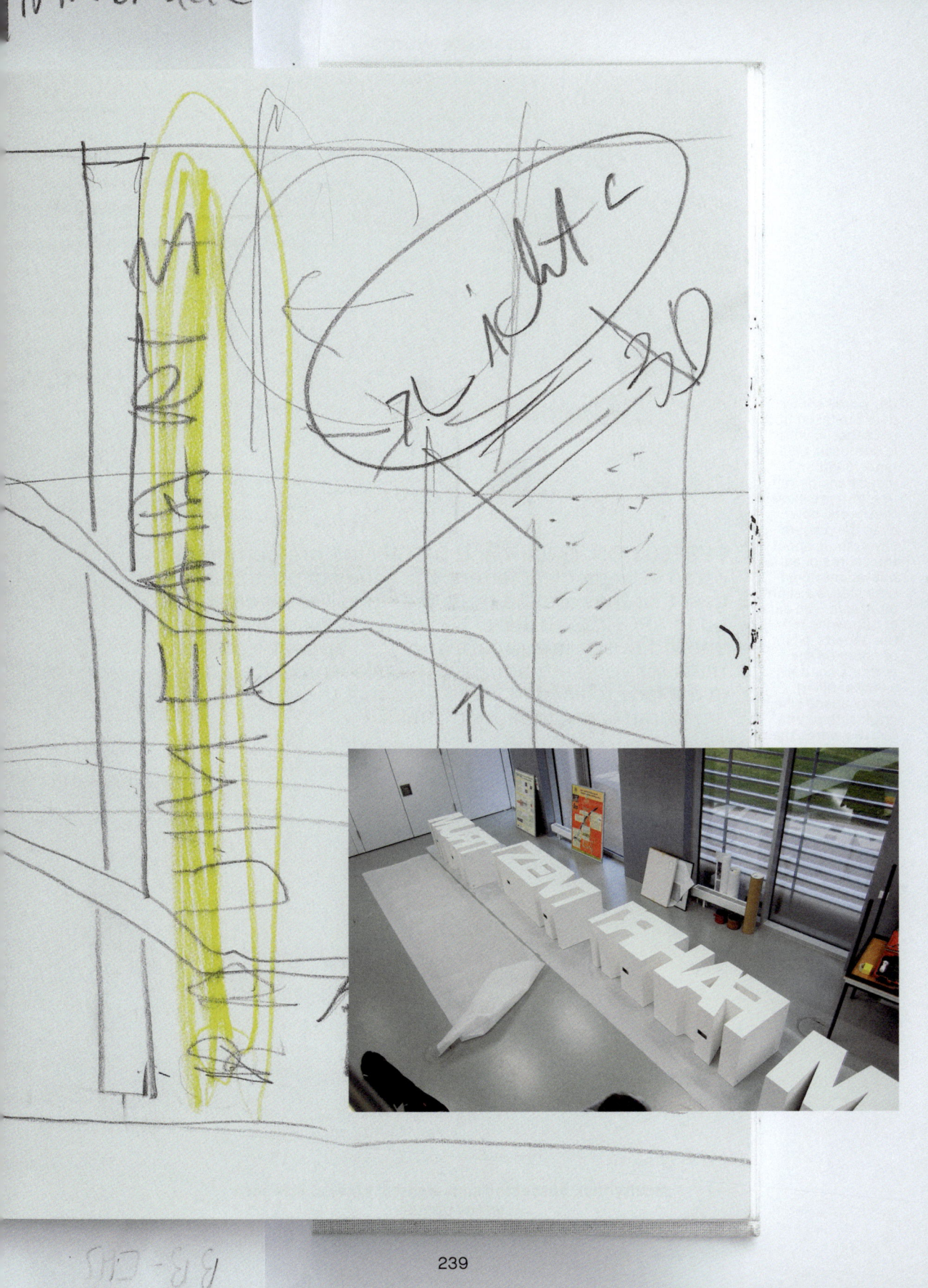

absolute words

the words shown here are taken from passages in which le corbusier, paul rand, jonathan meese and gerhard richter try to explain their work. however, the posters say nothing about the source or author. quotations sometimes leave a slight aftertaste – an aura of borrowing from the experts, a hint of riding on the author's coattails, a way of filling empty space when original thoughts fail. the words themselves are aimed at the students and teachers, challenging them to think for themselves. debate in place of footnotes; courage instead of outrage.

PERFECTION, ORDER and DISCIPLINE are communicated in large, clear letters. the series of posters suggest that they are the three prerequisites for creating good ARCHITECTURE or DESIGN. because this is not spelled out, it is a provocation, an appeal – please think for yourself! because the five words are a slap in the face to anyone who thinks that these two fields are warm, fuzzy, feel-good affairs.

faculty tour, düsseldorf university of applied sciences
event poster
2012

ktion

archit

gn

ordn

fa bella figura

viavai. the name itself conjures up the rhythm of people walking by. an image familiar from italian climes. whole landscapes arise before our inner eye, colours and shapes, the name reminds us of a familiar world and the design follows the mind-traveller into a typical local bar. the logo is created from the letters that make up the name. the shape is abstract, but familiar. it says: i am an italian bar. the colours are brown and violet, symbolizing elegance, fa bella figura. the clear, clean design effectively offsets the soft curves of the typeface: a playful, striking shape exuding nothing less than grandezza.

**viavai winebar
visual identity
stuttgart, 2004**

"what do you think of that?"

do you think it's okay for design to include disruptions, irritations or paradoxes? Take the eagle that serves as the symbol of the german bundestag, for example – is it acceptable to make it a bit on the chubby side?
i don't think things need to be slick or easy to swallow. i generally believe that everything that's obstructive, incomprehensible, irrational or subversive is better. when it comes to literature, i'll take hans henny jahnn over thomas mann any day. i actually prefer his brother heinrich mann, come to that. and the same applies to graphic design. i don't have anything against meticulous craftsmanship – quite the opposite. but that's a question for another day. otherwise i'd say yes, sometimes it's better when things are not set precisely in the middle, but slightly off centre.

alsterdorf [1]

the disruptive elements you mentioned can be deliberately planned; they help slow the process of aesthetic deterioration. you're probably familiar with our work for alsterdorf[1]. in the office we were thinking that we couldn't show it to the client because it looked really strange, ugly even. but then i realised that it might not be beautiful, but it's right and in its own way, without being slick, it works. when we presented it we said it'll take a few years to get used to, and it's now starting to grow on people. now about that eagle in the bundestag – it's really interesting that the sculptor ludwig gies, who created the plaster relief for the former plenary hall in bonn, actually built in a lot of imperfections. one shoulder is higher than the other, the feathers on the breast are not symmetrically distributed, and one of the four tail feathers isn't straight (see p. 217). later on a studio produced a "clean" fair drawing with all of the flaws taken out and the crazy thing is, at first glance you don't even notice. for the design competition we slimmed down the bird. and then, as the process continued, the owner of the copyright on the old eagle sculpture asked us to restore it to its former fat splendour, but leave out the other irregularities. to be honest, i have to say that the plump look and the crooked lines are better. the other design would have been as slick as a whistle. but we made something more subversive, something that doesn't go down as easily. the rotundity, the unwieldy shape, is also a more graphically pleasing form. so formally speaking, i think it's better. you could say that when something is unwieldy, it communicates better.

a different question: a signage system, like in a hospital, has to communicate things instantly. how would a disruptive element work here? does this type of design have room for paradoxes or incomprehension?
in a signage system for a hospital, you can write everything nice and neatly – high contrast, black and white, big letters for good readability – and position the right information in the right places. then you have zero errors, everything works, and you find the place you want to go. but i actually believe it doesn't work like that. what you get then is homogeneity of form; everything looks identical, everything is too slick. so you need to stir the pot. i think that even in cases like this, you have to bake in some disruption. disruptive elements help to

form contrasts, they send out a heads-up, they say look, here is some important information. this isn't a wall, this isn't an advertisement, this is something you need to know. we are working for a big hospital right now (see p. 184) and are doing something totally disconcerting. there are sixty, maybe eighty places you might want to go. and each one has its own pattern and colour combination. it's graphic overkill. but each visitor can look for the pattern they need and find it no matter where they are. and it works because it looks good. when you're in hospital, it's usually not for a happy reason – except for a birth, of course. and when even the signage is sombre and subdued, to keep it unobtrusive, you're left feeling completely alone. at least this way people can see that someone cared about what they were doing and that cheers them up.

you recently had an exhibition in innsbruck about, shall we say, graphic design in public spaces in innsbruck with a corresponding publication, the innsbruck alphabet. i'll cheekily assume that you didn't spend weeks in innsbruck doing research, but that you walked around the city with your radar homing in on graphic interruptions and irregularities, then documenting them. is this now a catalogue of successful public graphic design in innsbruck?
so first i'll agree that your question shows a lot of cheek. but yes, there are conventions, and the usual rule in graphic design is that you are supposed to research the subject thoroughly. however, it doesn't really strike me as necessary. we actually do very little research for our projects, and it's like you said – we went there twice, for a total for two-and-a-half days, and walked around the city together. one person took pictures and the other took notes. we also took in schlecker[2], although it really doesn't look good, but it's part of the city. some things dating from the middle ages also look bad, by the way, and are not even particularly well made. others were totally messed up, but somehow fun to look at. so we said, that's the stuff we want, make a note.

SCHLECKER [2]

we didn't work systematically; it was more like window shopping. the important question was what catches my eye? you could probably have sent out any graphic designer and they would have picked up on seventy or eighty percent of the same things. and in the end we can all agree that design not only can, but must, show some weakness – absolutely. i think it's horrible when everything is exactly right; pretentious design that suggests coherence where none actually exists. the fragile and the flawed are stronger, more robust, and more enduring.

viavai winebar • barbera d'alba 2006
denominazione di origine controllato
imbottigliato all'origine da addari
loredana • podere ruggeri corsini
monforte d'alba • italia • 375 ml
13% vol • lotto b1102

viavai winebar

wanted: communication barriers

the dealership is a drive-through sculpture. so the design of the signage system for vehicles responds by providing a guided tour. destinations appear in large black letters on white crash barriers: car wash, car park, service, sales. the familiar form of the crash barrier guides visitors to their goal. inside the building the barrier motif is echoed in different form. suspended white metal strips with black writing point to destinations; black metal strips with white writing indicate locations. the folded aluminium construction corresponds to the floorplan of the architecture. the strips are located above head height for optimum flexibility and legibility.

**car dealer pappas
signage system
salzburg, 2006**

1
2
3
4

the standard akzidenz-grotesk bold (1) is laid over the curves of an armco-style crash barrier (2). when you look at it – from any angle – the height of the letters is compressed by the curved surfaces because part of each letter lies at an angle to the eye. this makes the letters look vertically compressed. in order to restore the correct proportions, the letters were compressed horizontally by one quarter (3) and now, when they are applied to the barrier, they look just like the standard type (4).

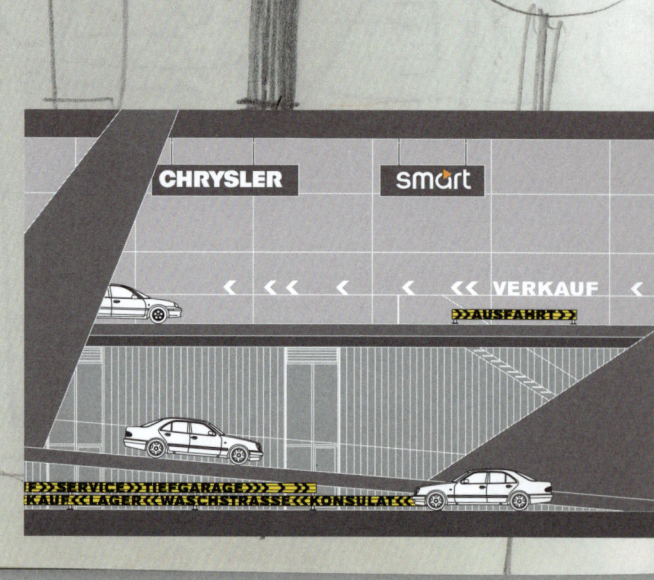

there's not much choice on the crash barrier market – you can have them with angular or curved profiles. on the angular version the lettering becomes illegible because a large portion of each letter is swallowed up by the deep corrugation at right angles to the onlooker. so the curved profile was chosen and legibility was tested with printouts attached to a roadside crash barrier.

lettering and identity

when you drive across the border, heading for france, you have to keep your eyes on the road, on the traffic, your route, the toll stations. but you still notice that something is different — the road signs have a different format and use a different font. even if you know nothing about typography, you can see that the public space has changed — the structure, colour, pictograms, arrows and lettering all add up to a different visual impression. when you drive across the border, you subconsciously perceive that the "typical" german din font has given way to an elegant, condensed, all-capital script.

![1]

travelling in the other direction, french visitors arriving in germany will note the stubborn charm of the din font with its precisely engineered lines and curves. and understand that although germans may love french food and wine, when it comes to designing fonts, machinery and vehicles, they know no mercy. solid construction will win over elegant appearance any day of the week.

as the typography and design of road signs change, so too does our perception of certain situations. signs in the usa communicate directly. "don't even think of parking here" is very direct and unambiguous, but also personal and humorous — completely different from the german bureaucratic language of dos and don'ts. instead of harping on about traffic regulations, this american sign with its verbal wagging finger tries to put itself into the shoes of the reader. what are people more likely to listen to? the sign citing chapter and verse, or an invisible third party with a sense of humour?

although many standards extend across borders in europe, when it comes to road signs there is plenty of latitude. these examples of different stop signs[1] show that every nation retains, or rather takes, its own design liberties. in keeping with regulations, the word "stop" is printed in white on a red background. so who's going to notice if we use a different font? it is a gentle form of rebellion against standards and rules, as well as an attempt to assert national identity, if only in such minor details — visible only to the expert eye — as the choice of font. subversive typography!

in small countries in particular, we always note how firmly typography is interwoven with identity. perhaps it is the desire to distinguish oneself from powerful neighbours and dominant languages? luxembourg has its own language and displays it on its road signs, but it doesn't stop there. lëtzebuergesch gets its own font, while gaelic receives a special style in ireland, and the transport heavy font used in iceland is supplemented by the special characters eth and thorn[2].

in the past, when designing signage systems countries often borrowed from other nations – greek road signs and italian number plates use a modified version of the german din font. the u.s. federal highway administration's standard alphabets for traffic control devices also serve widely as a role model. in modified form they are used in spain and in countries with an anglo-saxon heritage, such as canada and australia. on a superficial level and with no claim to scientific accuracy, this could be said to result in a typographical dominance on the part of the americans. connecting the dots between typography and politics is an audacious yet alluring mental exercise. signs reflect the spirit of the time in which they were created; political and societal upheavals are mirrored in seemingly unimportant everyday objects such as number plates. italian number plates from the 1920s – fa bella figura! – use a contemporary rectangular font that was replaced by an old-timey serif font in 1932.

of course it might be going too far to say that antiqua typefaces reflect an antiquated worldview, but it is one possible interpretation. so it follows that with the foolish duce gone, dolce tipografia made a comeback. starting in 1952, a no-nonsense, enlightened sanserif typeface could be found in the belle macchine designed by pininfarina, bertone and zagato. these sleek and purring works of art unfortunately sometimes drove into each other – italians are charming and fast drivers – which meant that the elegant road users had to be warned of this danger with a beautifully illustrated sign[3]. featuring an almost t-bone collision of two cars with comic-book-like rays indicating the "boom" of the crash, this sign is a belcanto of a road accident.

this small selection of examples shows that the need for distinctiveness, identity and regional independence is so great that it even manifests itself in seemingly insignificant things like road signs. the all-encompassing mantel of standardisation may save us from confusion and help us get our bearings fast in foreign countries, but it's the idiosyncratic details such as special characters, dialects, illustrative speech and communicative illustrations that help us – in a mosaic-like but clear-cut way – to answer the question "where am i?"

kunst = böse / design = lieb
(art = nasty / design = nice)

is art nasty? is design always nice? isn't nasty a nice word? do viewers like nasty typography better than a nicely-behaved typeface? are these questions just too black-and-white? the poster is an invitation to a lecture on the difference between art and design – and an invitation to make up your own mind. with a typeface so badly distorted that nasty becomes nice again, a vice becomes a virtue in the viewer's eye.

72h without art
exhibition poster
mannheim, 2012

KUNST=BÖSE
DESIGN=LIEB

72h Ohne Kunst Ausstellung
Hochschule Mannheim, Fakultät für Gestaltung
Projekt- und Abschlussarbeiten 2012

Ausstellungseröffnung: 14.6.2012, 19.00 Uhr
Mannheimer Kunstverein, Augustaanlage 58
Vernissagevortrag: Andreas Uebele

Sonntag
03.08.2014

16.30 Uhr

Finnisage
und Kuratorenführung

zur Ausstellung

„Geste,"

figures of speech

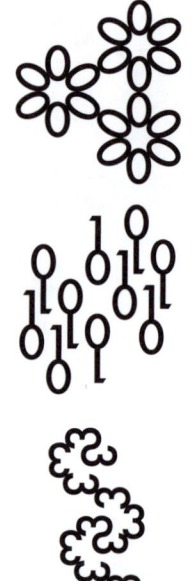

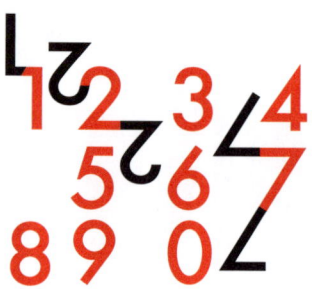

nineteen storeys, and nineteen times the same story: the same door, the same wall, the same floor. the only unmistakable element is the graphic wall-covering. the figures that make up the number of each floor are combined in graphic patterns that decorate the curving walls. they tell me: i'm at the right level.

paul renner's futura typeface is a geometric design. the figures have straight ends and can be readily combined to form patterns.

landesbank baden-württemberg, pariser platz
level designation
stuttgart, 2005

Ebene 5

Ebene 17

red-brown, caput mortuum, oxblood: walls painted in these dark tones convey a protective sense of security. red-brown is a rich colour. too much brown makes it dull, but if the red dominates the colour loses that special something. the beauty is in the fuzziness: the charm of this colour is the oscillation between warm brown and aggressive red, the wavering between loud and soft, the balance between alert and weary. that the name caput mortuum means "dead head" — reminiscent of the bloodstains after a beheading — is a striking image: a sudden flashback to archaic times.

does your training as an architect influence your design work?

acop, bem, far, gfa, nia, gea, sow, igcc, ffl, eer ... – as an architect you learn to think in structural terms.

how do I fall in love with my new corporate design?

ask klaus!
ask klaus!
ask klaus!
ask klaus!
ask klaus!
ask klaus!
ask klaus!

the corporate design's 25 different questions illuminate the diverse aspects of coaching and reflect the coach's working method. the "ask klaus" logo changes to adapt to the typeface in which the question is set. this adaptable visual identity references the fact that coaching is a living, changing process. the questions appear across a range of applications, describing situations that might make it necessary to approach a coach.

when people ask "what do you do?", the answer "communications designer" generally provokes a look of polite confusion on the questioner's face. adding in a swift footnote – "graphic design" – can help to prevent the small talk crashing to an abrupt end. other professions face the same problem: what does a gastroenterologist do? or a hermeneutist? but do we really want to know the details? anyway, in this particular case your resident communications designer didn't quite know how to manage the exuberant multifacetedness of one client's working life. how could his wide-ranging work as a coach be communicated in a brand? so reflecting this uncertainty, the corporate design asks questions. this is a brand without logos and emblems, but with questions galore – "how can i deal with uncertainty?" or "how can i embrace diversity?": small talk that communicates effectively, ideally leaving no questions unanswered.

ask klaus!
visual identity
stuttgart, 2015

feedback?

how can I cope with frustration?

ask klaus!

Klaus Haasis, Dipl.-Ing. Dipl.-Journ.
Personcentered Counsellor GwG
Systemic Coach DBVC

Rebhalde 7, 70191 Stuttgart, Germany
+49 170 63 13 193, ask@klaushaasis.de
www.klaushaasis.de

- how can I overcome resistance to change in my organization?
- how can I develop a new vision?
- how can I unlock my creative potential?
- how can I boost productivity in my team?
- how can I engage people with my ideas?
- how can I cope with the unknown.
- how can I become more solution-focused?
- how can I optimize my entrepreneurial performance?
- how do I introduce new ideas in my organization?
- how can I foster an ongoing innovation process?
- how can I improve teamwork and collaboration?
- how can I be agile when my organization is not?
- how can I be more productive?
- how can I create an appropriate context for change?
- how can I get more creative confidence?
- how can I provide feedback?
- how can I cope with failure?
- how can I improve my delegation skills?
- how can I strengthen team commitment?
- how can I balance my business and personal life?
- how can I reconcile with my organization?
- how can I network more effectively?
- how can I embrace diversity?
- how do I become more serene and mindful?
- how can I deal with uncertainty?

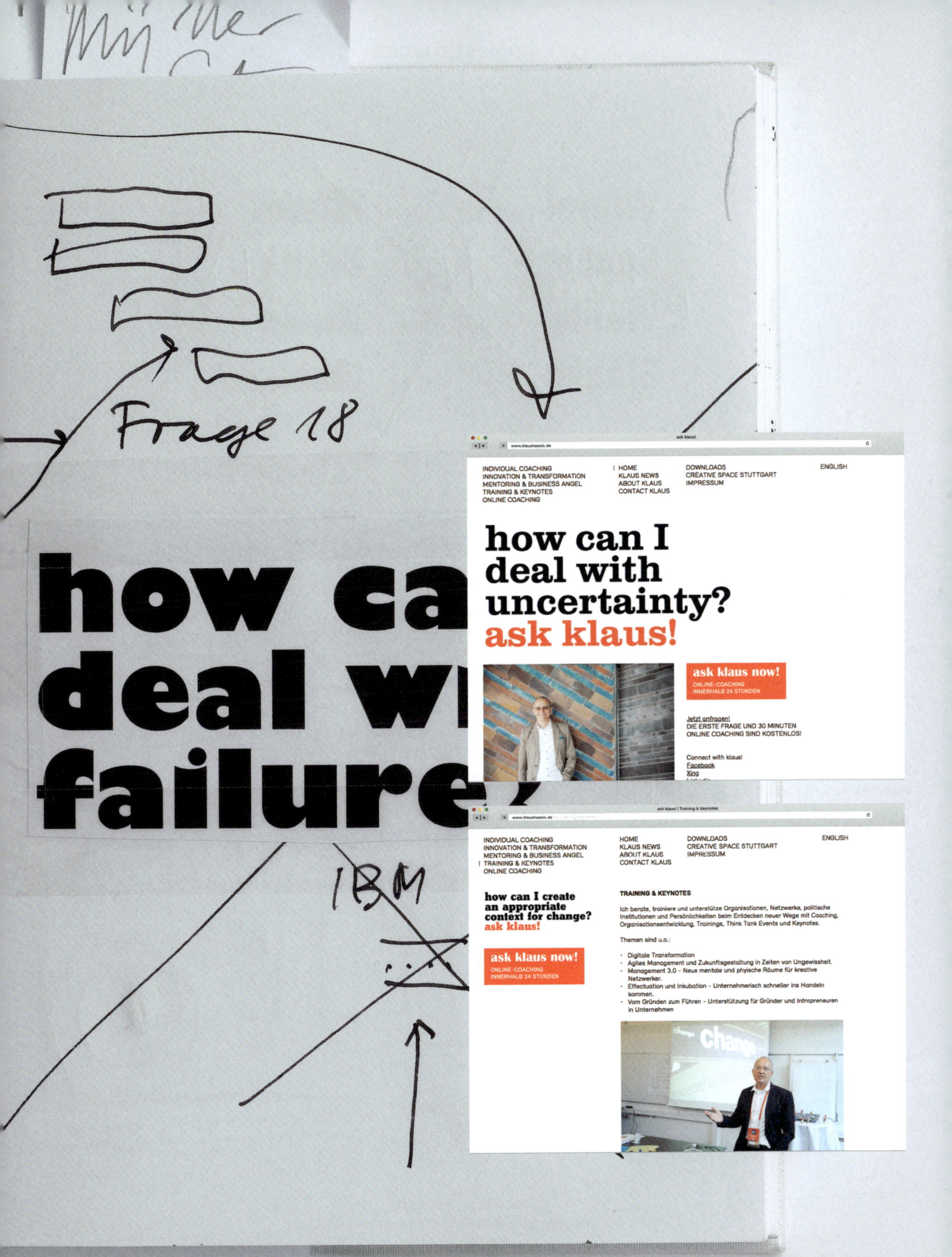

Frage 18

how can I deal with failure?

IBM

how can I deal with uncertainty?
ask klaus!

ask klaus now!
ONLINE-COACHING
INNERHALB 24 STUNDEN

Jetzt anfragen!
DIE ERSTE FRAGE UND 30 MINUTEN
ONLINE COACHING SIND KOSTENLOS!

Connect with klaus!
Facebook
Xing

INDIVIDUAL COACHING | HOME | DOWNLOADS | ENGLISH
INNOVATION & TRANSFORMATION | KLAUS NEWS | CREATIVE SPACE STUTTGART
MENTORING & BUSINESS ANGEL | ABOUT KLAUS | IMPRESSUM
TRAINING & KEYNOTES | CONTACT KLAUS
ONLINE COACHING

how can I create an appropriate context for change?
ask klaus!

ask klaus now!
ONLINE-COACHING
INNERHALB 24 STUNDEN

TRAINING & KEYNOTES

Ich berate, trainiere und unterstütze Organisationen, Netzwerke, politische Institutionen und Persönlichkeiten beim Entdecken neuer Wege mit Coaching, Organisationsentwicklung, Trainings, Think Tank Events und Keynotes.

Themen sind u.a.:
- Digitale Transformation
- Agiles Management und Zukunftsgestaltung in Zeiten von Ungewissheit.
- Management 3.0 - Neue mentale und physische Räume für kreative Netzwerker.
- Effectuation und Inkubation - Unternehmerisch schneller ins Handeln kommen.
- Vom Gründen zum Führen - Unterstützung für Gründer und Intrapreneuren in Unternehmen

linguistic looks

the system is adapted to suit a variety of applications, using different registers and volumes – a spectrum of measures from a whisper to a shout. all are feasible, and together they create a versatile toolkit for responding to the needs of the various spaces and rooms. the design of the furniture – reception desk, waiting areas and outdoor seating – follows the idea of the visible language, with individual words rendered in three dimensions. the x-height and ascenders of the letters form surfaces that can be used as seats or storage space as needed.

language is the shaping force. as ludwig wittgenstein said in his tractatus logico-philosophicus, "man possesses the capacity for constructing languages in which every sense can be expressed, without having an idea how and what each word means." words provide orientation and direction. the design of the interior and the wayfinding system draws upon language without subjecting it to inflationary use. language is given a visible graphic form – two- and three-dimensional translations of goethe's poetry – which resists erosion as the eye passes over it and is a pleasure to re-encounter every day.

goethe institute
structural corporate design, not realised
berlin, 2009

LINKS
KLASSENR
10 UND 11
TOILETTEN
MULTIME

СЛЕВА
КЛАССНЫ
ПОМЕЩЕН
10 И 11
ТУАЛЕТЫ
МУЛЬТИМ
ПОМЕЩЕН

manfred schmalriede

the interaction between environment and system is essentially based
on correspondences.

jórunn ragnarsdóttir
natural beauty and artificial beauty

in a barren landscape the question of beauty does not arise: here creation cannot be questioned, it simply is. it's very different with the things we make. every act of design can be regarded as a small-scale process of creation. here, as with comparable creative acts in music, painting or poetry, the technical aspect merges with a model for explaining our existence. this rarely succeeds as it calls for genuine expertise.

the three-dimensional communications concept responds to the diverse textures of the spaces with black-and-white furniture and graphic designs, referencing literature in a striking and succinct way. here, in black and white, is writing: the process of language becoming form. this narrative dimension is supported by a sparing use of colour on walls in spaces where people spend only short periods of time – for example the conference rooms, reception, foyer, cloakroom. coloured floors and carpets are used for rooms where people stay for longer, such as classrooms.

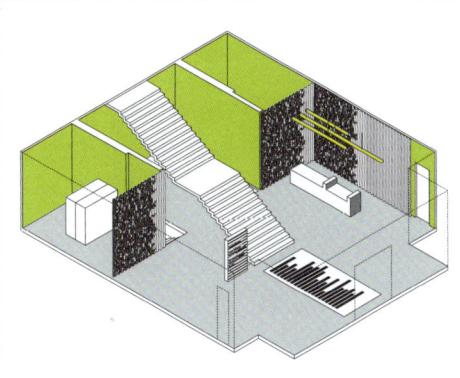

questions

which is the draft that's worth finishing? which typeface is appropriate? does it need colour? what does this poster show? and what's the onlooker supposed to think? initially the question as to what's "in the box" and/or what the poster shows remains unanswered. it's a surprise for the audience as well as for the guest designer, who's been invited to the "out of the box" series of events to talk ad hoc about objects that, at first sight, may have nothing to do with design. but isn't design omnipresent? the poster shows a collection of puzzling items. look closer, though, and you'll see that they are drafts, visualising the design process of the poster itself. that clears up the mystery: everything is possible. a draft can be good or bad, but design needs this element of mystery if it's to be surprising.

as so often in life, serendipity has a key part to play, a part that can benefit the designer. a casual glance at the screen where all the different versions of a draft are on show can be a gift, if you accept it. because then you not only see an image of the various options that can readily be generated with the help of your computer, but also an overall picture with a beauty of its own.

**out of the box
event poster
hanover, 2013**

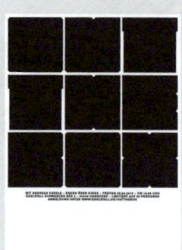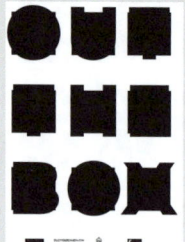

  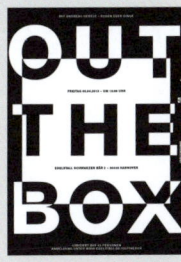 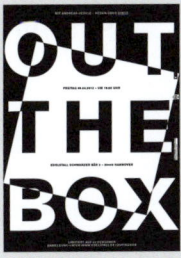  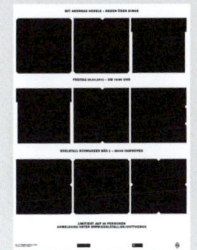
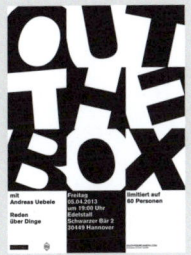 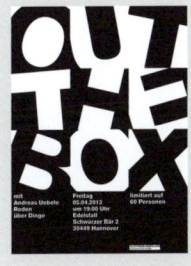    

  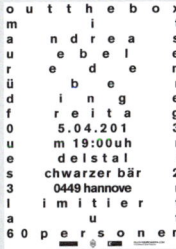 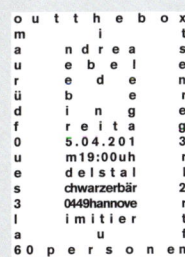  
   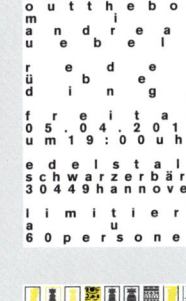 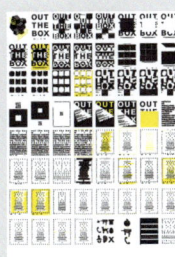 
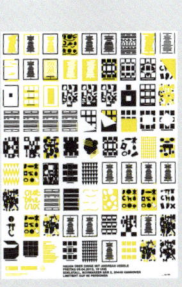 

contemporary witnesses

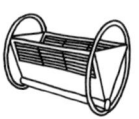

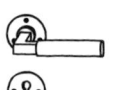

the term 'visual identity' captures the core of the matter very neatly: it's all about conveying – or rather translating – by graphic means the essence of a company or in this case a major museum and its collections. but what exactly makes up that essence? is it the principal actors? the architecture? the heritage? the location? the exhibits? in all probability it is a blend of all these factors. but the core of the whole thing – the identity per se – is the idea on which bauhaus was founded. this, we recall, is where the originals took shape that are etched on our cultural consciousness as "bauhaus". these iconic items, like the lamp, the chair, the door handle, were all designed and manufactured in weimar. the new design concept was manifested in architecture, in furniture and in a multitude of objects. clearly, then, these items don't just bear witness to the bauhaus style and philosophy: as it took shape in weimar, they actually form a key part of its visual identity. these contemporary witnesses are drawn by hand to emphasise the craftsmanship they embody; craftsmanship that was assigned such high priority in the bauhaus ethos. in this corporate design, it is the objects and their creators that take centre stage.

the shape of the wordmark is a tribute to the logo of the klassik stiftung weimar and serves as a visual reminder of its relationship to the bauhaus. the logo is set in neuzeit grotesk, a typeface designed by wilhelm pischner in 1930 just after the weimar bauhaus period. it is structured around circle, triangle and square and is an attractive reminder of its roots in – and the stories told about – weimar. the use of lowercase letters in the logo creates balanced, equally high and calmly flowing ribbons of typography. the wordmark is always shown in combination with an illustration, although their relative sizes can vary depending on how and where they are being used.

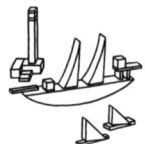

bauhaus museum weimar
visual identity
2015

**bauhaus
museum
weimar**

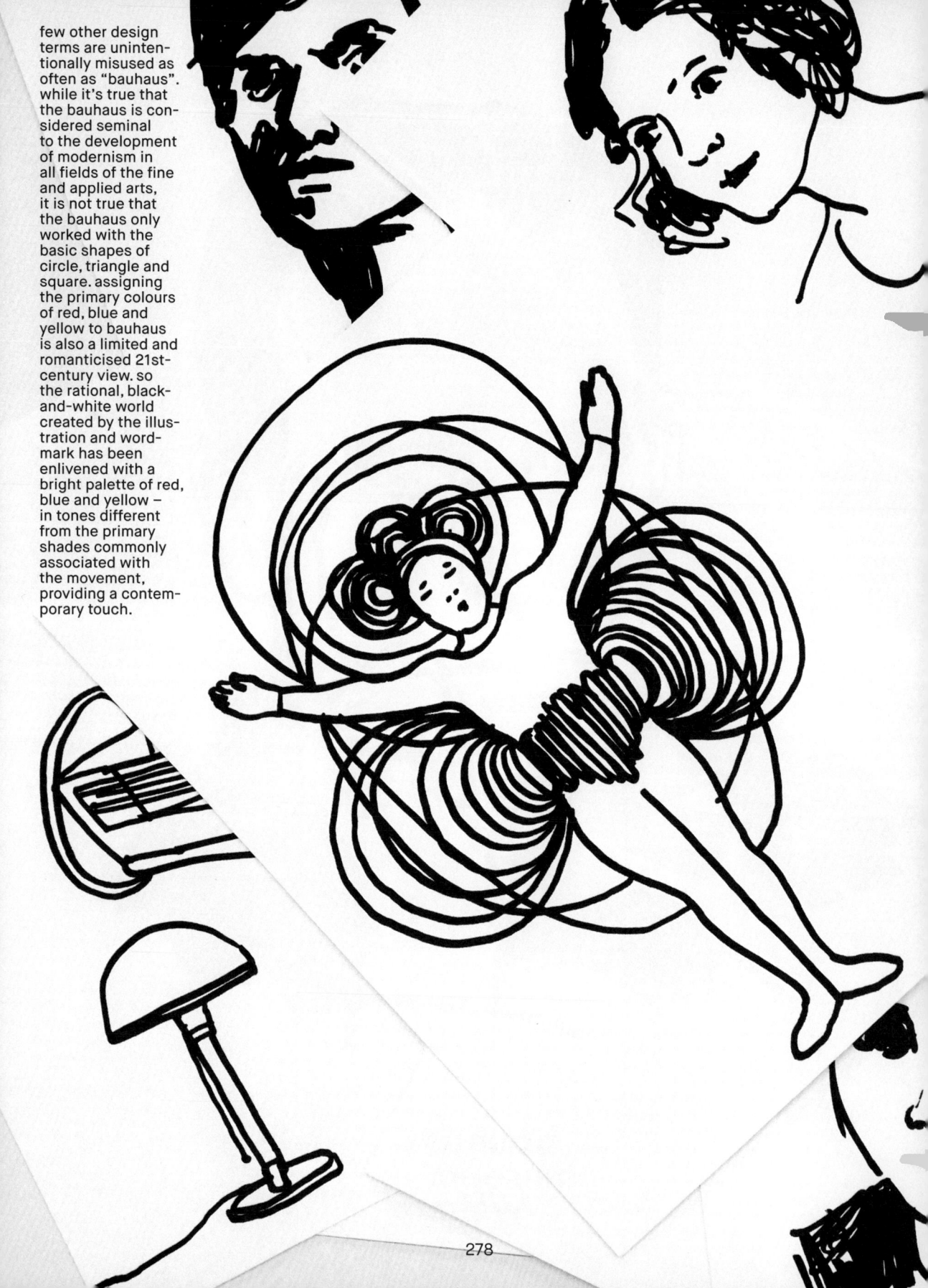

few other design terms are unintentionally misused as often as "bauhaus". while it's true that the bauhaus is considered seminal to the development of modernism in all fields of the fine and applied arts, it is not true that the bauhaus only worked with the basic shapes of circle, triangle and square. assigning the primary colours of red, blue and yellow to bauhaus is also a limited and romanticised 21st-century view. so the rational, black-and-white world created by the illustration and wordmark has been enlivened with a bright palette of red, blue and yellow – in tones different from the primary shades commonly associated with the movement, providing a contemporary touch.

on ashtrays, or the difference between design and art

art is nasty. no one needs art. art is for bored, sated, upright citizens. they pay their taxes and on sundays they wander around state-subsidised art museums. art is collected by law offices and banks. they bask in the acquired reflection of their good taste – or put on a public display of patronage that promises them absolution for profits perhaps not always earned with a clear conscience. people need toilet paper, washing-up liquid and nutella. they don't need art.

if a city has the good fortune to host an art museum designed by a star architect, it can expect a significant jump in tourist numbers. instead of investing in the sort of serious urban planning that would improve the lives of local residents, the holders of the public purse pour money into an endless series of big-ticket shows that are guaranteed to draw the crowds – monet, blaue reiter, and drawings by rembrandt and his contemporaries (because a solo show by rembrandt would overtax the budget). art satisfies our longing for inefficiency and nonconformity in a world where all of our thoughts and actions are shaped by a kind of capitalistic, dictatorial self-exploitation that is all well and good for those who have the chance to partake in it. because the alternative is to be left sad and depressed as we realize we would have much preferred to be part of the game than to stand on the sidelines, entirely unexploited.

dabbling in art derives from a romantic longing for emotion and expression. pictures are hung on the wall to add value. ceos like to have their portraits taken sitting at a desk; in the background, modern art. in bygone days company directors and captains of industry were photographed pen in hand. now these corporate heroes simply relax and stare into the camera. why not show them surrounded by elegant objects or sophisticated devices? by good design, in other words? why not a desk lamp by richard sapper as a display of edgy (that is, good) taste – although perhaps that's not fair on this well-designed lamp? why don't all these powerful people have themselves depicted with a walter zeischegg ashtray on their desks? or, in the interests of political correctness, why not an ashtray by philippe starck[1]? at least its form doesn't betray its function. it looks less like an ashtray and more like a piece of abstract sculpture. and an ashtray disguised as art would turn the tables, making for an artistically correct piece of provocation.

1

this ashtray forms a counterpoint to the proper, well-designed ashtray by walter zeischegg[2] mentioned above, which always keeps the cigarette positioned in the hollow where it belongs. this is no accident, but the will of the designer. the design of his ashtray borrows from the mathematical principle of the sine wave. its form is defined by these curves, which aren't just attractive, but effortlessly produce a beautifully choreographed movement when several ashtrays are stacked. Place a cigarette on the slanted surface of the ashtray by phillipe starck, by contrast, and it will invariably roll into the open slit, or else end up with the mouth-end on the ashy ledge, which is slightly disgusting. and when you're ready to pick it back up, you have to be careful where you grasp it, because otherwise the slender object of desire will simply roll away. you can't clean the thing either, because although its jumbo-jet-like wing can be lifted to let the ash tip out, it actually tips over the hand that is holding the flap open. but it is a thing of beauty; it is an enchanted, icy block standing there on your desk.

so in design, wrong can also be right in certain cases — such as this one. and since our train of thought has been diverted to these ashtrays, maybe this somewhat esoteric example is a good way to explain something that frequently leads to misunderstandings: the difference between art and design. people who feel that art is their calling but are rejected by the academy often go ahead and study design, which, after all, is much the same thing — colours and all that. and this is exactly how we end up with trained designers who don't understand or haven't been told that art and design have absolutely nothing to do with each other — and yet still have something in common. but this can only be understood once people have grasped what design really is.

the difference between art and design can best be explained in the contrast between good and bad design — the distinction between artisanal kitsch and intelligent composition. artisanal kitsch can be found both in design and in art. and maybe these ashtrays can be used to illustrate the dichotomy.

bad design has something to do with the desire to mix design and art. design is an objective and conceptually coherent approach to fabricating objects that people can use. design applies logical criteria. art doesn't have to do any of this, although it would be the place of the artist to deny the idea that the creation of art is bound up in emotion.

the zeischegg ashtray is an example of good design and is familiar to everyone. it has mass appeal because it's cheap, which is one criterion for good design — it's supposed to be affordable, because the more buyers who can afford good design, the better. it's also ecologically correct, because the few drops of petroleum that are needed for its manufacture are invested in a long-lasting product. this object is design brought to perfection. the material is made of heat- and age-resistant melamine and is easy to clean — warm water, a quick wipe with a cloth and you're done. it is functional and attractive, timeless and contemporary, shatterproof and light. its colours harmonise with any and all surroundings. it is modest and unassuming. it is not art, but product design. zeischegg taught at the ulm school of design, and what was invented and conceived there almost 60 years ago still applies today. and is often better than many of the modern things thought up by designers who seem to have confused themselves with artists.

being an artist is sexy. but without wanting to be unsexy, designers also shouldn't try to be artists or harbour delusions of grandeur. graphic designers, for instance, have a job that consists of positioning and repositioning a bunch of letters. and if they want to play above the middle leagues, they also need to use their heads. that's it. they shouldn't try to elevate or overinflate their work through artistic pretentions. good craftsmanship is an art in itself, in the sense of well-honed skills and a quality product. and this applies to both ashtrays. thirty years passed between their creations: zeischegg's cute curves date to 1967; starck's winged wonder to 1996.

the zeischegg ashtray can still be bought today and, at 50, isn't showing its age. the starck ashtray is 21 years old and also doesn't look outdated, but is no longer in the shops.

when you see the ashtray by philippe starck on a table, clearly it is (almost) a work of art. it has no rationally comprehensible design vocabulary, no logical lines, no functional aspects. the selection of the material was solely down to the appeal of the polished aluminium with its matte shimmer. by all other criteria the choice seems slightly frivolous, because although aluminium is easy to recycle, it is also very energy-intensive, and therefore expensive, to produce. this concern has nothing to do with ecology, but with good design, which demands the selection of a suitable material that is as good for the environment as possible. the polish, which shimmered so seductively at the time of purchase, has become increasingly matte over the years. the material has been discoloured by wear and tear and corrosion. the ash sticks stubbornly to the surface. but it is beautiful, and it has its justification. the irrational, emotional and narrative moment, the nonchalance of its form, stand in star(c)k contrast to the german desire for durability and the teutonic obsession with cleanliness. it is good that there are objects that call the perfection of things into question!

beauty can certainly be explained, like with the zeischegg ashtray. because, as nature teaches us, the right form is always beautiful. this french, unnatural, artificial and artistic object, on the other hand, when viewed through the functional lens of the ulm school, is wrong, wrong, wrong. but it is still possible to find it beautiful, because it questions the ideas of right and wrong and illustrates how an attractive object enriches our lives.

is this art? no, definitely not. it is consummate product design. the problem is that while there are objective logical grounds for this conclusion in the case of zeischegg, there may also be in the case of starck but they lead to misunderstandings. because in the world of design, there are far too many ashtrays like this. just not as beautiful as the one by philippe starck.

2

now let's add a third ashtray to the mix. it's the arty sort, the kind you find in better museum shops. designed in 1912 by vlatislav hofman[3]. it belongs to the czech cubist movement. this ashtray was purchased because it is beautiful. but in contrast to its two predecessors, it doesn't come anywhere near being a design object. it is a touch on the nasty side, because it fills up fast and you have to get up to empty it after a single cigarette. it is an ornament that sits there and collects dust. hofman applied the cubist repertoire of shapes and forms to furniture and objects, taking formal language from the world of art and forcefully imposing it onto ordinary household items. this doesn't usually work — in the best case you end up with handicrafts. this has nothing to do with art and nothing to do with design, either. this ashtray is a charming object, nothing more. art doesn't work, art is nasty. design has to work, design is nice.

quite simply, the majority of design objects are unspeakably nice and meaningless. well-intentioned stuff — graphics, products, fashion — that has been shuffled back and forth. in communications design, this means hapless layouts of lines, letters and spaces, clunky texts, silly and ingratiating language, careless spacing, incorrect indentation, english-style quotation marks instead of the correct german or french, and attractive letters made ugly by the typesetting. it means a dreary attempt to knuckle under to business and softly and gently meet the expectations of marketing. "we can't afford to lose the contract, and after all, we're just a service provider." saying no, my dear enablers, is also a service – but it requires taking a stance.

3

the creative economy (an idiotic name, and therefore fitting) produces well-intentioned nonsense to the tune of 12 billion euros each year. design competitions reward submissions that directly translate rather than transcend the brief – with no visual message, no surprises, no narrative, no sense of humour. and this direct translation is executed in cheap graphics. ghastly, but true. and there's no sign of improvement. or is there? the situation could be saved if all design students and teachers would pay regular visits to the mannheim art association – and while they are at it, to the mannheim art museum as well. and not just in mannheim, but also in mindelheim and mühlheim.

as a designer, you have to learn to see. you have to learn to observe. you have to learn to look very closely, to be perceptive and (discerningly) receptive. art teaches us to do this. it is not a supermarket where we go in and help ourselves to whatever we want. it is more like an opticians. you go in and get your glasses, and afterwards you can see clearly and wonder how you could have stood looking at the world without them for so long. because without nasty old art, design is just plain nice – and how dull is that?

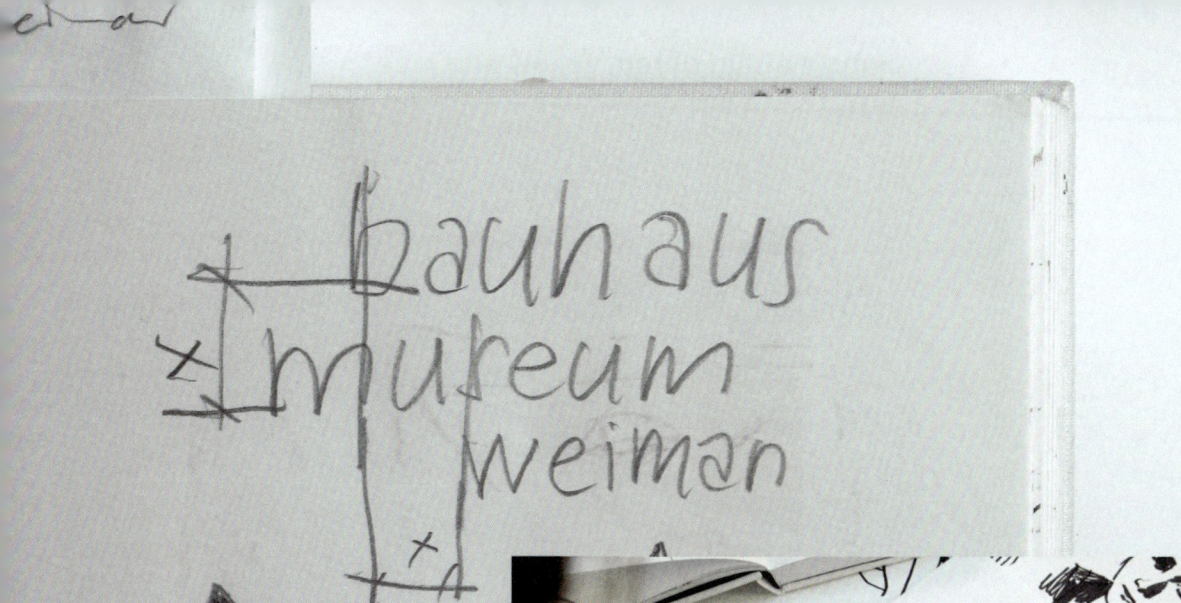

"who's afraid of red, yellow and blue"

where to, and where next? visitors to the new stuttgart region chamber of commerce and industry building are welcomed and guided to their destination by cheerful bands of colour. even if their route leads up a hidden staircase, visitors can tell at once where they are heading: from the two-storey foyer they can already see the colourful signs on the floor above. clear information is presented on multi-coloured wallpaper – the layered stripes blending in naturally with the architecture. at each new wayfinding point the pattern of bright colours is configured differently, reflecting and representing the diversity of the stuttgart region.

stuttgart region chamber of commerce and industry
signage system
2014

EBENE 5

→ KONFERENZRAUM 506
← PRÄSIDENT
HAUPTGESCHÄFTSFÜHRUNG

**a term for the lesikon
"design depth"**

depth in design is achieved by deep diving – immersing yourself in the subject and the work. the visible surface invariably expresses a deeper form, which is manifested in the design. if it's right, then it's beautiful.

does the craving for individuality generate ever more diversity and complexity we then have to navigate? are individualisation and functionalism mutually obstructive?

now and then
time and again
out of the question
no way
here and there

a design is a vessel into which the most disparate aspirations are poured. if they're conflicted they can produce a pretty murky mixture. the designer's task is to clarify, ensuring that the various ingredients relate to each other in the right proportions and are properly blended. good design is a clear solution and has an internal logic. it is the manifest result of weighing up all the ingredients. if something works well, if, for example it's easy to grasp or understand, it's beautiful. yet an object can also be beautiful if it's not easy to grasp but compels the viewer to take a closer look. in the design for the chamber of commerce and industry, we took care to ensure that all the different elements were in harmony. not just beauty and functionality, but beauty and accessibility and ease of maintenance and readability and functional efficiency and clarity.

the colourful stripes not only communicate the region's diversity but also help to send a strong, clear signal to visitors, one that's visible from afar: look, it's this way! or: here's some information for you. these signage elements were developed to work over large distances, confirming destinations or marking the places where different routes intersect. their design stands out against the calm structural background. they also provide a striking feature that people with visual impairments can identify – one they can easily distinguish from other parts of the building. the main font size used is much larger than normal, with a cap height of 45 mm, which provides good readability for the visually impaired. the letters are set in white on black, without any blend effects, ensuring optimum contrast, which also supports readability. a few destinations are signalled with especially large type – over half a meter high, which even visually impaired visitors can read comfortably from a distance.

EBENE 2

KONFERENZRAUM 202–252
WOLKE BLAU

monsters for little monsters

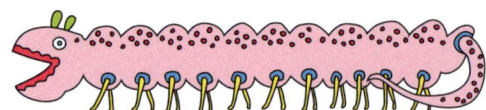

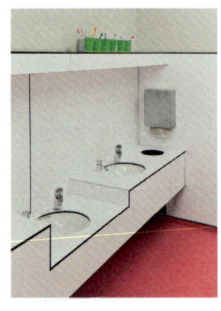

a space for children. the pure white fixtures are outlined by an orthogonal network of lines formed by their bevelled black edges, designed to guard against scuff marks. such concessions to rationality are embedded in colourful spaces that are bright, but not garish. nuances of colour give each room a unique look, and each is marked with its very own imaginary friend that helps the children find the right group. these fantastic creatures also guide grown-ups through the different storeys and hallways of the day-care centre to reunite them with their own little monsters – oh, sorry – children.

a signage system can take on many different forms. instead of putting up the usual sign reading "preschool" or "school", the façade design says what the building is all about. the utilitarian annex to the gründerzeit mansion was "camouflaged" by painting it with black-and-white geometric patterns. the building blends in and sends out a clear signal – this way!

silcher school, heidenheim
signage system
2012

of easily readable fonts and a lift for the leaning tower of pisa

… this is a beautiful, readable font …". stop, stop right there. it's a phrase we often read, one — admittedly — this author has also been known to use. guidelines for font readability (or legibility****) are seriously misguided. we know virtually nothing about it, and what we do know is outdated, wrong and incomplete — or simply trotted out parrot-fashion, without verification.

we know what makes a font beautiful: it has to please us. the factors that produce this effect are soft ones. we also think we know what makes a font readable. these factors or attributes are hard: open counters, large x-heights, etc. yet if we examine the issue of readability in detail, we realise that even this is nonsense. after all there are arabic fonts that are perfectly legible. but if we're unfamiliar with arabic then we're going to find arabic fonts hard to read. some people, similarly, find helvetica less readable if they're used to times. this is where the whole business of readability rules falls down. because if we're thinking about legibility and wanting to test it, we need first of all to know about our test subjects' habits and experiences. a beautifully decorated handwritten letter from a loved one may be illegible scrawl, but the happy recipient will take infinite pains to decipher it. there are many factors behind font legibility. the reader's attitude (bliss! letter from loved one!) is just one of them.

when our office was working on the corporate design for the german parliament, we were asked by disability representatives to make our designs disability-friendly, a politically and socially justified and just desire, perhaps, but one we initially resisted, because what interested us was what really makes a design accessible. to get to the heart of the matter we spoke with eye specialists at berlin's charité hospital and with the dbsv, germany's umbrella organisation for visual impairment support charities. they explained to us that serif fonts are less easily readable for visually impaired readers than sanserifs — and that antiqua fonts should be avoided altogether as a result. given that we had won the competition with a serif font and that the assignment was nearing completion, it seemed to us impossible to comply with this requirement without potentially undermining two years' work.

we responded to the objection to using serif fonts with a simple test: we presented the dbsv with sample texts, including one in the bauhaus typeface — a sanserif font, but one that's clearly difficult to read — and were able to refute the assertion that sanserif fonts are always readable and serif fonts are always difficult to read, which featured on the organisation's website as a recommendation — a recommendation it subsequently withdrew.

at a later meeting it was clearly demonstrated to me — by giving me glasses that simulate a visual impairment — that serifs do indeed make things more difficult for the visually impaired. the joint solution we ultimately reached was that a corporate design needs to assist those with disabilities in other ways.

after all, planning an entire corporate design (or wayfinding system) exclusively on disability-friendly grounds brings with it massive creative limitations which — in our view — are unacceptable.

this attitude was shared by the individuals involved, some of whom themselves have a visual impairment.

a sanserif font was therefore off the agenda. which left the question of which serif font would be better: times, which had been used previously, or melior, which we were proposing. a meeting was arranged with a visually impaired german parliament employee to test our new design. we had prepared several printouts: a short piece of body copy in 11 pt melior and another in 11 pt times. the visually impaired employee was to say which typeface he found easier to read. our view was that the melior should be equally readable, or even – based on the criteria mentioned above (open counters, x-height) – easier to read. the first text we gave him to read was set in the previous typeface, the one he was familiar with (times); after this came the text set in the new house font (melior). just as we suspected might happen, he said that the times was much easier for him to read and that the new font gave him real difficulties. there was a lot at stake, of course: many people with decision-making powers were present. and yet in the tension of the moment i'd made a mistake – i'd unintentionally mixed up the two printouts. the story ended happily for us: the new font was accepted. we find it easy to read what we're used to reading; and even easier to read what we're motivated to read.

this little story shows how difficult it is to assess typeface readability objectively and rigorously. yet one aspect that's inadequately considered in all these investigations, in my view, is aesthetic quality. it may sound cynical, but it's hard to imagine the leaning tower of pisa being fitted with a disability-friendly lift. as a designer i allow myself the freedom to advocate that sensible and justified accessibility measures on behalf of those with disabilities are to be offset against aesthetic viewpoints, which in our view are equally justified.

calls for supposedly more easily readable fonts are doubtless justified. yet one thing above all remains irrefutable: if something looks good we'll be more likely to read it.

kramrettel

this lettermark illustrates how discovering the world is something we can always do from different angles: we can view things from above or from below, from the left or from the right. the logo is a symbol, referencing the playful way children get to grips with life, exploring it in order to understand it better. the children and grown-ups alike will enjoy solving this little puzzle. the apparent disorder of the letters conjures up a sense of lively interaction – and creates a memorable and distinctive brand.

**kinderwelt
visual identity
heidenheim, 2012**

Kinderwelt

KIN
DER WE
LT

KINDERWELT

all squared away

this system guides the visitor through the company at two levels, providing both physical wayfinding and an introduction to the brand. both tasks are handled by a square module that varies in size, colour and angle, depending on its role. bright red squares bear short sweet messages: upholstery; leather inspection; future. these signs accompany visitors as they enter the brand world, passing through the various buildings dating from different centuries. these red signs made of solid aluminium and set at 20 degrees to the vertical point to the brand's hallmark blend of high-tech production and traditional craftsmanship. they also pose little red riddles along the path through the brand world. the solutions to these riddles are close at hand, printed on large reflective surfaces. these texts on high-gloss aluminium panels explain, for example, how a machine works or the importance of the human hand, eye and mind in inspecting the quality of the leather.

test sequences illustrating potential angles at which the squares could be set. the individual angles should be easy to distinguish, but retain their identity as part of a series.

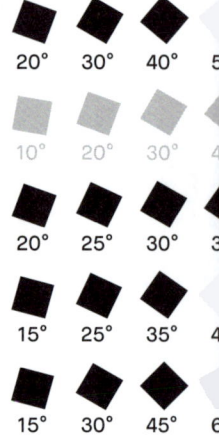

walter knoll
signage system, brand world
herrenberg 2007

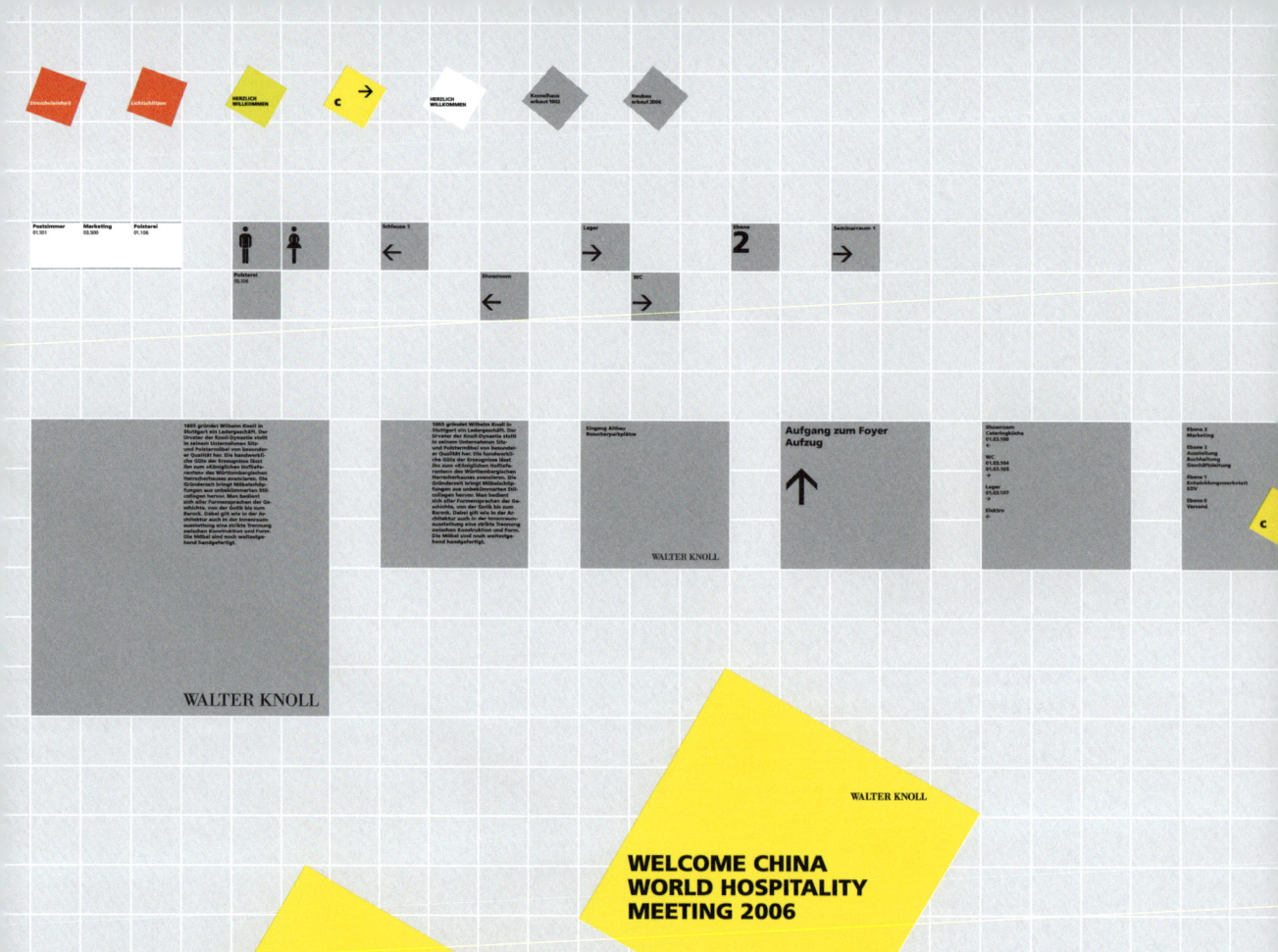

**WELCOME CHINA
WORLD HOSPITALITY
MEETING 2006**

**WILLKOMMEN
WELCOME
BIENVENUE**

the signs pointing the way through the buildings take the form of white type on aluminium plates of different sizes, polished to a high gloss. locational and directional signs appear large and small; the squares follow a matrix structure and figure in different combinations in line with their architectural location. the cool sheen of the polished metal reflects the discreet understatement of the brand. the precision finish of the surface communicates the company's technical expertise.

what mistakes or "traps" should a young designer avoid when working on an identity system?

do not execute the exact brief of the client. as a designer you need distance. don't research too much, it makes you prejudiced.

how do you define intuition?

in the design process there are different kinds of intuition. hardly ever do you get the bolt-from-the-blue kind of idea – "that's how we could do it!" – and even when you do it's not at the start of the design process. and even then this "having an idea", this visitation by the muse, only happens after some pleading: please please come! but what's an idea anyway? aren't these ideas often accidents waiting to happen? fragile, superficial solutions, because they haven't undergone the process of evaluation? visually these "creative ideas" very quickly wear thin, they are pitiful, insubstantial work – unless you roll your sleeves up and apply yourself to developing them, testing them, changing them, and then re-assessing, rejecting, or recycling them.

often intuition is like a light bulb that switches itself on after you've tried out various options and had to conclude: "this isn't working". at this point you still don't know what does work, but at least you've eliminated one option – which is helpful in itself.

intuition is listening to your inner voice, it is your feeling for artistic matters speaking to you directly – though the criteria by which it judges are eminently subject to rational explanation. this instinct or sensitivity for artistic matters is a gift. it can be trained: over time, the accumulation of multiple training experiences evolves into gut instinct.

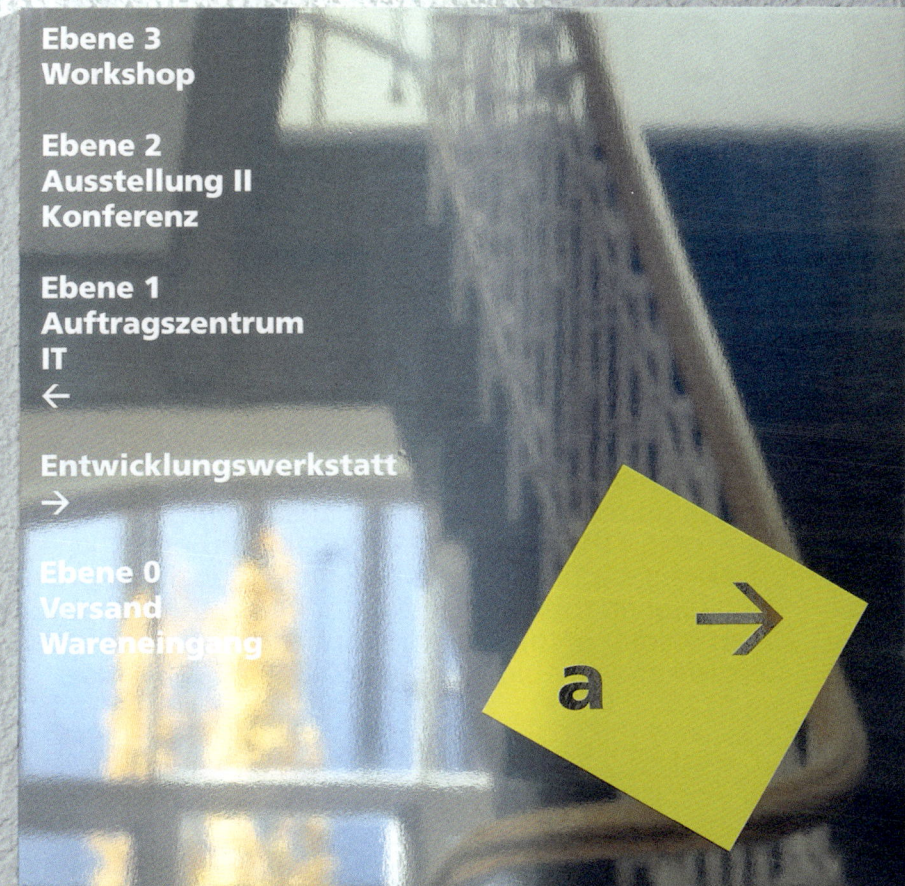

the clean design stands out against the various background surfaces, while the mirror-like material reflects the style of the architecture: bricks from the gründerzeit, wooden panels in the joiner's shop and fair-faced concrete in the latest building. in all, the system merges with its surroundings without surrendering its identity. white and yellow squares speak to the visitor. temporary signage is handled by yellow squares set at an angle of 30 degrees to the vertical. these are held in place at the correct angle by hidden magnets milled into the reverse face of the backing plate.

samba da fonte

A B C D E F G H I O K L M
N O P Q R S T U V W X Y Z

the company's name is formed from the initials of its founder, vilson hardt. typographic construction creates a lettermark that visualises the company's activity: designing and building houses. simple procedures – rotating the letters and interlacing them – have generated a striking and memorable logo. its expressive design is the balanced outcome of the constructed character of the pressura font and the cool anthracite-grey and sky-blue colour scheme.

**vilson hardt construtora e incorporadora
visual identity
curitiba, 2013**

model planning

the signs feature ornamental edging inspired by the historic architecture of the town. the ornamentation is patterned after its parapets, arches, façades and window frames.

the signage system is invisible. its forms are woven into the warp and weft of old and new, architecture and landscape, and borrow from what came before. its patterns are familiar to the town, not foreign. yverdon's trick of mounting its road signs as if they were hanging pub signs has an endearing quality. the system builds on this approach to supplement the existing signage. differently shaped signs already point the way, attached to lighting masts, road-sign fixtures and historical lamp posts. red, white, blue and yellow signs are a familiar visual element in this urban landscape. their colours signify their function: red for cycle paths, blue for the main roads. the rich variety of this graphic moment was captured and carried forward in a system which seamlessly integrates the new into the old. the graphic design of the new signs clearly marks them as a municipal initiative. the different colours and arabesques provide subtle guidance. no two signs are the same, but all are clearly part of the same visual scheme.

la ville d'yverdon-les-bains
signage system, not realised
2009

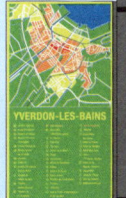

the official typeface of the town of yverdon-les-bains is the timeless and attractive neue helvetica font, which also includes a weight suitable for signage. the neue helvetica condensed 77 bold font offers good legibility without taking up too much space, optimised by slightly increasing the spacing of the characters. seven different font sizes were selected for the different sign formats. two different font sizes solve the problem of signs to destinations with names that are either very short or very long, harmonising with the existing signs to leave a suitably urbane typographical impression.

peter zizka

that making an image could be something sacrilegious is something not even bob ross could have imagined, the man whose tv show "joy of painting" democratised the concept of genius with a real sense of mission, his presentation style both mainstream-friendly and unintentionally funny; and that we in the design world have thrown out the concept of genius altogether is – in a bewildering communications universe characterised by mass participation on the one hand and autocratic exclusivism on the other – a tremendously good thing. today we can combine real and virtual labyrinths into readable content, we can shape discourses, in doing so helping to explain the world, at least in part. whether in the process we're pursuing a democratic principle or losing ourselves down blind alleys of economisation and extravagant dogmatism is determined solely and uniquely by our creative integrity. as goethe said, "all our thoughts point forwards, like flags and streamers" – and he was right.

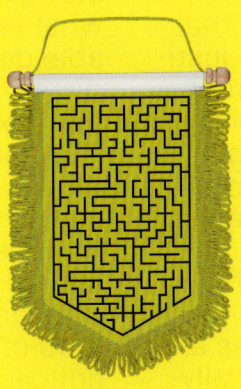

klaus klemp
typography becomes architecture and more

if you find yourself in architecture where andreas uebele's been involved, you're likely to have letters flying around your head. surely few other communications designers have realised as many signage systems in buildings as he has. and in buildings of all kinds – from museums, universities and hospitals to the german parliament, mercedes-benz, a gelatine manufacturer, a space centre, a psychiatric unit, the adidas design centre and even motorway toilets. some 40 locations in all.

none of these projects are similar and virtually none of them are subtle. but can a signage system in fact be subtle? after all, a signage system that you have to hunt for – as is often the case, sadly, in public buildings – isn't really a signage system at all. uebele is always present, in the building and on the building: on the walls, on the floor, on the ceiling, inside and outside – sometimes even with letters floating in space. which could be a nightmare scenario for architects – and yet miraculously these typographies always combine effectively with the building, be it in harmony or through contrast. the typography itself becomes architecture. which means that there's no longer any need for the kind of art that was once tacked on to buildings – justified, in the days of cold, post-war functionalism, not just in terms of subsidising the arts but in order to bring a touch of cultural warmth to those washed-concrete façades. uebele's typographies-in-space are art works, though not in the sense of "fine art" – a notion that's apparently in the process of being redefined and that often sees itself as a kind of sociologically-, psychologically- or politically-motivated investigative act. what we see with the designer andreas uebele, by contrast, is what we might call "applied visual art" – but it really won't matter to him whether it's labelled as art or as design.

andreas uebele originally studied architecture and in the 1990s worked for the behnisch & partner architecture practice – who at the time doubtless offered one of the most intelligent approaches on the "postmodernist" scene, capable of combining functional construction with a poetic sensibility. and this former architect is clearly someone who feels at home in the architectural world – he understands spaces and knows how to use them effectively.

yet typography has become his core medium. uebele, who describes himself as a self-taught designer, moves far beyond mere signage here into a world of concrete poetry. wordplay becomes typographic play, and vice versa. he has found his own very distinctive formal language that draws on art and design history, connecting both with the past and with the future. his posters have long since appeared on gallery walls and he has, as a matter of course, published numerous graphic editions – a subject he actually studied at the stuttgart academy of art and design. what we have here is a versatile, capable designer whose works always display a lightness of touch, a freedom from excess, which is notoriously hard to achieve.

"design is attitude" said the austrian-japanese typographer helmut schmid. andreas uebele stands for a design attitude that brings together – in a multitude of ways – usability and aesthetics, critical discernment and seriousness, play and pleasure, conjuring and promoting a fertile communication culture. or, as he would put it himself: "it works and it's beautiful".

the flow

an eon is an indefinite and very long period of time. the word "strom", in german, can refer to both electricity and a river – stream, in english, has the same etymological roots. it's a lovely image – electrical current flowing through time and space, like a river. a river is subject to constant change. it shapes spaces and flows through landscapes. there's the same type of metaphor in english, of course: electricity is a current, from the latin currere, to run. ever since the 18th century, electrical energy in many languages has been described in terms of flow and this dual meaning underlies the communicative concept of the e.on signage system: streams, currents flow through the different levels of the building. customers, visitors or employees may find their home town or country on one of the walls. the rivers themselves are not named but can be identified from the names of towns, descriptions of the landscape, stories and poems that appear on the glass partitions. together they form an associative space that helps with the process of psychological orientation. what river is that? talking to each other, visitors and employees might say: "i'm sitting under the loreley", or they will walk upstairs to see a colleague who works "in vienna".

the river motif that runs through the different levels is taken up again and developed in the colour concept. each level and each section of the building features from four to six shades of colour. the colour scheme flows uphill from level one to level five, and from south to north – from warmer tones to cooler shades. the double-glazed office partitions add their own notes to the symphony of colour. the brightly coloured stripes, produced by high-transparency screen printing, are applied alternately to the inside and outside of the glass. to the moving eye of the passer-by, the outcome is chords of colour.

**e.on headquarters
signage system
munich, 2014**

the colour is incorporeal, its tinted shadows paint the walls and fittings, refining and defining the space which drifts through shifting moods as the day runs its course. each room is a unique, unmistakable colour zone.

Niederrhein

Ich will dir
kein verlogenes Loblied mehr singen.
Dein geborgtes Sonnenlicht
soll mich nicht mehr blenden,
dein Reichtümer schleppender Buckel
mich nicht mehr bestechen.

Du bist weit gekommen. Du bist tief gesunken.
Du kamst von heiteren Weinhöhen
und sankst in dumpfe Niederung.
Die Dome und Burgen sind längst
entsetzt stehengeblieben.
Schwefelrauchend, rußrülpsend und ölkotzend
drängen sich Kamine, Waschtürme
und mannsdicke Rohre
an deinen betäubten Strand.

Willy Bartock

white walls are spun with a silver web, like graphic sketches of expanses of water rippled by currents, breezes and raindrops. each floor of the building is endowed with its own visible identity, aiding wayfinding.

»Ihr seid spät auf der Bahn«, sagte er, »habt Ihr Euch nicht gefürchtet, in so dunkler Nacht durch den Spessart zu reisen? Ich für meinen Teil habe lieber mein Pferd in dieser Schenke eingestellt, als daß ich nur noch eine Stunde geritten wäre.«

aus »Das Wirtshaus im Spessart«
Wilhelm Hauff (1802–1827)

the coloured stripes are reminiscent of shimmering light glancing off water, facilitating wayfinding by "painting" the various parts of the building in different colours. while the spatial distribution of the colours follows the principle of assigning each part of the building its own colour, the two-dimensional distribution on the walls is aligned with a musical principle. the colours are combined like notes in a chord: adjacent, overlapping and at intervals.

on the walls opposite the rivers are signs that can be understood en passant. they are designed to give you information while you're on the move, i.e. they repeat themselves and don't have to be remembered. they provide information about the buildings and their different levels and infrastructure and how to navigate them.

beautiful is right.
right is beautiful.

you can tackle a design task in one of two ways. the first is guided by reason and takes account of all project-related points of view, like the history of the company and the people involved, or the mission and function of the corporate entity. you factor in the owners, the customers and the products, or the setting, the architecture and the visitors. if you manage to strike a harmonious balance and meet all of the objective criteria, the design will stand as a coherent whole. this conceptual approach doesn't usually require a lot of back-and-forth with the client. you don't have to explain your choice of colour, because it was based on the internal logic of the project. nor do you have to justify your choice of font, because it was dictated by formal or substantive considerations which the client can understand. it is a rational, objective way to approach a project.

or you can take the opposite approach, one that has nothing to do with logical thought. this is the way to go when you've considered all the aspects mentioned above – and yet no form emerges. or when the solutions developed by rational thinking still don't fit the bill. then you tackle the project with the sole intention of designing something beautiful. you focus on form; you try to solve the puzzle by creating a surprising colour scheme or a visually arresting typography. this is a creative process which defies explanation. the form feels its way along the paths of rightness, accuracy and coherence, or reveals itself as unwieldy, insubordinate and atavistic. it is an irrational approach which relies on intuition. this process asks different questions. is the form right? is this curve or that colour scheme beautiful? unconventional? or even outlandish? you set aside your usual tools and look at the task from a different perspective. if you can allow this to happen and still adhere to the rules of design, you can develop solutions with a distinct and special power. they are beautiful because they are unique. and people can see that this beauty has its own rightness – which in turn can be explained by reason. just like we acknowledge the beauty of intelligent design because it is coherent and right.

how important is the financial side?

good design costs more than bad design. low budgets are no excuse for bad design.

INTERIOR THINGS

orderly spaces

we not only came up with the company's name, interior things, but also designed its abbreviated form. this monogram, the brand's smallest communicative unit, can be depicted even where space is at a premium, like on an injection moulded part.

product designer wolfgang hartauer designs accessories for desks – in the office or at home. and for bathrooms. for all those places, in other words, where even the neat freaks among us tend to run out of ideas: what to do with all those fiddly bits and bobs, the rubber bands, that favourite pen? this elegant system uses a u-shaped aluminium profile as a simple solution for creating order, providing a uniform structural base for a range of spatial configurations. we adopted the same principle for the interior things logo, using angled characters to add structure and create a distinctive look. and all those capital 'i's are neatly cleared away. tidiness rules!

**interior things
visual identity
holzminden, 2015**

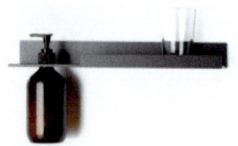

Das Warten hat ein Ende
Meterware jetzt als Wandprofil verfügbar.
Produkte ansehen

Meterware Wandablage
(Mit) Leichtigkeit an die Wand gebannt
Produkte ansehen

/NTER/OR TH/NGS

Meterware Zubehör
Dinge können sich verändern
Produkte ansehen

Temporär verfügbar
Meterware Zubehör in amerikanischem Nussbaum. Solange der Vorrat reicht.
Kontaktieren Sie uns.

Das Unternehmen Interior Things
Wo innovatives Design und handwerkliches Können eine leidenschaftliche Liaison eingehen ...
mehr über das Unternehmen lesen

Interior Things | Meterware Wandablage
www.interiorthings.de/produkte/meterware-wandablage

/NTER/OR TH/NGS

Produkte
  Meterware Tischablage
  Meterware Wandablage
  Meterware Zubehör
Unternehmen
Händler
Kontakt
Warenkorb (2)

AGB
Versand und Rücksendung
Bezahlung
Datenschutzerklärung
Widerrufsbelehrung
Impressum

Wandablage
Schwebezustände

Manchmal sollen Dinge einen festen Platz haben und trotzdem leicht zugänglich sein. Einzeln gehängt, locker über die Wand verteilt oder auf Linie gebracht zeigt sich **Meterware** von seiner leichten Seite.

Ob Sie Ihren Wohnraum zur wandelbaren Galerie machen oder im Flur eine formschöne Ablagemöglichkeit für Schlüssel, Smartphone und Allerlei kreieren: Die Kompositionsmöglichkeiten der **Meterware** Wandablage sind so vielgestalt wie Ihre Ideen.

Für Ihr Badezimmer ist das Profil alternativ mit einer Lochbohrung versehen. So können Sie Flaschen mit Dispenser elegant in der **Meterware** Wandablage verankern.

Apropos Verankern: Sie werden die Ablage mit Leichtigkeit an die Wand bringen. Denn sie verfügt über eine innovative und ausgesprochen smarte Befestigungslösung: Einfach justierbare Klemmhalter, deren Geometrie optimal auf die verdeckte Nut an der Profilrückseite abgestimmt ist, halten das Profil stabil an der Wand und gleichen sogar kleinere Unebenheiten aus.

Material: Aluminium extrudiert (Materialstärke 5 mm)
Oberfläche: pulverbeschichtet
Maße: siehe Artikelvarianten
Herstellungsland: Deutschland
Design: Wolfgang Hartauer

Die Wandablage ist in einer Länge von 100 cm sowie mit Lochbohrung in der Länge von 40 cm erhältlich.

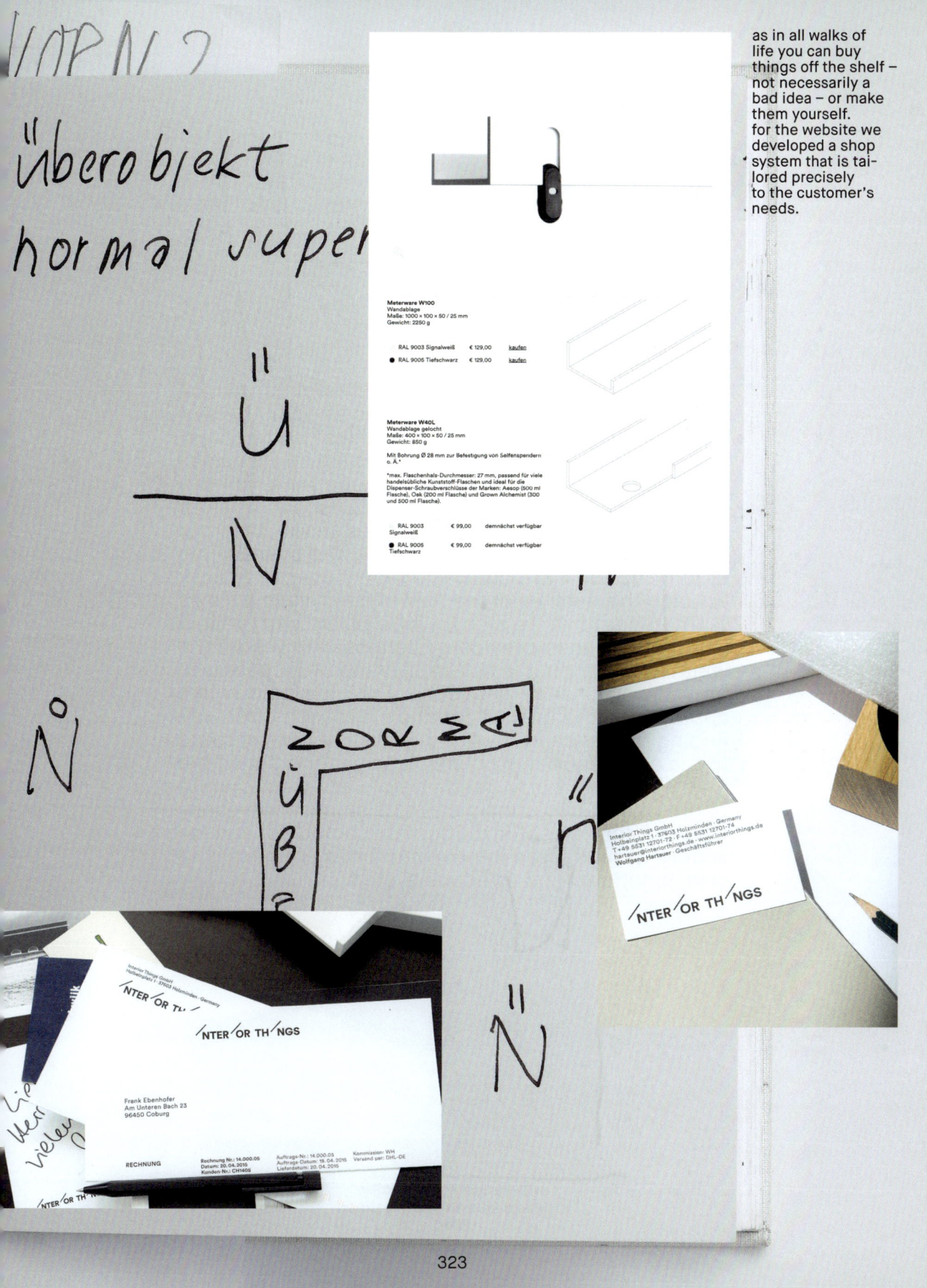

as in all walks of life you can buy things off the shelf – not necessarily a bad idea – or make them yourself. for the website we developed a shop system that is tailored precisely to the customer's needs.

fractal order

the signage system references the masterplan, which views the hönggerberg campus as a town. the system is an unpretentious but aesthetically refined version of a street sign. the destinations are street names and building numbers, offering scope for a high degree of flexibility, permitting different uses in different buildings. the connective tissue takes shape: the information infrastructure seems chaotic. the overlayering of information tiers creates a blurry overall effect – echoing the outlines of the "town" itself. yellow masts with grey and white signs, white pillars with yellow and grey surfaces, grey constructions with yellow and white information. the self-replicating order seems to follow its own natural sequence, a precise logic. where appropriate, the grey information level can offer wayfinding guidance in black on white. the yellow route to the congress centre is visible at every point where a delegate in a hurry needs help – on yellow, white or grey signs. this principle avoids an overload of any single colour or construction. the colourful appearance – with its three interwoven tones – hosts a precise, functional and effective system.

eth zurich science city
signage system, not realised
2010

what's your own approach, in terms of the way you work?

form is good, if it's protected from idle conceits, compromises and coercion. you have to let things be and observe them. they'll tell you where they want to go.

should the media increasingly see themselves as a forum for discussing social and economic alternatives?

we are the media

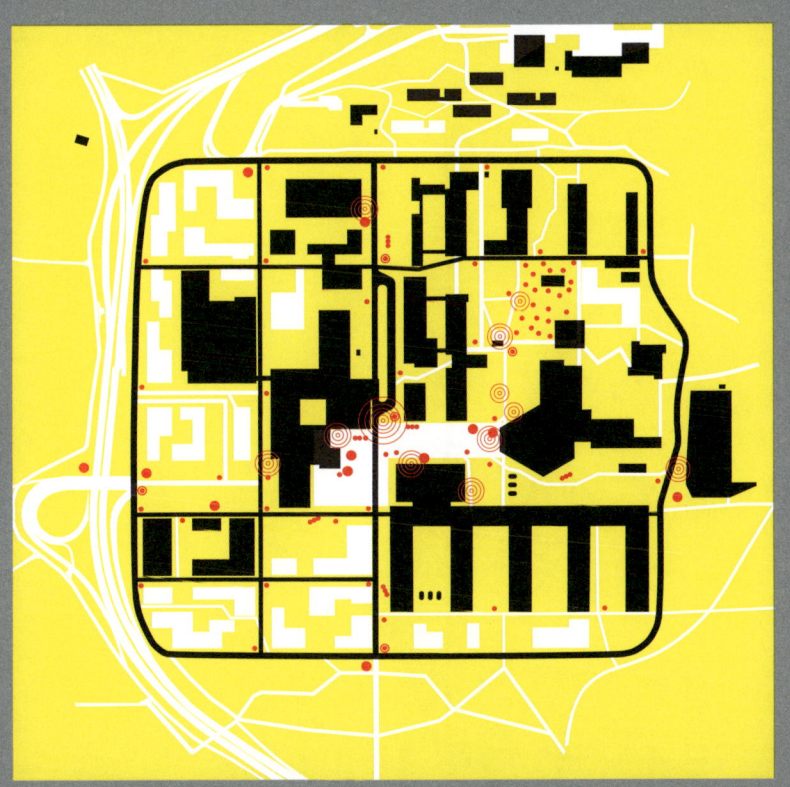
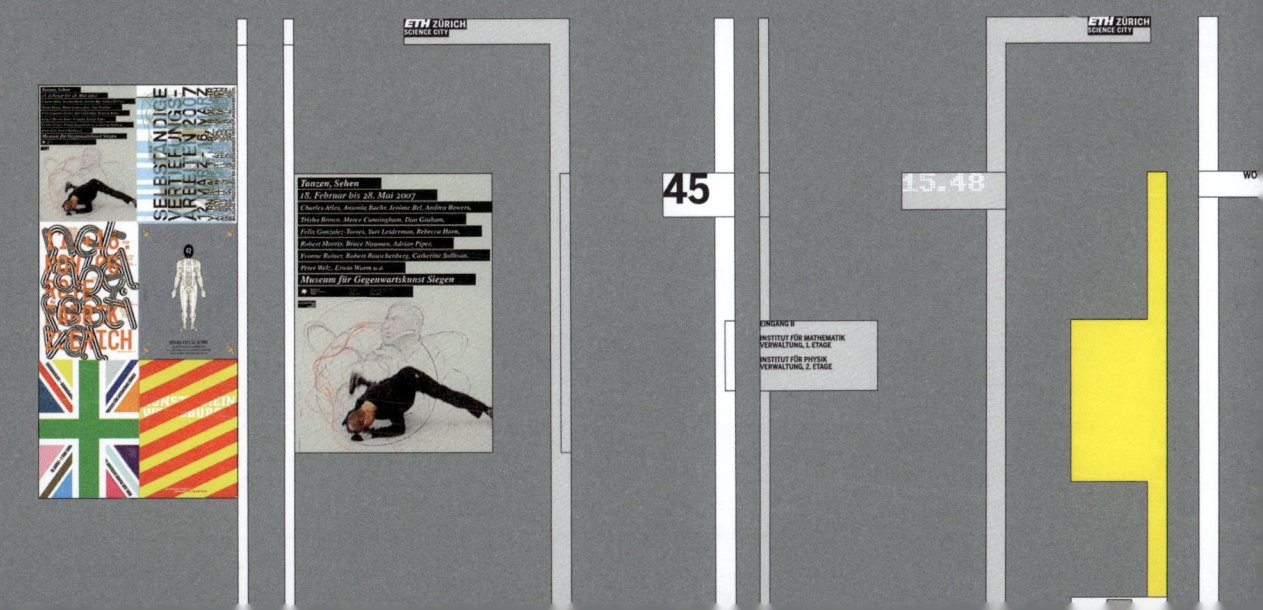

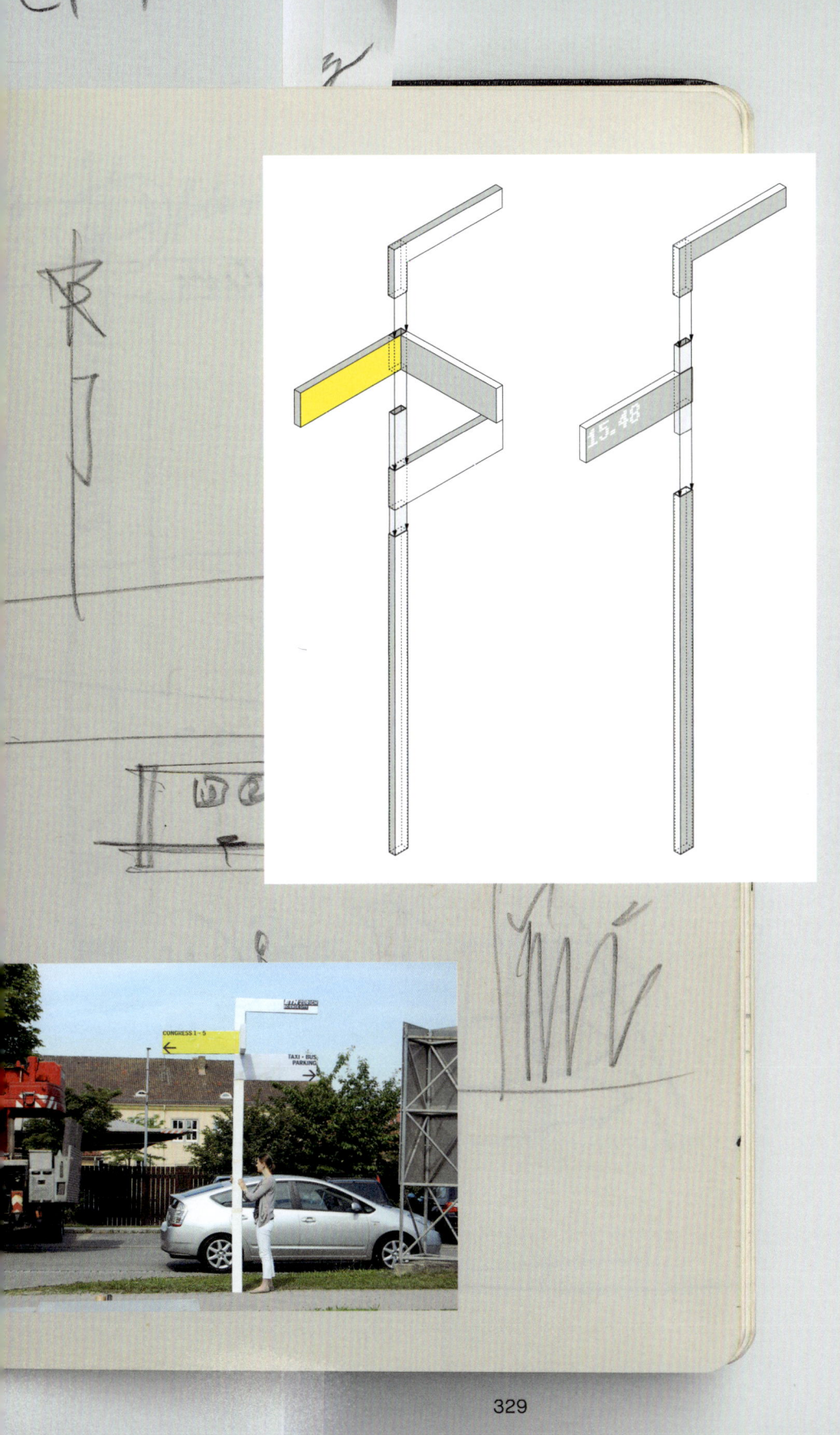

on the very narrow column – just 6×12 cm in cross-section – the mast and the sign itself are connected by means of an internal rectangular profile. this construction makes it possible to change, supplement or remove specific elements with a minimum of fuss. the sharp-edged system elements are firmly interlinked without the need for any visible connecting units.

a book is a book is a book.

but this report on the activities of a company is three books in one: technical publication, documentary report and narrative tale. at the first level the reader finds images depicting large sections of buildings. the photos reveal details of the indoor-climate technology that impact on the shape of the building, becoming part of the architectural design. at the second level there is an essay on the history of human habitation. the copy underpins the photos: open any page and read it in isolation, leaf through from back to front, or read page after consecutive page. at the third level photo captions and a glossary explain the details. the technology is packaged in a stream of words and images. the reference list of projects is hidden yet highly visible on the cover.

transsolar climate engineering
monograph
stuttgart, 2004

Wasser

Grundwasserkühlung 151
Regenwassernutzung 27
Raumluftfeuchte 209
Verdunstungskühlung 181
Wasserkraft 59
Wasserwand 21
Wolke 183

arum wird die Luft nicht durch nen Erdkanal gelenkt?

Eine einläufige Treppe verläuft im Fassadenzwischenraum der Doppelfassade vom Erdgeschoss bis in den nördlichen Dachgarten. Die Anordnung von Erschließungen in witterungsgeschützten, aber ganzjährig unbeheizten Bereichen nutzt konsequent die Potentiale thermischer Pufferzonen.

Wolken bilden sich durch Kondensation der mit Feuchtigkeit übersättigten Luft an Kondensationskernen wie zum Beispiel Staub, Rußteilchen oder organischen Verbindungen.

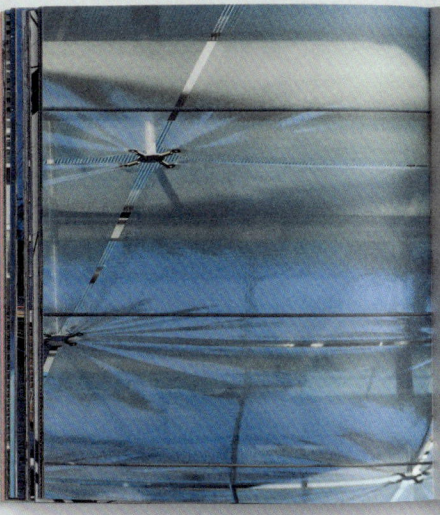

Wie lässt sich Licht bestmöglich nutzen?

Um im Winter Kälteabfall vom Glasdach zu vermeiden und ein Abführen von Wärme zu ermöglichen, hängt unter der Glasfläche eine transparente Folie. Die Mikroperforation dieser Folie verbessert die Akustik, die Bedruckung von Folie oder Glas den Sonnenschutz. Der zweischichtige Aufbau mit einer Beschichtung auf der inneren Glasoberfläche verbessert zusätzlich den Wärmeschutz.

Thermischer Spiegel Glas reagiert auf verschiedene Strahlungsarten sehr unterschiedlich: Sichtbares Licht wird zum großen Teil durchgelassen, nicht sichtbare, aber fühlbare Infrarotstrahlung dagegen fast vollständig absorbiert. Diese Wärmestrahlung kann darum ein Glashaus nicht verlassen. Der Fußboden eines beheizten Atriums gibt im Winter Wärmestrahlung ab, die vom Glasdach absorbiert wird. Dadurch steigt die Temperatur der Glasschicht um einige Grad, der Aufenthaltsbereich verliert aber merklich Energie. Ideal wäre ein Material für die Bedachung, das die Wärmestrahlung zurückwirft: ein thermischer Spiegel.

Metalle weisen diese Eigenschaft auf: Zwischen 85 und 97% der auftreffenden Wärmestrahlung werden von metallisch beschichteten Oberflächen reflektiert. Von der Wärmeschutzverglasung her seit langem bekannt, können jetzt auch Kunststofffolien entsprechend beschichtet werden. Die Folien, Glas- oder Kunststoffscheiben bleiben für sichtbares Licht dennoch transparent, wirken zum Raum hin aber als thermischer Spiegel.

gender diversity action plan

the unsystematic design of these pictograms – with the outline of the body sometimes described by a line, sometimes by the outer edge of a solid shape – may cause graphical problems, but it does allow for a wide range of depictions. different clothing, different skin colours, different accessories such as belts, glasses and necklaces, and different hairdos portray an amusing array of different personalities.

**tu berlin
signage system
2016**

in terms of your work, what does the expression "overdesigned" mean to you?

in german we would say "verschwenderisch", which has a nice double meaning: splendid luxury on the one hand and wasting for example your time or energy on the other. to me design always means creating something both beautiful and fragmentary that has both depth and surface. overdesign is only possible when the foundation is solid. it needs a hard working structure that is "invisible". we always try to develop a clear and functional structure for our work and to overlay it with the impact of typography, colour and form, which i suppose you could call overdesign.

what makes it good?

a signage system is good when it tells a story about the place or the company, when it engages in a dialogue with the architecture by responding to it. a system is good when it is designed with self-confidence. it can form a contrast to the architecture or harmonize with it and integrate seamlessly. in any case, whether loud or muted, it must be independent, innovative, surprising.

a system is good when the lettering isn't merely legible, but also has something special to offer. this can mean that it is rendered in an unusual colour, one that is completely and utterly unexpected in that location. or one that has a specific connection to the place. the lettering might also take on physical form – large, larger, much too large! – so that it seems like a sculpture and not just the necessary labelling of a building.

a system is good when it frees itself from the formal restrictions of design, the usual expectations of how lettering should appear in space and is developed based on real-world parameters such as cost, infrastructure, traffic, surface structure and the like.

a system is good when it provides more than the things people would normally expect of it – legibility, logic, clear guidance, systematic construction and durability. for example, the lettering might be visually alluring, just as the column in the barcelona pavilion by mies van der rohe does more than is actually required of it. it bears the weight of the ceiling, but at the same time it is coated with a beautiful, lustrous material that distracts from the hard work it is doing. form follows function? yes, because beauty is also a function!

a system is good when it responds to the architecture instead of simply being imposed upon it. this means that this system can only exist in this way in this particular place – it is only possible and meaningful here.

spring/summer collection

kaleidoscopic colours, rhythmically transposed blocks: this website is like a sample book, where you can turn over one of the cards and discover the various projects they conceal. the blocks in the menu change colour, showing that colour isn't just a surface add-on, but can be used to give spaces very distinctive moods. just as the colour blocks contain particular projects behind them, so the concept of "interior design" – the client's specialist field – contains within it the task of creating specific atmospheres.

zieglerbürg büro für gestaltung
website
stuttgart, 2012

} schw
} grau
} weiß

projekt

> Architektur)

> Frühling<
(2)

NAVI PROJEKT

variations on a theme

the symbol conveys the essence of the museum: a collection of different objects and subjects under one roof. the letter logo is an s, its internal form varying from collection to collection, while its outer form remains constant – like the museum's constant central theme: its relationship to the city. both parts of the museum's german name begin with an s, and the letter logo is constructed so as to create an outer s and an inner s. the outer s can be read as standing for the place and the building, the inner s for its content, the objects. these two letter shapes vary in form for each application, the variations conveying the diverse scope of the collections and demonstrating that this museum is a living entity.

**stadtmuseum stuttgart
visual identity, not realised
2011**

hannes böhringer
sweeping

sometimes something slips out of my hand, a key, and i pick it up and stick it in my pocket. but a glass that is accidentally knocked off the table shatters into pieces. breadcrumbs on my trousers are easily brushed off. they fall to the floor. sauce drips onto my shirt. i rub the spot with warm water and soap. no joy. the shirt has to go into the wash. and maybe the stain will be permanent.

cleaning the floor is no different, wet and dry, swept, scrubbed, mopped. in the end, everything lands on the floor; everything falls downward. the advent of electricity brought us the vacuum cleaner and banished brushes and brooms from our living space to the basement and the backyard, to the street and the pavement. they stir up dust and leave us with no doubt that we'll never get things completely clean. every attempt to clean up produces a new mess. we simply push the dirt to the side and out of sight, or rearrange it, sweeping it across the floor and swirling it into the air. the vacuum cleaner produces its own pollution in the form of noise.

by making and using things, we create dirt, produce waste. if we don't touch things at all, they collect dust. we see how the dust stirred up by our movements settles on their surfaces. at first it is nothing, but as it collects it robs the objects of their freshness and shine. so we vacuum them clean. the vacuum cleaner, however, just hovers over objects and floors. unlike the broom, it never really touches them.

we don't usually pay attention to the floor, even when we are standing on it. sweeping the floor means taking its solidity seriously. there are two types of sweeping implement, the flat brush and the long-handled broom; there are brooms with short and long bristles. the flat brush scratches and scrapes over the floor, the broom whooshes and wipes. and wiping leads us to damp and wet mopping. sweeping is good for rough floors, mopping for smooth ones. department stores and airports love smooth, shining floors. so they are mopped to give them a flawless sparkle.

sweeping and mopping are quick, decisive motions. all evidence of mopping completely evaporates and disappears. sweeping, on the other hand, leaves traces on the floor and in the air. when you sweep, you have to exert just the right amount of pressure on the floor at just the right angle. brushes and brooms aren't supposed to stall in mid-sweep or brush too much or too little off the floor. sweeping calls for just the right touch.

cleaning is just as necessary as tidying up. it's a never-ending task. it creates dirt and stirs up dust. when i tidy up, i create a clear space, a patch, a spot where i can linger. i have to brush, sweep and mop this spot. the spot will never be truly clean. it remains a spot, but a place to stay all the same – as long as i look after it.

joachim blüher
andreas uebele on a 2015 scholarship at villa massimo

the question of whether design is art mostly only occupies designers who would like to have been artists. artists, even unsuccessful ones, would never ponder the same question in reverse. design always needs a reason and an objective. art can have a reason and an objective, but doesn't need one. what characterises art is its freedom from directive – its freedom in general. design encounters requirements at every turn. but is that really the question?

villa massimo is an academy, a place where art has been made for more than 100 years. visual arts, music, literature, architecture. and as soon as we come to architecture, what i've just written starts to break down, because architecture always has a reason and an objective. so is it art? more of a noble craft that is considered art because of its complex formal structure.

so our narrow definition increasingly no longer applies. today more than ever, art is often so infused with technology or practical concerns that one person simply cannot do it all alone. just like architecture.

that's why i launched the creative scholarship program at the villa massimo in 2008. it is open to designers, bakers, basket-weavers, singers, actors, stonemasons, dancers, potters, photographers, trumpeters, and, and, and. we no longer draw a line between the fine arts and their less sophisticated cousins. it's no longer a valid parameter. instead, what the residents who live and work together here have in common is that their work is exemplary. and even though what they do, and how they do it, may be extremely disparate, it all articulates the face of our country. and our face looks different than that of other nations – something that first becomes clear when we leave germany and become aware of how others see us.

this results in an attitude that no longer grows out of one specific genre, but from the understanding that we can articulate a shared vision of our country through the individuality and uniqueness of our work. and so it does not matter if we are artists or designers. what unites us is this attitude. what separates us is hubris.

by combining the nine different outer s shapes with 18 different inner s's we have created 162 distinct symbols and use the 32 most aesthetically pleasing for the corporate design.

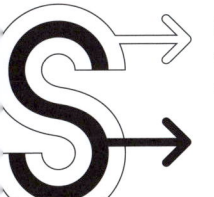 STADTMUSEUM
 STUTTGART

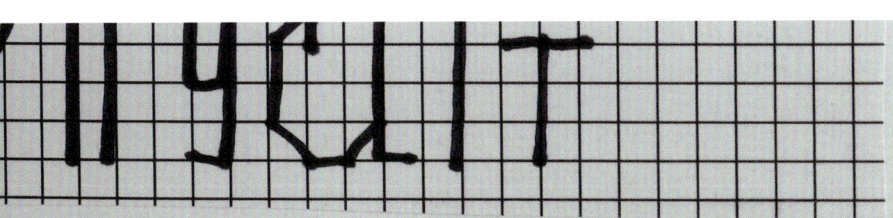

multiple ambivalence

the künstlerhaus poster leads a double life as a leaflet. the typeface for the poster is too small, the volume of text too large. the result is a typographic pattern. for the leaflet the format is too bulky, the lines are too long. both versions demonstrate, in an absolutely literal, straightforward way, the scope and dimensions of the spaces – both literal and figurative – offered by the künstlerhaus itself.

**künstlerhaus stuttgart
poster, leaflet
2004**

... IM KÜNSTLERHAUS ... GREIFEN PRODUKTION ... PRÄSENTATION ...
... EINANDER UND VERKNÜPFEN SICH WECHSELSEITIG. SEIT DER GRÜNDUNG 1978 WURDE DAS HAUS DURCH VIELFÄLTIGE EXPERIMENTELLE AUSSTELLUNGE
... INTERNATIONAL BESETZTE SYMPOSIEN UND DURCH KRITISCHE DISKURSE ZU FRAGEN DER GEGENWARTSKUNST NATIONAL WIE INTERNATIONAL ANERK...
PRODUKTIONSSTÄTTEN FÜR NEUE MEDIEN UND DEN TRADITIONELLEN WERKSTÄTTEN ERMÖGLICHT DAS KÜNSTLERHAUS PERMANENT EIN KÜNSTLERISCHES
... DEN UNTERSCHIEDLICHSTEN FORMEN. JEDES JAHR VERGIBT DAS KÜNSTLERHAUS VIER ATELIERSTIPENDIEN AN KÜNSTLERINNEN, KÜNSTLER ODER KÜNS...
ZUSÄTZLICH ZUR NUTZUNG EINES RAUMES HABEN DIE STIPENDIATEN FREIEN ZUGANG ZU ALLEN WERKSTÄTTEN. EINE PERSÖNLICHKEIT AUS KUNST ODER
... WISSENSCHAFT WIRD VOM KÜNSTLERISCHEN BEIRAT BEAUFTRAGT FÜR ZWEI JAHRE — MIT DER OPTION AUF VERLÄNGERUNG — DAS PROGRAMM DES INSTI...
... TION DER KÜNSTLERISCHEN LEITUNG EIGENVERANTWORTLICH ZU GESTALTEN. DAS INTERNATIONAL ANERKANNTE KÜNSTLERHAUS HAT SEIT 1984 SEINE R...
... EM FABRIKGEBÄUDE, DAS ZU BEGINN DES LETZTEN JAHRHUNDERTS ERRICHTET WURDE. DIE WERKSTÄTTEN, DIE ATELIERS UND DAS PROGRAMM DER KÜNS...
... TUNG SIND SELBSTVERWALTET.

PRODUKTION
DAS REICHHALTIGE WERKSTATTANGEBOT DES HAUSES, SIEBDRUCK-, LITHOGRAPHIE-, FILM-, MULTIMEDIA-, VIDEO- ODER AUDIOWERKSTATT STEHEN D
... ERN GEGEN EINEN UNKOSTENBEITRAG ZUR VERFÜGUNG. DIE TECHNISCHE AUSSTATTUNG DER WERKSTÄTTEN REAGIERT NACH MÖGLICHKEIT AUF DIE KÜNS...
... OJEKTE DER MITGLIEDER. DIE ANGEBOTENEN KURSE BIETEN SOWOHL EINEN EINSTIEG WIE AUCH EINE SPEZIALISIERUNG IN DEN JEWEILIGEN TECHNIKEN...
KÜNSTLERINNEN UND KÜNSTLERN GELEITETEN KINDERWERKSTATT KÖNNEN DIE KLEINSTEN UND ZUKÜNFTIGEN MITGLIEDER DES KÜNSTLERHAUSES IHRE
... LEBEN UND ERSTE KÜNSTLERISCHE ERFAHRUNGEN SAMMELN.

PRÄSENTATION
DAS PROGRAMM DER KÜNSTLERISCHE
SETZT SICH AUS ASPEKTEN KÜNSTLERISCHER PRAXIS UND THEORETISCHEN ANSÄTZEN ZUSAMMEN, DIE EIGENSTÄNDIGE POSITION ERMÖGLICHT EIN DIFFE
... D KRITISCHES VORGEHEN, DAS SICH MIT AKTUELLEN TENDENZEN IM ZEITGENÖSSISCHEN KUNSTDISKURS AUSEINANDERSETZT. NEBEN DEN KLASSISCHEN...
... ELLUNGSFORMATEN SIND FILM-, VIDEO- UND PERFORMANCEVERANSTALTUNGEN VERTRETEN, DIE DURCH THEMENGEBUNDENE WORKSHOPS ERGÄNZT WER...
IHRE LOKAL HAT DAS KÜNSTLERHAUS STUTTGART 2004 SEIN VERMITTLUNGSPROGRAMM ERWEITERT, UM DEN DIALOG ZWISCHEN DEM HAUS, SEINEN MITGLI
... UND DEN BESUCHERN ZU ERWEITERN. KÖNNEN MITGLIEDER IHRE ARBEITEN IM RAHMEN SPEZIFISCHER PLATTFORMEN PRÄSENTIEREN UND ZUR DISKUS...

REFLEXION
KÜNSTLERISCHE LEITUNG EINERSEITS UND ENGAGIERTE MITGLIEDER ANDERSEITS REALISIE
... SCHIEDENEN AUSSTELLUNGEN, VERANSTALTUNGEN ZUR VERMITTLUNG MIT VORTRÄGEN UND SYMPOSIEN ÜBER FRAGEN UND TENDENZEN DER AKTUELLEN
PRODUKTION. ÜBER DEN ZEITRAUM VON BISHER 25 JAHREN WURDE DURCH DIE JEWEILIGE KÜNSTLERISCHE LEITUNG, ERGÄNZEND ZUM VERANSTALTUNGS-
... NE ÖFFENTLICH ZUGÄNGLICHE BIBLIOTHEK UND MEDIATHEK ANGELEGT. DER BESTAND UMFASST EINE REIHE NATIONALER UND INTERNATIONALER PUBLIKA...
... N SOWIE ZAHLREICHE KÜNSTLERVIDEOS, DIE AUCH VOR ORT GESICHTET WERDEN KÖNNEN. IM ARCHIV DES KÜNSTLERHAUSES KÖNNEN FAST ALLE 600 AUS...
PROJEKTE UND AKTIONEN, DIE SEIT 1978 VERANSTALTET WURDEN, RECHERCHIERT WERDEN. DIE REIHE VISIT ERÖFFNET DEN KÜNSTLERHAUS-MITGLIEDER
... CHKEIT EINE ABEND- ODER WOCHENENDVERANSTALTUNG ZU GESTALTEN. DAS KONZEPT DIESER REIHE SIEHT VOR, AKTUELLE KÜNSTLERISCHE POSITIONEN...
GEN IM ZEITGENÖSSISCHEN DISKURS ZU HINTERFRAGEN.

AUDIOWERKSTATT
DIE WERKSTATT BIETET DIE GELEGENHEIT ALLE GÄNGIGEN DIGITALEN UND ANALOGEN MEDIEN UND TONTRÄGER ZU DIGITALISIERE
HRSPURIGES DIGITALES ABMISCHEN ERMÖGLICHT DER MIT PRO-TOOLS AUSGERÜSTETE G4 MACINTOSH. EIN MIDI-KLANGERZEUGER FÜR MIDI-DATEIEN IST
... LS AUSGABEMEDIEN STEHEN CD- UND DVD-BRENNER ZUR VERFÜGUNG.

COMPUTERWERKSTATT
DIE AUSSTATTUNG DER COMPUTERWE
... DER DIGITALEN BILD- UND TONBEARBEITUNG. DIE ZWEI VORHANDENEN ARBEITSPLÄTZE VERFÜGEN ÜBER DIE HERKÖMMLICHEN PROGRAMME, DIE ZUM
... IG, DEM ERSTELLEN VON DVD-MULTIMEDIAPRODUKTIONEN, VIDEO- UND AUDIOEDITING UND FÜR DAS KLASSISCHE DESKTOP PUBLISHING NOTWENDIG SIND
UND EIN AUDIO-ZUSPIELGERÄT ERGÄNZEN DAS ZUBEHÖR.

FILMWERKSTATT
DIE FILMWERKSTATT BESITZT EIN VOLLSTÄNDIGES EQUIPMENT FÜR DIE REALISIERUNG KLEIN
... TTLERER FILMPROJEKTE. UM DIE PRODUKTION VON NO- UND LOWBUDGET-FILMEN ZU FÖRDERN, KÖNNEN DIE GERÄTE ENTLIEHEN WERDEN. IN DEN ARBEITS...
EN WEITERE NUTZBARE GERÄTE ZUR VERFÜGUNG.

S/W-FOTOLABOR
IM FOTOLABOR DES KÜNSTLERHAUSES LASSEN SICH PROFESSIONELLE S/W-FOTOS REALISIEREN. DAS INVENTAR BESTEHT AUS ZWEI VERGRÖSSE-
SGERÄTEN FÜR KLEINBILD UND EINER LANGBAHNENTWICKLUNGSEINRICHTUNG. NEBEN NEUEREN TECHNISCHEN GERÄTEN BESITZT DIE WERKSTATT AUCH
BARY-TROMMELTROCKENPRESSE.

BUCHDRUCKWERKSTATT
IN DER BUCHDRUCKWERKSTATT DES KÜNSTLERHAUSES KÖNNEN TEXTE IN
... ATZ, FLIESSTEXT ODER FLATTERSATZ ZU GEDICHTEN ODER KURZTEXTEN GESETZT WERDEN. ZWEI TAG-HANDDRUCKPRESSEN UND EINE KNIEHEBELPRESSE
... EXT ZU PAPIER. ZUSÄTZLICH KÖNNEN HOLZ- UND LINOLSCHNITTE, MATERIALDRUCKE UND HELIOGRAVUREN HERGESTELLT WERDEN. EINE REPRODUKTIONS-
KAMERA ZUR HERSTELLUNG DER FILME FÜR DIE HELIOGRAVUREN IST VORHAN

LITHOGRAPHIEWERKSTATT
DIE IN DER LITHOGRAPHIEWERKSTATT VORHANDENEN STEINE KÖNNEN MIT GRAPHISCHEN KREIDE- UND TUSCHEZEICHNUNGEN
... WERDEN. GEDRUCKT WIRD AUF EINER MANUELL BETRIEBENEN STEINDRUCK-REIBERPRESSE. DIE FARBWALZEN UND TROCKENPAPPEN DER WERKSTATT ST...
... IEDERN ZUR VERFÜGUNG.

RADIERWERKSTATT
IN ZWEI SEPARATEN DRUCKRÄUMEN
RAUM KÖNNEN ALLE GÄNGIGEN TIEFDRUCKTECHNIKEN, WIE KALTNADEL, ÄTZRADIERUNG UND AQUATINTA AUSPROBIERT WERDEN. NEBEN EINER ELEKTRIS
... ND ZWEI WEITERE DRUCKPRESSEN UND EINE VORRICHTUNG ZUM TROCKNEN DER DRUCKE VORHANDEN. IM ÄTZRAUM BEFINDEN SICH SÄUREWANNEN UND
KOLOPHONIUMKA...

SIEBDRUCKWERKSTATT
IN DER SIEBDRUCKWERKSTATT KÖNNEN PROFESSIONELLE SIEBDRUCKE
STELLT WERDEN. DIE WERKSTATT IST MIT EINEM GROSSEN LEUCHTTISCH, EINEM BELICHTUNGSTISCH UND EINEM DRUCKTISCH AUSGESTATTET. ABLAGEN FÜ
ND EINE HOCHDRUCKREINIGUNGSANLAGE STEHEN EBENFALLS ZUR VERFÜGUNG. DIE FÜR DEN DRUCK NOTWENDIGEN SIEBE KÖNNEN ENTLIEHEN WERDEN

KERAMIKWERKSTATT
IN DER KERAMIKWERKSTATT WERDEN ZWEI VERSCHIEDENE DREHSCHEIBEN UND ZWEI BRENNÖFEN ZUR VERFÜGUNG GESTELLT. HIER KÖNNEN OBJ
UKERAMIK UND WANDBILDER IN MAJOLIKATECHNIK HERGESTELLT WERDEN. MIT DER GLASUR- UND ENGOBETECHNIK KANN EBENSO EXPERIMENTIERT WER
IK WERKSTATT BEFINDET SICH NICHT IM KÜNSTLERHAUS, SONDERN IN DER LESSINGSTRASSE 3B.

KINDERWERKSTATT
DIE KINDERWERKSTATT BEFINDET SIC
TTELBARER NÄHE ZUM KÜNSTLERHAUS. UNTER DER ANLEITUNG FREISCHAFFENDER, PÄDAGOGISCH ERFAHRENER KÜNSTLERINNEN UND KÜNSTLER KÖNNE
ERSCHIEDENE GESTALTERISCHE TECHNIKEN ERPROBEN UND INNERHALB DER GRUPPE NEUE SOZIALE KONTAKTE KNÜPFEN. BEI INTERESSE MELDEN SIE SIC

the architecture and its little gucci bag

VITRA HOUSE COLOUR BLACK

TEMPORARY SIGNS LIGHT RED

EXIT YELLOW

PARKING BLUE

the campus, characterised by its contrasting architectural styles, needed a neat, compact structure for its signage system, restrained in both height and form; one that wouldn't compete with the architecture's own style statements – some of them gestural and expressive. even so this system makes a clear statement of its own, self-assured but calm in its expression. the straightforward design is based on a modular, flexible lettering system and technically intelligent details. it's easy to use, making the client independent of external suppliers. the dimensions of the modular structure forming the body of the sign are determined by the similarly modular typeface, which is used in a number of different sizes. the majority of the sign structures are 72 cm high, and integrate visually with the campus in a very natural way, leaving the architectural scene uncluttered. the predominantly black-and-white colour scheme references vitra's house colours and sits comfortably with the understated approach of the design as a whole. the only colours are bright red, yellow and blue, used here and there to highlight specific applications or destinations. taller sign structures – 216 cm high – are used in places where it's ergonomically appropriate and won't disturb the silhouette of the architectural landscape.

invited international competition, not realised
photos: julien lanoo, © vitra

vitra campus
signage system, not realised
weil am rhein, 2011

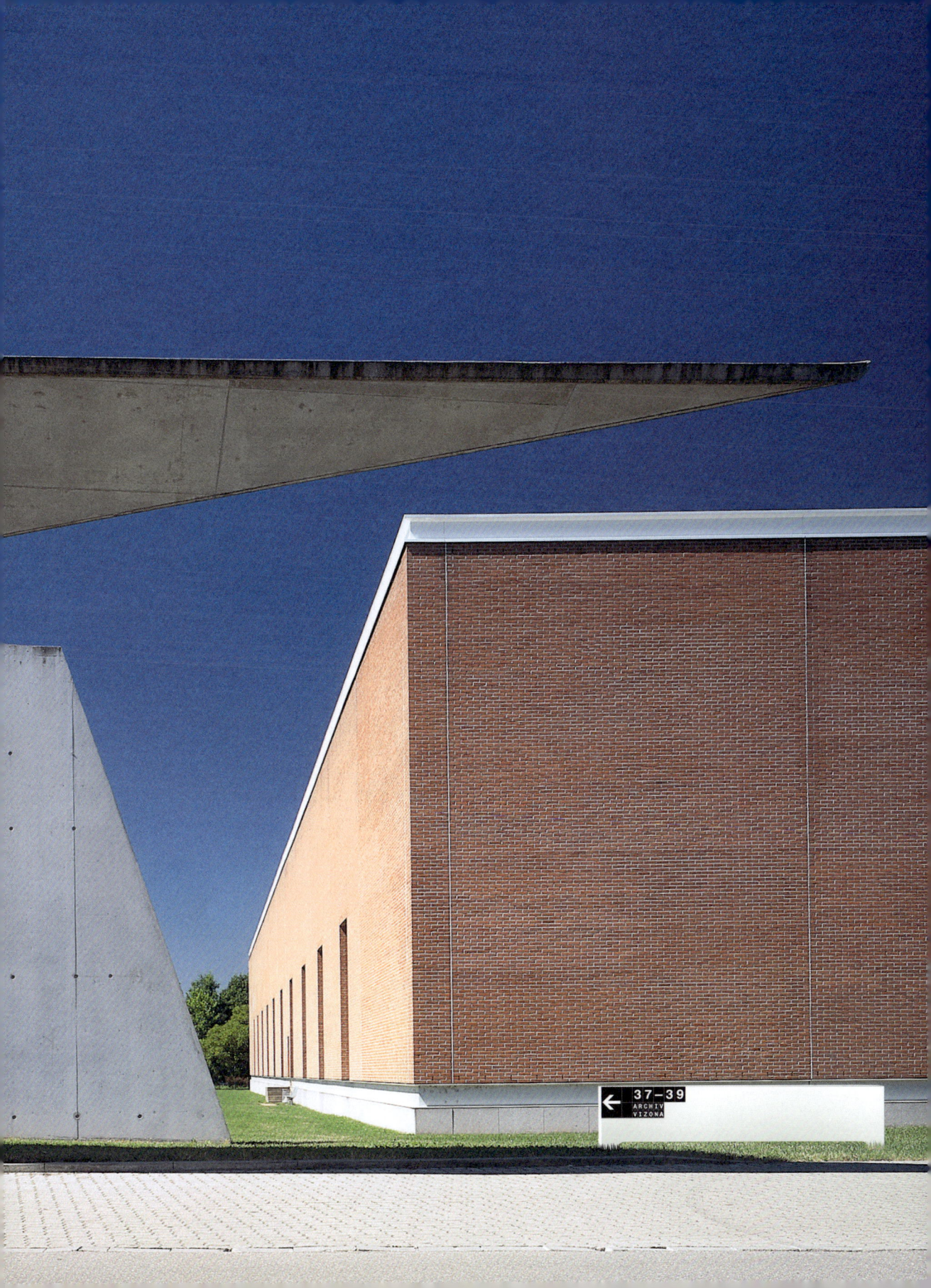

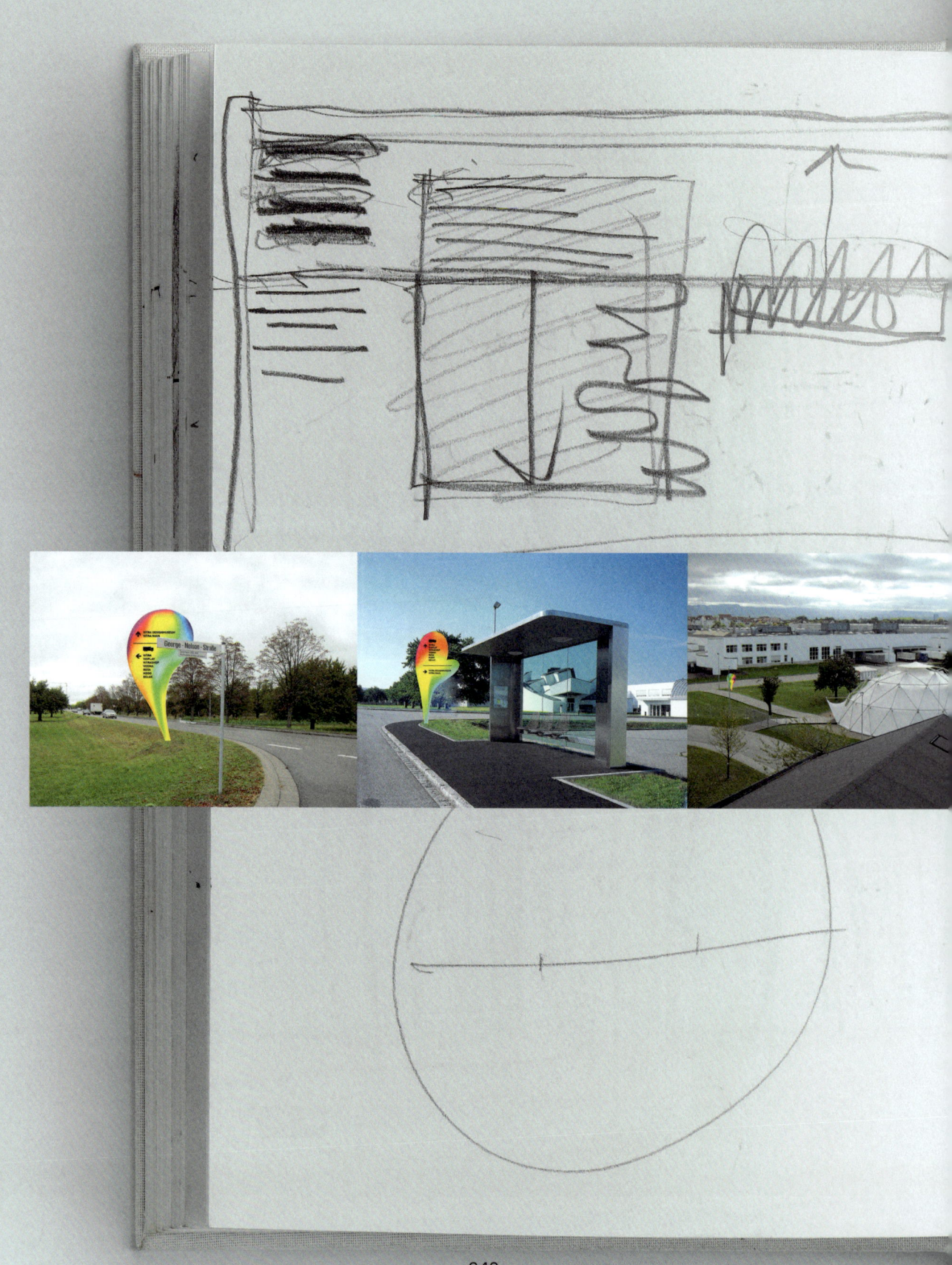

Vitra

← VITRAHAUS
HEUTE GESCHLOSSEN
CLOSED TODAY

↑ AUSFAHRT EXIT   P →

↑ 17–55   VITRA VISPLAY
  60–70   VITRASHOP
           VIZONA REGA
           MODO BELUX   STOP

WELCOME TO THE VITRA CAMPUS
ART BASEL 2012

"we're seeing a trend in which art is being appropriated by the private sector and lost to society in consequence." would you agree with this statement?

art = establishment

in your creative process do you use a particular method to bring your powers of intuition into play?

dialogue is one method. it's an important tool at the start of a project; it is the idea-conjuring machine. when you talk you're no longer bearing the weight of responsibility on your own — it takes the pressure off. there's someone with you at the table; you can try out ideas, you can even give yourselves specific roles (e.g. a is in a good mood and having brilliant ideas, b had a rough night and is grumbling). this dialogue is like making bread: as the dough gets warmer and warmer it eventually yields pretty bubbles full of insights.

```
A B C D E F G H I J K
L M N O P Q R S T U V W X Y Z
1 2 3 4 5 6 7 8 9 0
! ? *
```

monospace 821 by max miedinger is a reworking of the successful helvetica ideally suited for modular lettering purposes, combining good readability with an aesthetically idiosyncratic, highly distinctive design.

this system can have lettering on both front and back and the text modules can be affixed to justify on the left-hand or right-hand margin. each sign can serve four different directions, which keeps the number of signage elements on the campus to a minimum. the different font sizes are sorted hierarchically according to readability requirements: signs for pedestrians and truck drivers, for opening times and announcements – each have appropriate font sizes available. black-and-white delivers optimal contrast for reading even when weather conditions make for poor visibility. exit signs are set on yellow, making them easy for drivers to spot. a vibrant light red is used for temporary announcements, distinguishing them from texts that serve as wayfinding aids. signs with blue backgrounds guide visitors to the car parks. the text modules can be changed quickly and simply, making the system flexible – and also easy to expand as the campus grows.

the system includes large panels constructed on the same principle. their surfaces are covered with images – brand/advertising visuals; or images promoting exhibitions, events or other special occasions. the modular lettering system can be superimposed on these digitally printed decals and quickly and easily changed as necessary. this information system is part of how vitra communicates with its visitors, setting the mood for the vitra campus experience.

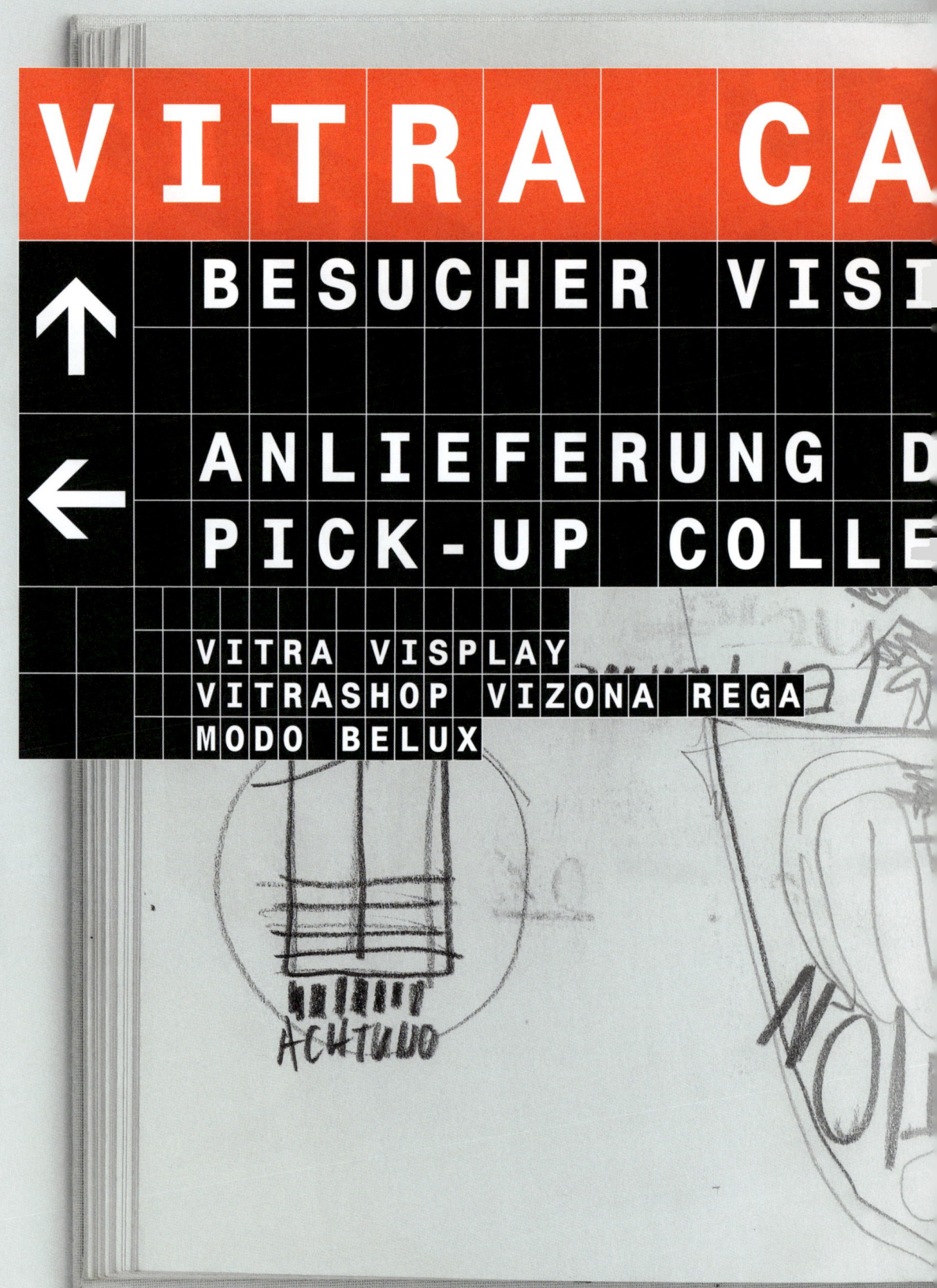

VITRA

muito legato

hardt is a manufacturer of high-quality furniture fittings. these small metal parts forge the links between doors and hinges, windows and frames, cupboards and doors. it's a role that's reflected in the company logo: sidled up snugly like fitting and frame, individual letters are run together, like the a and r or the d and t – and links don't come much closer than this: they actually form typographic ligatures. this simple solution has two decisive benefits: on the one hand these "elective affinities" mirror the company's products. on the other they shorten the brand name, making for clear legibility even in tight spaces, like when embossed on a little hinge.

**hardt
visual identity
curitiba, 2014**

strawberry red

strawberry red: even the words sound like summer. it's the heaviness of the shimmering midday heat that drains the sharpness from this colour; the heat that slows our movements to a sultry elegance. it's the muted blue shadow of a cloud passing across the impulsive flickering red, calming and placating. yet even so this is still red — powerful, but not aggressive.

**a term for the lesikon
"attraction distance"**

attraction distance: each letter attracts the next one, joins with its neighbour to form a word, creating meaning. at the same time each character needs enough space to be read clearly; the black needs the white. without the right spacing — the braking distance between characters — there will be a collision. sensitive braking is beautiful.

Projektseite   Sakenzahl
                Titel
                Kennzeichnung Textseite

Begleittexte   Vorsele   ①   Papier ?
                          ②

Tex
Im

Marseille, Aix en Provence

Baggio Schiavon Arquitetura
Rua Pasteur, 804
80250-080, Curitiba

10 30 2013

Bem-vindo a Curitiba

Pagina 1

Do Parana com o Litoral. Feita em cinco anos (1880-85), a ferrovia e uma das maiores obras da engenharia nacional, gracas aos irmaos engenheiros Antonio e Andre Reboucas. Utilizou grandemente a forca de trabalho dos imigrantes, chegados em massa desde meados dos anos 1800.

Curitiba se beneficiou, no inicio do seculo, com a riqueza oriunda dos engenhos de erva-mate. Seus proprietarios, os "baroes da erva-mate", construiram mansoes para moradia na capital, em boa parte preservadas em dois conjuntos significativos, nos bairros Batel e Alto da Gloria.

O ciclo economico seguinte foi o da monocultura do cafe, que semeou cidades no norte do Estado do Parana, com reflexos evidentes sobre a economia da capital. Castigado pelas intemperies, o cafa foi sendo aos poucos substituido pela soja, ata sua completa erradicacao apos a geada negra de julho de 1975.

A cultura mecanizada da soja expulsou trabalhadores do campo. Curitiba recebeu grandes contingentes de migrantes. Precisou de decisoes rapidas para evitar o caos urbano e antecipar demandas futuras. Investiu no planejamento urbano e na gestao municipal centrada no homem, ou seja, nos 1.587.315 habitantes recenseados em 2000.

No Brasil também chamado de Nononono (eu sempre me pergunto se tanta energia negativa não acaba influenciando o cliente). É aquele que vai nos layouts simulando o texto final. Ou seja, não é para ser lido. Serve apenas como decoração, não vale nada, muito menos o que está escrito. Bom, então vale tudo: errar, escrever palavrões (cu, ah, ah), bobagens, falar mal de quem você quer, sacanagens, usar várias vezes a letra zzzzzzz, contar piadas como aquela: uma índia norte-americana que engravida durante uma temporada num college e, depois de comunicar ao pai-cacique, volta para a tribo. Ao cumprimentar o pai, diz: "How", ao que o pai replica: "How I know, I want to know who", falar bem de mim mesmo (que cara legal!); enfim, ninguém vai ler este texto mes-

Hardt Importadora e Distribuidora Ltda.
Rua Frei Gaspar Madre de Deus, 830 B11, 81050-590 Curitiba PR Brasil
c. +55 41 9973 1862, t. +55 41 3022 11871
info@hardtimport.com.br • www.hardtimport.com.br

turbocharged typography

movement is the essence of sport – and movement also defines the design language: turbocharged typography runs through the new adidas design centre. it is also reflected in the typeface of the signage system: fast and light, it leaps and bounds across walls and balustrades, its form vibrating and altering in the process. words identify places, become coloured surfaces, reliefs and sculptures. the building is a functional place, in black and white, offering employees a neutral setting for the company's colourful products. in the meeting areas on the upper floors the white lettering appears to have been frozen in mid-movement, forming a mural relief. on the glass balustrades of the high walkways that criss-cross the interior of the building, the letters look as if they have been stamped into superfine, transparent gauze. the outlines are made of highly reflective film, creating a shimmering effect. in certain locations the letter forms solidify into abstract surfaces or create a screen, a reception desk, a staff entrance.

adidas laces
signage system, spatial design
herzogenaurach, 2011

do you prefer commissions from the cultural sector?

"cultural sector" sounds like "eastern zone" – coincidental? is this impermeable demarcation justified? what is culture, or the cultural sector, anyway? if a bank supports a cultural event doesn't it also become part of the cultural sector? if an entrepreneur has their head office built by a good architect aren't they producing culture? if the director of a state-funded literature festival gets a ridiculously underpriced corporate design by some self-exploiting outfit in berlin, is that supporting culture?

mission: designer

it is a huge luxury to be able to decide for yourself how and when you work. it is a kind of self-fulfilment, which provides you with a living along the way. it's not a mission; it's about the pleasure of making things. that we can only be happy when we're working is perhaps a very protestant way of seeing things.

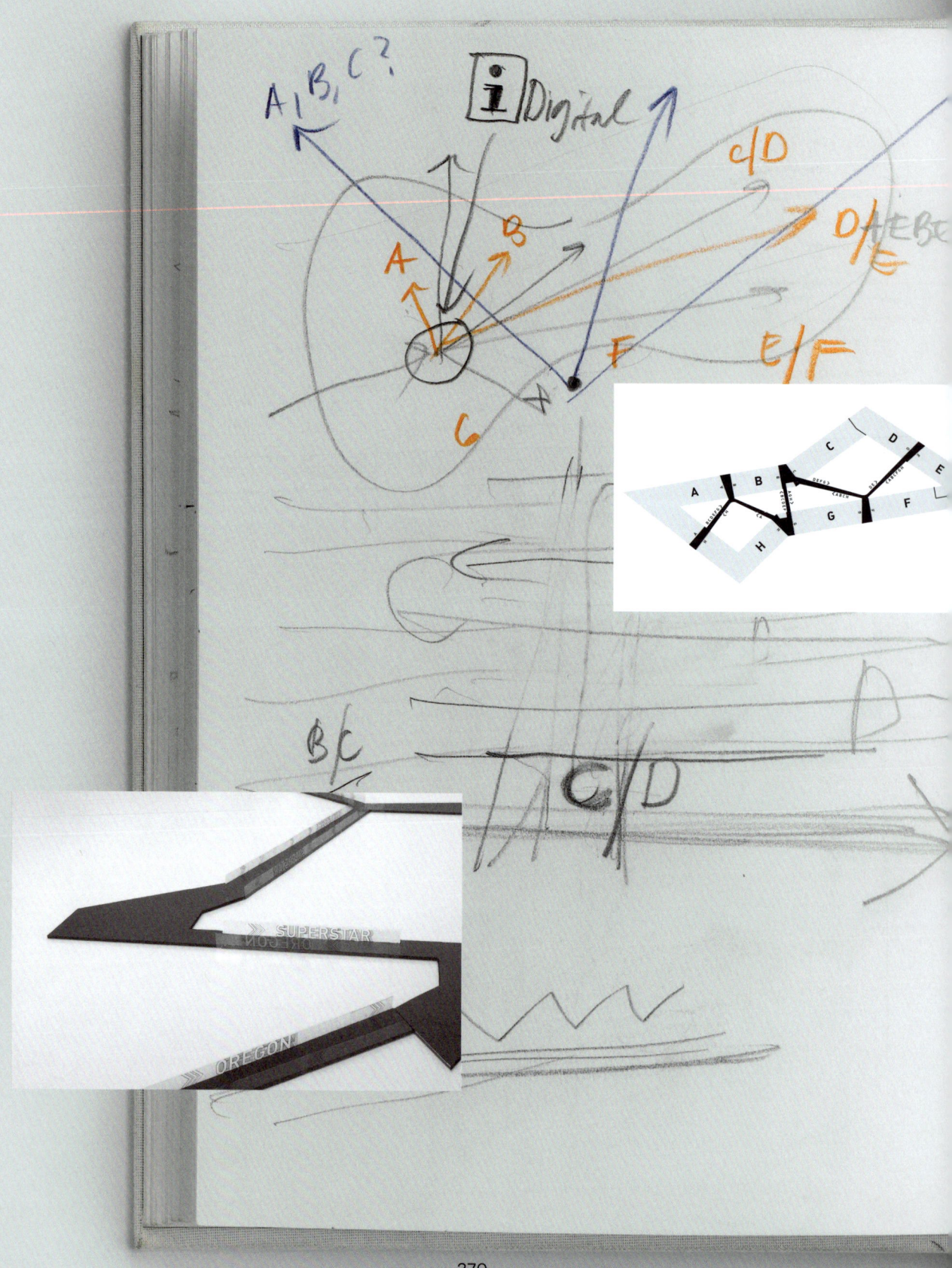

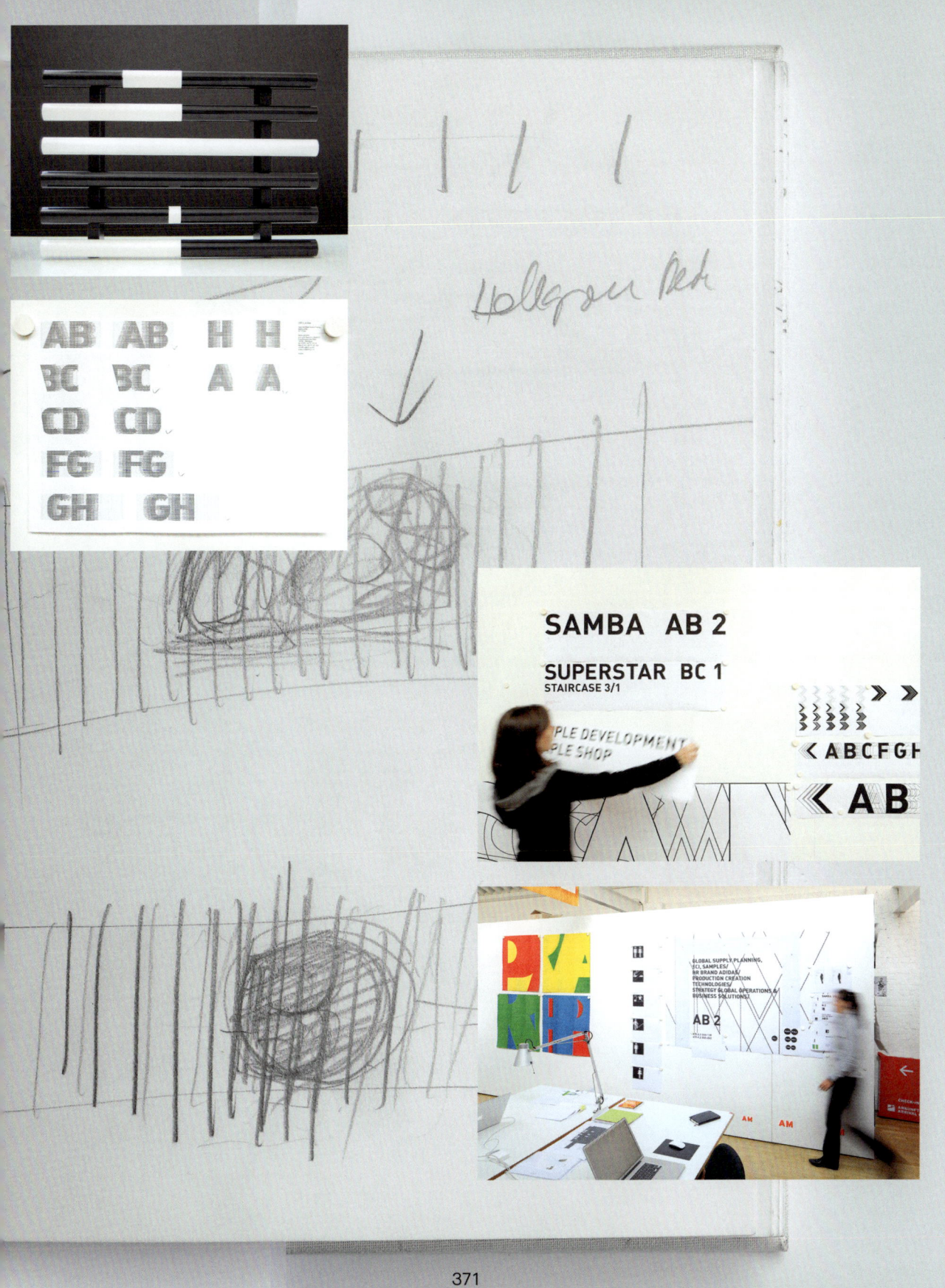

is beauty or form more important than function?

form is an expression of function. the purpose of an ashtray is to catch ashes, which is why it is shaped like a bowl. so is a wineglass. both are vessels. and both of these vessels can be crafted. you could take a lump of clay and press and pinch it to form a hollow. you could then use your creation as an ashtray. you could probably also drink wine from it at a pinch, but the wine would dribble out to the left and right of your mouth. that might be why, at some point, we start striving to unite artistic vision with functional principles. we want to move from functionality to a perfectly functioning form. for example, a riesling glass has a tulip-shaped bowl and a thin lip along its rim. this lip fits pleasantly against our lips. and not only does the liquid glide smoothly from the glass to the throat, but the organic form speeds the flow of the wine and directs it to the back of the mouth, where some of the more important taste buds are located.

form and purpose are a single entity and are bound together, indivisible. think of a slide projector: what makes a kodak carousel special is that the slides fall into place. in other projectors they are pushed and can jam because as they are pushed, they rotate lengthwise. in the kodak carousel, there is an opening that allows the slide to automatically drop into the right position. the tray holds eighty slides rather than fifty, and you can let the projector run in an endless cycle. form follows function, and suddenly the product looks wonderful. this applies everywhere.

some problems, however, are purely questions of form. the shape of corners or edges often has no bearing on function, for example. in automotive design, surfaces often present a challenge. when you look at classic cars you can see how much our body-mass index has changed over time. these cars have a lower waistline, and don't have such vast expanses of metal on the sides, and the resulting form is sleek and attractive. i think it was pininfarina who once said that these surfaces look bad when they get too big, and the large "unstructured" areas need to be broken up by character lines that catch and refract the light. this is strictly a question of form and has nothing to do with function. so there are also problems related to form alone that designers resolve – simply by making things beautiful.

as a designer is it your primary aim to get a message across, or to call things into question and foster change?

as a designer you should at least make the world a better place. better still – a revolutionary thought! – would be to make it more beautiful.

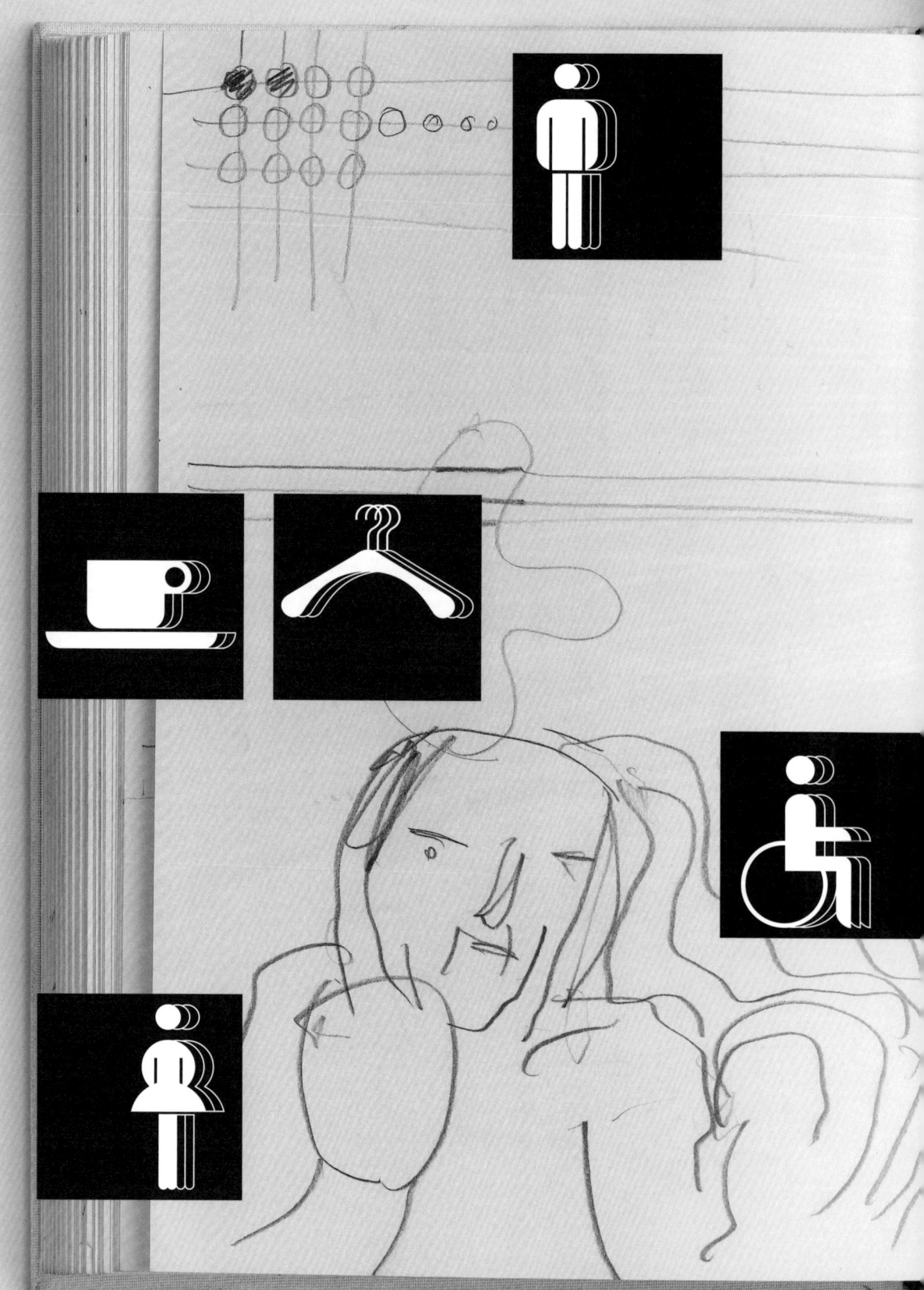

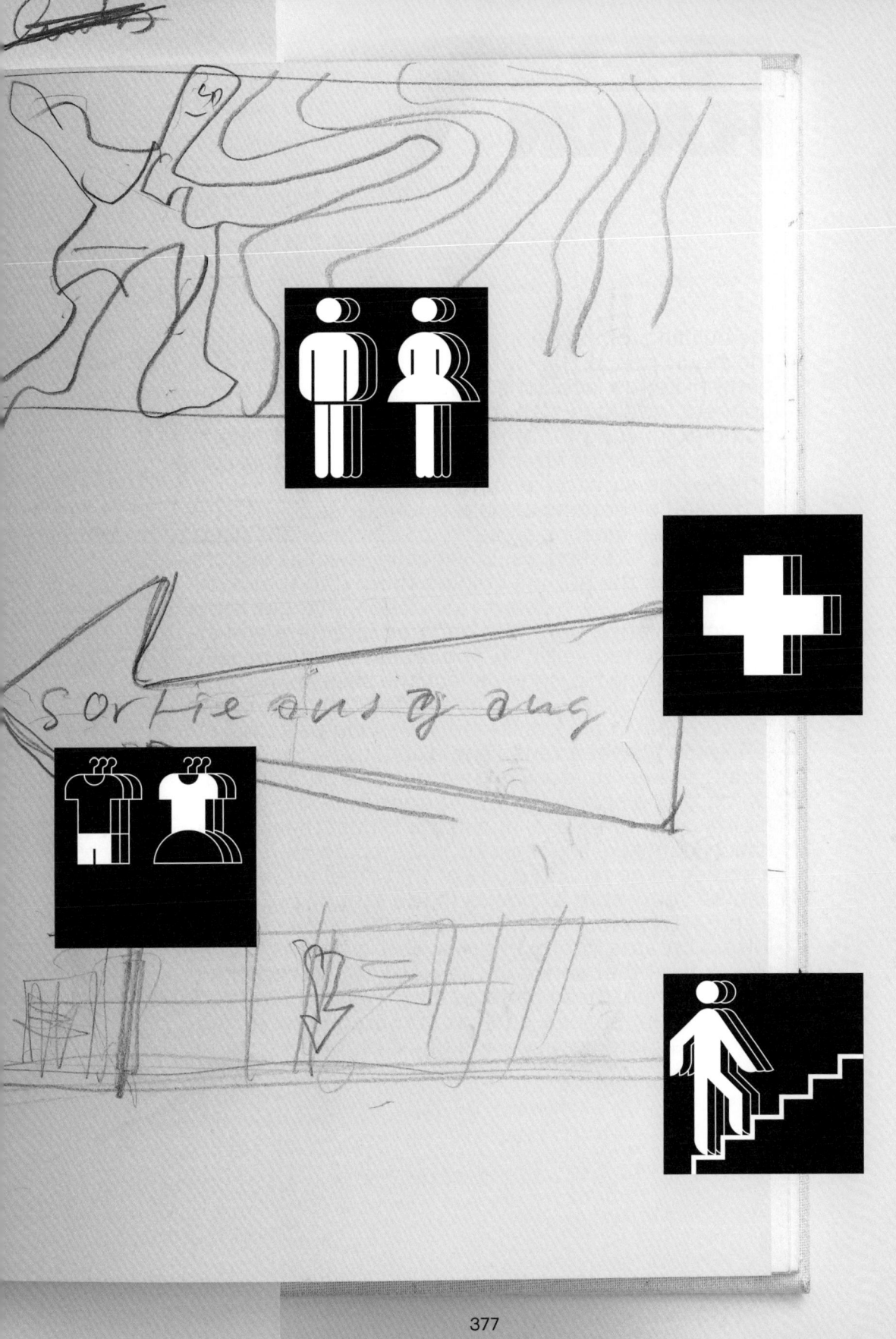

the building forms a loop. suspended walkways cross the atrium space, "lacing" the building's structure together like the laces of a sports shoe. the walkways connect individual departments within the building complex, making for greater proximity and preventing the disruptive effect of people walking through offices. the signage system supports this function, providing directions at hubs and intersections. the names of the meeting areas are displayed on the glass balustrades, creating a subtly mobile effect as visitors look across the atrium, helping them find their way.

the corporate typeface, a variation on ff din, is dynamically varied here. the outlines of letters and arrows are shifted vertically and repeated rhythmically, creating a dynamic, sporty effect. the shimmering characters – for all the world as if frozen in time-lapse photography – are combined in varying patterns, offering the viewer a varied and distinctive echo on the "laces" theme. to identify destinations an alphabetical code is displayed at the entrances of the departments. at ground level and in the atrium these destination identifiers are outsized, and incorporated within a screen-style façade made of thin steel tubes. they can be seen from all points in the atrium, providing a self-explanatory wayfinding aid. the motif of living letters creates interesting, intricate patterns – lace-like, in the other sense of the word. though abstract at first glance, these patterns clearly identify the various different spaces, such as conference room, restaurant, athlete services and brand archive.

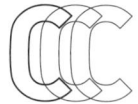

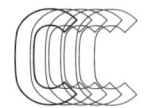
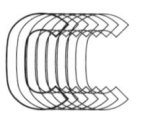
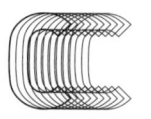

are cultural institutions more open to new ideas than private-sector clients?

the ladies and gents of the private sector are of course conservatives and the bad guys (commerce! yuck!) and the people from the art scene are the cool ones, lovely people (did you get to art basel?). believers in this fairytale include, notably, many designers, who regard it as especially desirable to allow themselves to be exploited, on an entirely voluntary basis, by cultural institutions. the private sector generally pays well and expects performance to match. if you're paying a designer a proper fee then you also respect their opinion. but let's get away from these over-simplifications: in statistical terms, good clients are probably represented, sector by sector, in exactly the same proportion as good bakers or good butchers. there are just as many good private-sector and good public-sector clients as there are good clients in the business world or the cultural sector.

what does design mean for you?

design in german is gestaltung — which translates, literally, as shaping or forming. every product and form is shaped; design is consciously providing or creating a form. you're giving something its form, creating its figure, its shape in the world. gestaltung is a good, precise word. the term design lacks precision, designer has a vagueness about it, all-embracing and unspecific. gestaltung is always about inner qualities and attributes, too. it's not about styling or making a product look good. gestaltung means deriving things from their content, their functionality and their environment; shaping them — giving them form — in context. which is why design should be part of the curriculum, just as much as english. why is music taught in schools and not design? why is fine art taught while the applied arts are not?

each of the 28 lounges is assigned one of five colours that is then used for the furniture and curtains, as well as in the kitchenette, which is given total colour immersion, with floor, wall, ceiling, sideboard, cupboards, work surfaces and even the towel dispenser in all-blue, black, red, yellow or green. these bold colours shine through the serving hatch into the white space of the meeting area beyond, promoting intuitive wayfinding. the curtains in the meeting rooms are also coloured on the inside but white on the outside; if the colour is felt to be intrusive it can be pushed aside. this use of colour adds a splash of brightness to the black-grey-white architecture.

the walkways that criss-cross the atrium lead to informal meeting lounges with adjoining kitchenettes. these have a key function as communication forums during the product design process. their importance is signalled by striking floor-to-ceiling reliefs along the walls. portrayed here are the names of iconic products like "gazelle", "rom", or, as in our photo, "burner". they give these open spaces not only a name but also their own distinctive identity, making them a wayfinding aid.

SAMBA SUPERSTAR OLYMPIA
SUPERNOVA FORZA CONQUEST
STREETBALL TORSION ADICOLOR
RESPONSE TANGO TEAMGEIST
PREDATOR GALAXY GAZELLE
RESCUE BOUNCE ROSSA
WORLDCUP MARATHON COUNTRY
FREESTYLE MONZA BURNER
ROM COPA RAC PUMP

at basement levels the typographic reliefs of the meeting lounges are translated into two-dimensional coloured wall designs.

to what extent do cultural institutions interfere in the design process? more or less than other clients?

interfering isn't the problem. the cardinal sin for clients is faint-heartedness. feedback, arising out of a clearly-defined approach, is always welcome.

what does timeless design mean to you?

the balance between
the still and
the shrill,
the coarse and
the calm,
the right and
the wrong,
the soft and
the strong,
the cracked and
the intact.

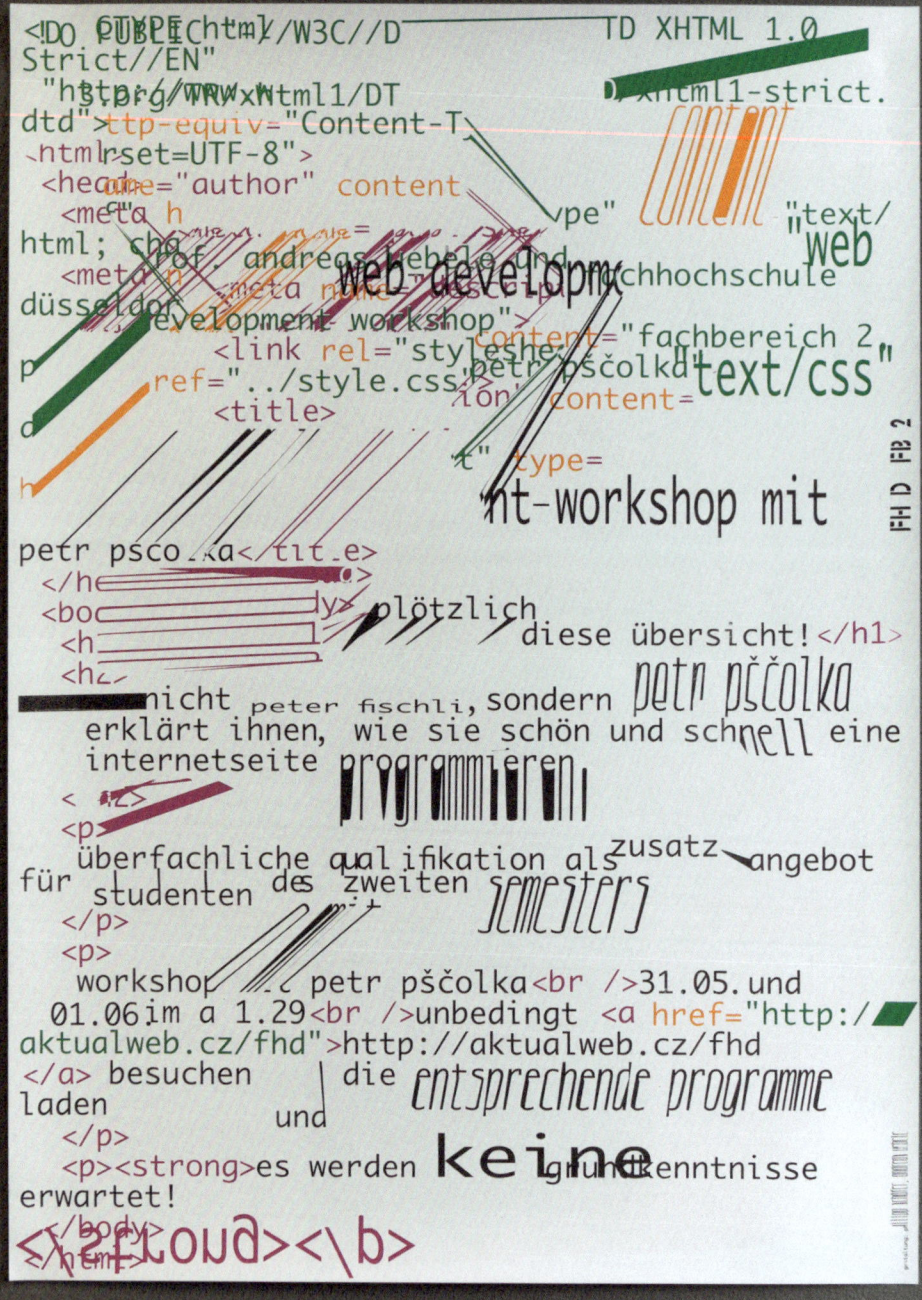

coincidentally remastered

this cheerful dance shares both its country of origin – the czech republic – and its name with the speaker: petr pščolka explains – quick-quick-slow – the rules of programming to design students. the typeface has been twisted into two-four time, too, communicating the need for design to hold sway over technology, taking the lead as it promenades its partner: hand-in-hand, hands-on-hips, hop and skip.

**html-polka
event poster
düsseldorf, 2012**

the buck hops here

the roebuck is an appealing and unmistakable heraldic animal. it's a popular and familiar figure, which is why it has been retained as the key visual element. the new drawing is businesslike but still has emotional appeal. the roebuck is leaping, it's dynamic and this motion is a visual representation of the innovative and open style the community of rechberghausen has targeted. the new form of the buck has none of the severity of its conventional heraldic counterpart, instead becoming a friendly and eye-catching logo. the colours of the community's traditional coat of arms – red, green and silver – are given a fresh makeover. silver is now rendered by white. red is associated with motion, a suitable choice of colour for the active community of rechberghausen. but since many logos and coats of arms already use this colour, a special shade of red was selected for rechberghausen: a red with a typical bluish shimmer – a truly distinctive tone. then the search was on for a special typeface for the community. it was to be warm and yet businesslike, unpretentious but not boring, modern without being fashionable. the avenir font was designed in 1988 by adrian frutiger. its precise characters and rounded nature go well with the clear lines of the logo.

why is the roebuck shown leaping to the left? because all heraldic animals face left. a mounted knight would hold a weapon in his right hand and a shield on his left arm. by facing left, the heraldic beast on the shield would be looking in the direction in which his horse is moving. and while that may mean it faces right from the knight's point of view, seen from the side or the front it's facing left. another interesting observation in this context is that, when an animal is drawn by hand, its head always faces left. the artist's wrist, to the right of the pencil, lies on the page like an obstacle. to the left, meanwhile, the fingers have space to move the pencil as they draw. of course this only holds true for right-handers – but they're in the majority. maybe that's how a tacit agreement was reached that heraldic beasts always face left?

**community of rechberghausen
visual identity
2004**

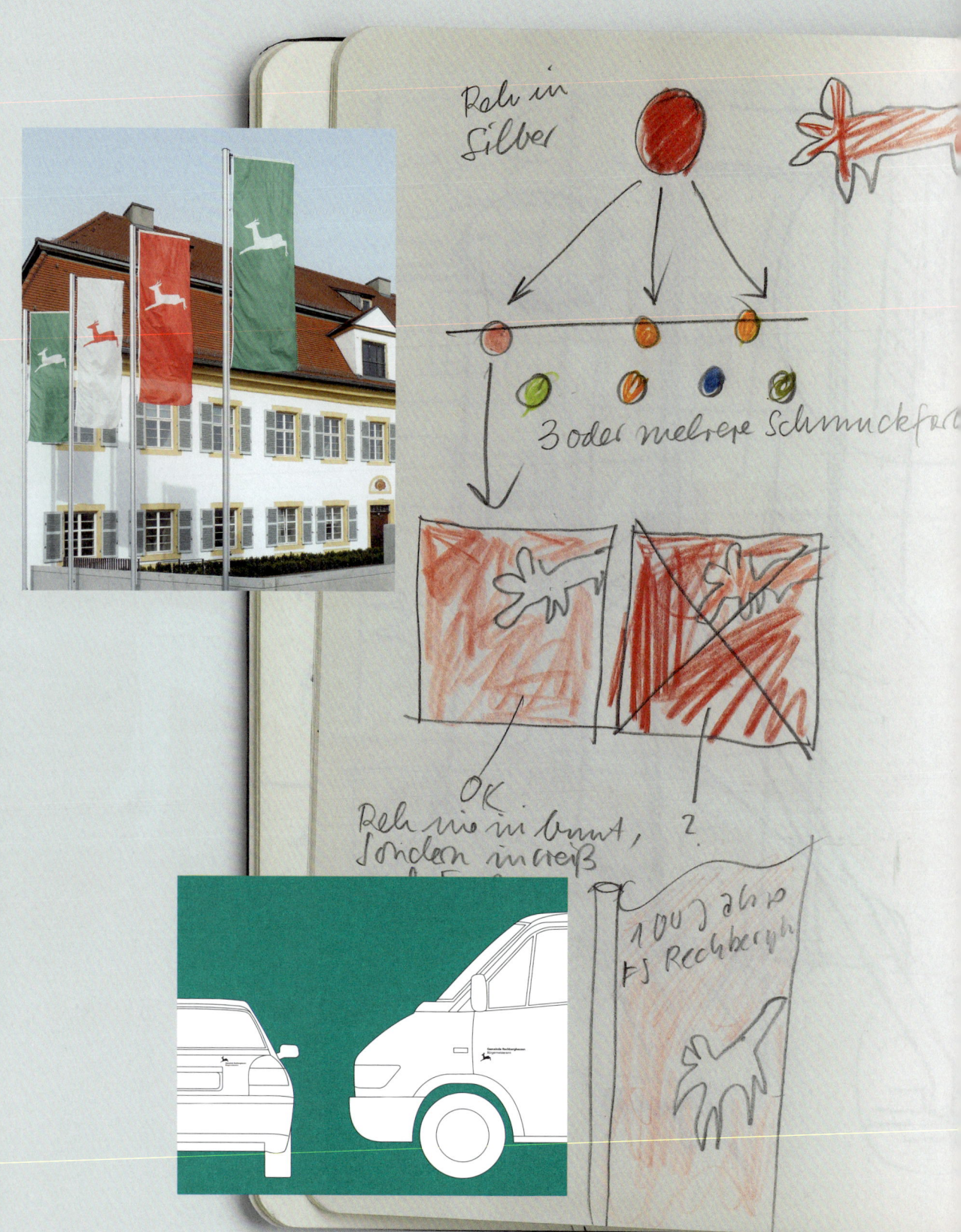

do designers need to be good writers?

write away

writing is thinking. writing a thought down makes it visible. letters, cast upon the page, form words and sentences. a design is outlined. now it can be subjected to scrutiny. precise words, fluent sentences, tell you if the idea they describe is any good. what's written down can be re-written, over-written, written out, written off. you can write something into being: gather yourself, lose yourself in thought, put your thoughts in writing. the written text is a formulation, it illustrates a form. designers who write have a sensitive tool at their disposal. they can write things up, write them down, they can hand-write, type-write, ghost-write, get it write.

your word for the future?

uninhibited

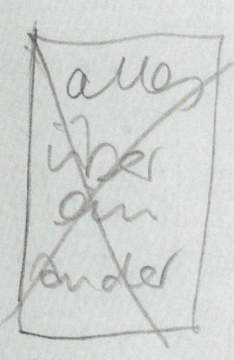

a leaping roebuck. asked to describe a picture, no one would say that it shows a roebuck about to leap, or about to land. it's simply a leaping roebuck. what counts is that it's in motion and not standing still. the actual phase of the leap is not so important. for the design of this roebuck we chose a shape that shows the animal about to land. of all the conceivable natural positions of the drawn figure, we chose the one that offers graphic stability and balance.

if you see what i mean

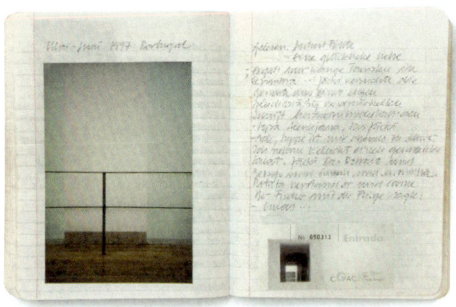

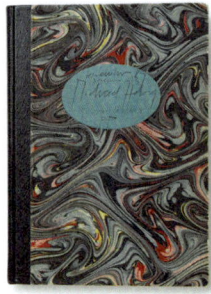

michael held was a man of letters. he recorded his thoughts in notebooks where he made a collage of them with tickets to exhibitions and all kinds of little treasures: there are photos clipped from magazines, of items of clothing, bicycles, tables and above all houses. this book presents his work in the same way that his diaries are arranged: as a multifaceted architectural landscape comprising narrative elements, drawings and colour. a collection of plans, computer drawings, sketches, original artworks and photos has been collaged in blank "diaries". the quality of the reproduction has been deliberately sacrificed to maintain the impression of a diary, which aligns well with michael held's approach as an architect for whom perfection was less important than the story, the image or the atmosphere, which is not, of course, to detract from his painstaking attention to detail when planning his buildings. this report on his oeuvre is complemented by articles from architects, engineers and artists whom he held in esteem and whose work, he felt, added value to the buildings he created.

no detail, michael held, 27 houses
monograph
stuttgart, 2011

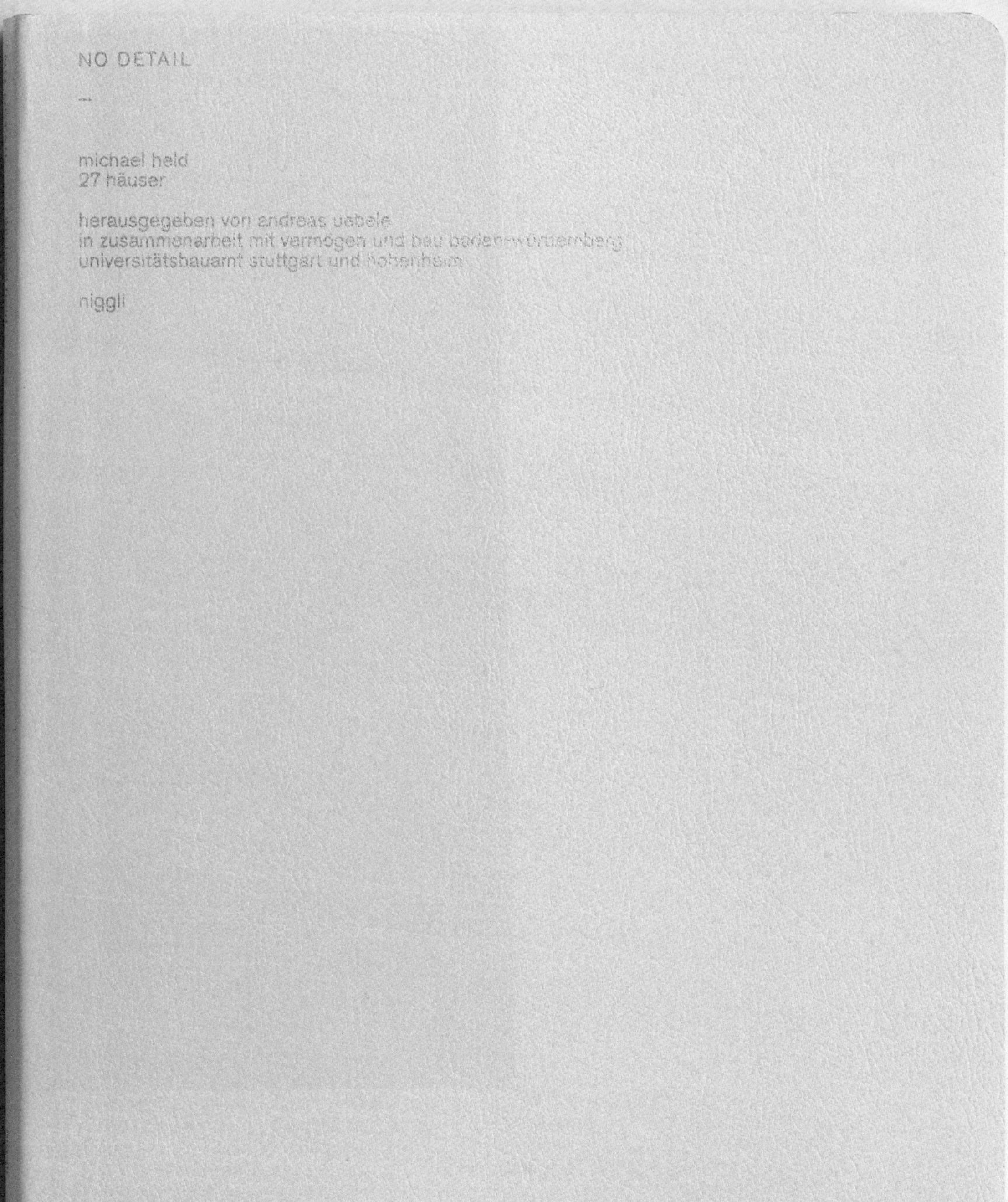

NO DETAIL
—

michael held
27 häuser

herausgegeben von andreas uebele
in zusammenarbeit mit vermögen und bau baden-württemberg
universitätsbauamt stuttgart und hohenheim

niggli

eti 2 ist ein gebäude für lehre und forschung; der überwiegende teil des raumprogramms besteht aus forschungslaboren, der kleinere teil aus seminarräumen und büros. da das gebäude im rahmen eines e budgets erstellt werden sollte, wurde bei allen konstruktionen auf eine äußerste sparsamkeit des mittel einsatzes geachtet. bekannte, bewährte und weitestgehend industriell gefertigte teile wurden im detail feinert und zum ganzen gefügt. eine besondere aufmerksamkeit wurde bei diesem bauwerk dem umga mit dem tageslicht gewidmet. das einfallende licht wird weitergeleitet (luxaclair), gebrochen, gestreut u gespiegelt. die glasbausteintreppenhäuser streuen das licht bis in das untergeschoss, die hochglänzen flurwände spiegeln nicht nur das licht, sondern auch die farben der jahreszeit in die tiefe des gebäudes die materialien sind naturbelassen, beton, glas, glasbaustein; faserzement für die flurwände, die dem li abgewandt sind, hochglänzendes resopal für die dem licht zugewandten teile. die sehr zurückhaltend verwendetete farbe unterstützt die materialien und den raum – schiefergrau für glasrahmen, caput mort und grafitgrau für stahl.

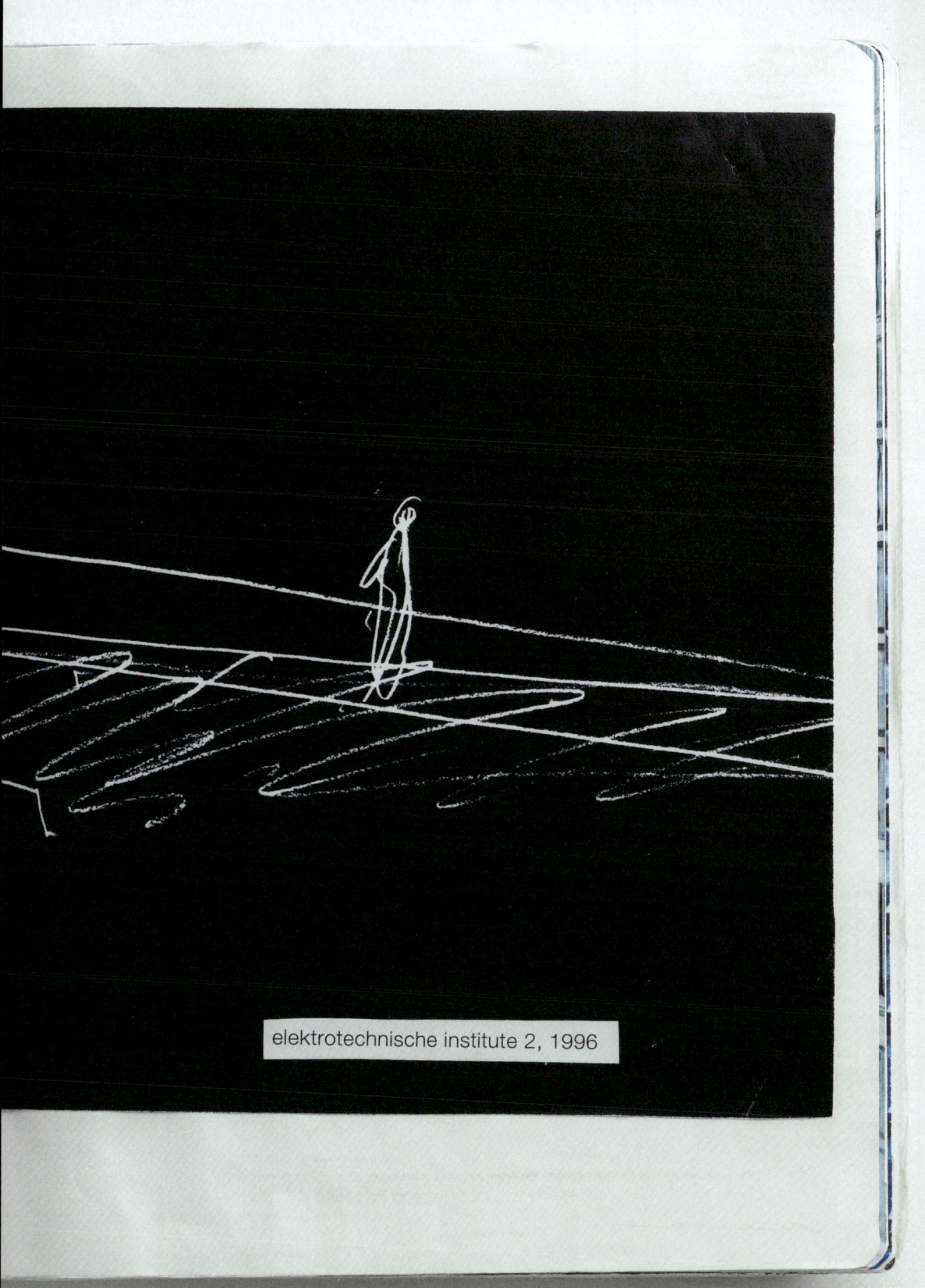
elektrotechnische institute 2, 1996

MA
—

je m
stut
la c
l'un
lité
avo
em
de
bou
me
éco
et
il é
un
sou

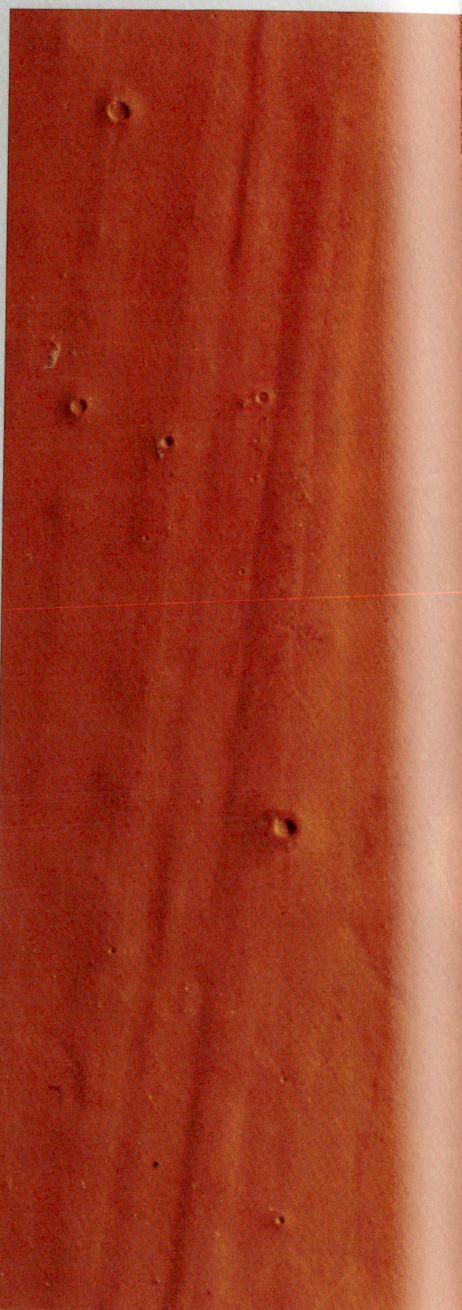

heliogenblau-königsblau   irgazinorange

**please classify your style:
how would you describe your work?**

structure and poetry

when did you first realise that you wanted to become a designer?

it happened by coincidence at the age of seventeen. when writing hopeful love letters it became clear to me that my messages got better results when they were well designed. i designed the envelopes and then i realised that design is something that suits me.

na-vita-grün   madder-lake-rot

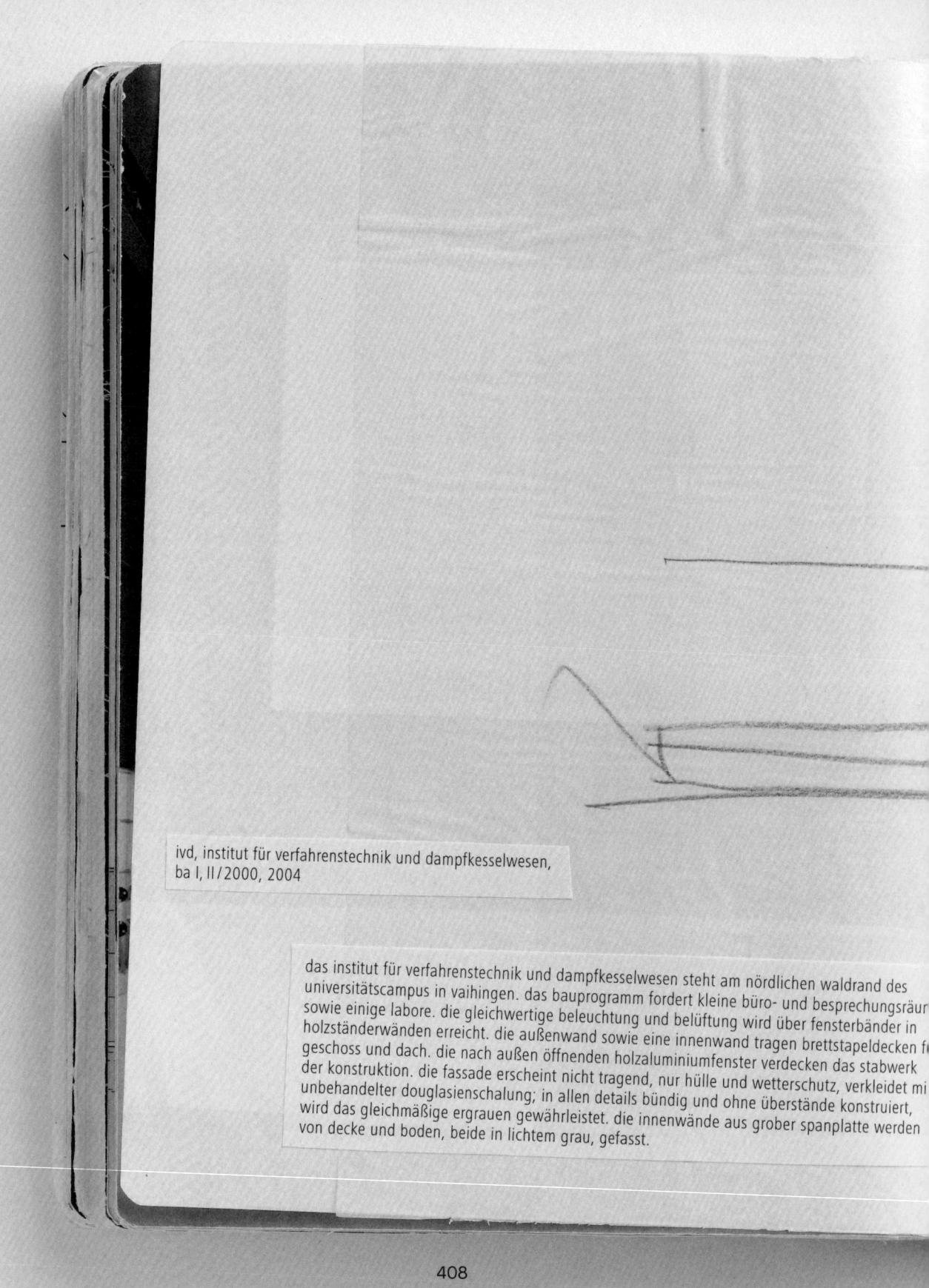

ivd, institut für verfahrenstechnik und dampfkesselwesen,
ba I, II / 2000, 2004

das institut für verfahrenstechnik und dampfkesselwesen steht am nördlichen waldrand des universitätscampus in vaihingen. das bauprogramm fordert kleine büro- und besprechungsräum sowie einige labore. die gleichwertige beleuchtung und belüftung wird über fensterbänder in holzständerwänden erreicht. die außenwand sowie eine innenwand tragen brettstapeldecken f geschoss und dach. die nach außen öffnenden holzaluminiumfenster verdecken das stabwerk der konstruktion. die fassade erscheint nicht tragend, nur hülle und wetterschutz, verkleidet mi unbehandelter douglasienschalung; in allen details bündig und ohne überstände konstruiert, wird das gleichmäßige ergrauen gewährleistet. die innenwände aus grober spanplatte werden von decke und boden, beide in lichtem grau, gefasst.

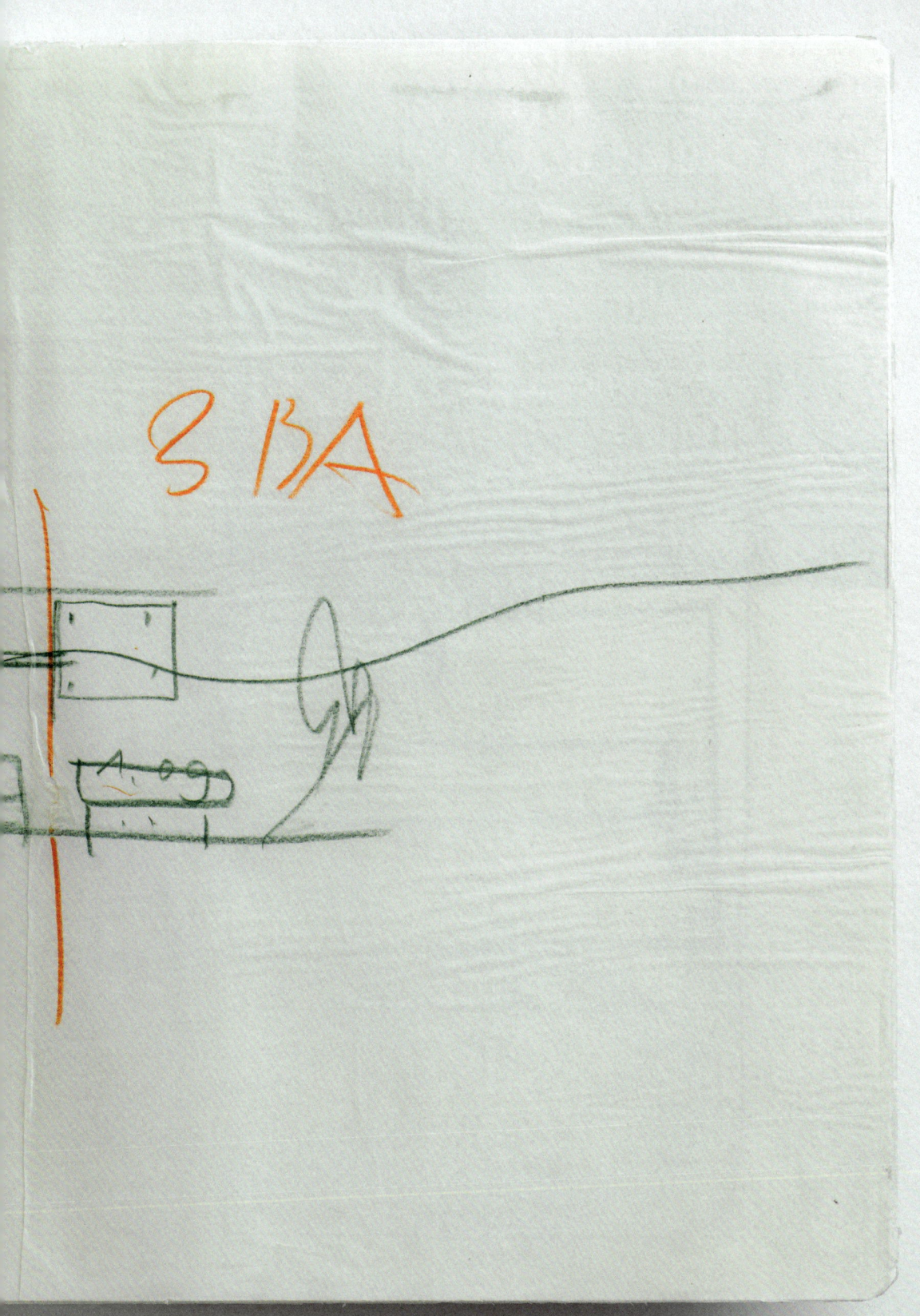

Architekturpreis Beispielhaftes Barrierefreies Bauen 2003

hindrance and help

the plaque and the certificate feature a zig-zagging line that forms five triangles of differing size. the triangles decrease in size from bottom to top, creating the illusion of a horizon. the line shows the natural path that people select to overcome an obstacle. you don't forge straight ahead on the most direct route, and you also don't try to completely circumnavigate the object. you feel your way along the hillside. the serpentine path combines the gentlest possible gradient with the shortest possible distance, making it the most effective route. the graphics don't try to cosy up to the topic of disability, but rather use an aesthetically pleasing form and generally applicable metaphor to show that obstacles can be surmounted.

architectural award for exemplary accessible building
certificate, plaque
stuttgart, 2003

harald f. müller writes backwards

harald f. müller was bored at school and so he taught himself to write backwards. this brief anecdote formed the basis for the simple and highly individual typeface that defines his corporate design. because in life as in art it's often the little things that matter and that we need to attend to.

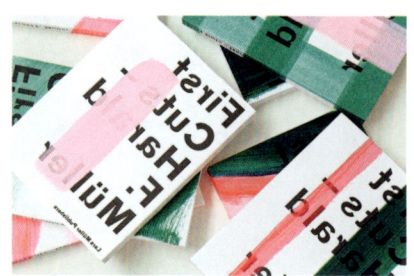

harald f. müller
visual identity
öhningen, 2012

**what approach do you take when
developing a visual identity?**

identity is something you read in someone's eyes as they're speaking, communicating. you listen to what they say and you read in what is said or shown what the other person wants to see and what you have to read from the outside with your own eyes. a visual identity has to suit the individual or organisation, but it also needs to be comprehensible for outsiders, looking in. how a brand is widely perceived is often different from how clients would like it to be seen or indeed how they would like to be. their unfulfilled aspirations then become mission impossible. meanwhile the simple, more far-sighted solution is clear to you and fits like a well-tailored suit – which likewise is not something you modify to suit what the buyer has in mind. their spontaneous delight when they see the figure they cut in a new light is a measure of how well you've done your job.

why do you do what you do?

it's about doing what you do best and loving what you do: surface marking, sheet folding, paper cutting, paint mixing, brush dipping, line drawing, type setting, line breaking, rule breaking, character shifting, form finding, concept clarifying, layout organising, system articulating, space attuning, solution seeking, wish fulfilling, wishful thinking, nuance grasping, error fixing, plan changing, dogma dodging, issue simplifying, brand building, language compressing, word weighing, first drafting, pencil sharpening, number crunching, digit designing, conformity rejecting, potential unlocking, idea recalling, perspective shifting, expectation meeting, perfect ending the book is upside-down, turned-around, topsy-turvy. in a word, it's all mixed up. here, top is bottom, back is front, it's all twisting and turning. the numbers look like they've been scattered randomly about the margins, the images – all of them – are tipped at right angles to the text. and the text is set in a wild and crazy way. why? is this art's intrinsic anarchy breaking through into book design? not at all. in fact this wild (dis)order is coolly calculated – everything's in its place. a limited edition was produced with the artist harald f. müller in which 120 uncut printed cover sheets were painted by hand before being bound and trimmed to the book blocks. this process generated new and unique cover designs: first cuts.

This is especially evident from the image of the Brussel music pavilion that is known as the Philips Pavilion (page 147). The theme's architectural dynamism arises from the intimation of maximum tension, similar to a rocket just held back from shooting skywards. It is as if that rocket is restrained from further flight solely by the structure of the fabric of the building's outer skin. In this image of the pavilion, as in all the First Cuts, the phallic theme of progress and the penetration of the cosmic matrix is present, albeit to a restrained extent.

In the Philips Pavilion there are at least two levels to reading this tension: The symbolism of rocket and net is an allegory not only of the battles of the sexes but also the rivalry between science and art. Both the conservative compensation theories of the school around Joachim Ritter and the Marxist-inspired theories of the project of Modernity of Jürgen Habermas and Marshall Berman emphasized precisely this side to Modernity's self-healing powers: the propensity of technological-scientific Modernity to resort to violence needs to be pushed back and constrained by cultural effort.

Technologically speaking, the First Cuts are simply sheet metal, given a raster by the different sizes of circular holes made by digitalized punching – only from a greater distance can you discern the themes. The metal sheets are glued to noise-absorbent, black foam. The themes arise from the changing configu-

41

written in light

how should the dead be remembered? how can their names be displayed, in a dignified and appropriate manner? the memorial is a peaceful place, and the "inscription", likewise, exhibits the utmost restraint. the names are projected digitally, while the technical act of projection remains invisible. the names shine out on a concrete wall, written in light. the mystery of how light brings life to this dense matter expresses, by the simplest of means, eternal questions of life and death. the memorial consists of a substantial, brightly lit colonnade-like structure and a cella, or inner chamber, a place of quiet contemplation which is entirely black and lit only from above, by a skylight. displayed on the end wall over the entrance, in regular succession, are the names of all bundeswehr personnel who have lost their lives. the names appear in a disembodied text made of light, which penetrates the concrete of the chamber wall. the display is created using an led display located behind translucent concrete in the ceiling slab.

the depressing fact that the roll-call of fallen soldiers isn't a static entity but a constantly increasing number is accommodated by a dynamic display in which technology plays an entirely unobtrusive role. silently, in the background, an led panel solves the problem. the names appear and fade away in a sequence that's choreographed for calmness of effect, giving visitors ample time to read each name.

armed forces memorial
spatial design
berlin 2009

ACQWX
Ö˜1368.

for this special digital application, type designer lucas de groot developed a unique typeface (photo on opposite page) based on gill, which is used on the golden wall. this rather simplistic-looking pixel font was specifically designed to closely approximate the gill, in formal terms, when illuminated by the panel's led grid. the pixel font was also optimised to ensure that it remains clearly readable across the irregular pattern of glass fibres in the translucent concrete.

massimo vignelli

among the young generation i think that andreas uebele holds a very significant place. the excellent quality of his design is reflected in every project that he has done, from the graphics for the reichstag to the signage for the adidas headquarters. his experimental work leads to interesting and innovative solutions that are gradually inserted in the reality of some projects. his work is strong, elegant and appropriate and it stands out for its clarity and lightness. he seems to bring forward the language of modernism to reflect our times much better than other designers who are still anchored in the muddy waters of the postmodern era. uebele design is the logical continuation of the modern movement, showing attention to materials and new technologies, in the most responsible way.

durs grünbein

writing is a paradoxical process, composition and decomposition rolled into one. through writing we grow closer to ourselves and yet more distant. the written word is a high-resolution means of expression.

bright radio(logical) waves

the colourful accompaniment all the way to the doctor helps to dispel dark thoughts. light blue welcomes patients and guides them to the door. pink walls provide a warm embrace for bare skin in the changing rooms. the waiting room bathes its occupants in sunshine yellow. green circles dance along the walls like waves, spreading good vibrations.

**radiological practice dr. heinrich
signage system
stuttgart, 2007**

private banking

the whole building says: this is a private space. visitors are received like guests – and courteously accompanied by their host – to the dining room, through the library, to the door. no one would think of leaving a visitor to wander alone through the building. signs on the walls would, in any case, make the place look public and thus impersonal. the signage system handles this task like a well-trained butler. the design language is quiet and restrained. the information accompanies visitors who have no need to go looking for it, because it's quite literally right at their feet. there are no panels or constructions to impair the architecturally sensitive ensemble – bright metallic characters are inlaid into the terrazzo and granite floor, connecting with the buildings in a way that's both natural and assured.

private naming: the names of the conference rooms point to those of the neighbouring roads and squares providing additional orientation within the building. but quite apart from that, these names are so much more attractive than the uninspired monikers that otherwise decorate conference rooms – madrid or rome, daimler or bosch. some of the rooms here are named after the architect; the western door is known as the salvator door, while the meeting room uses another local street name: löwengrube – the lion's den.

**hypovereinsbank board building
signage system
munich, 2005**

words in large type show locations, telling you where you are. words in small type indicate destinations. the polished letters reflect the sky and the colours of the building.

Grosses Atrium
Maximiliansaal

Kleines Atrium

the polished steel
letters reflect the
light back again,
casting words onto
the walls where
they progress with
the movement of the
sun, travelling like
comets.

Grosses Atrium

**is handwriting still relevant for
a contemporary designer?**

the art of writing

handwriting is a personal notation, a manuscript, like a musical score. the writer gets to decide how it will sound. will it break free from standardising convention, or will it conform to a structure of spontaneously defined design features? writing drawn by hand can be extra-bold or scratchy-thin, softly flowing or crunchily variable. the writing implement sets the tone. the surface is occupied, letters — rebelliously — packed in right up to the edges, signalling a direct, unaffected — apparently haphazard — command of the space. it's a powerful, unprettified image. the flow of the lines reveals the ease, the effort, the power, of the writing hand, which thinks and sees simultaneously. a handwritten letter or notelet is a special form of communication. the time and effort devoted to painstakingly forming the letters signal the writer's esteem. handwriting is an art in itself. it is a contemporary form of communication.

mirror

the mirror speaks: come closer, my beauty, beyond the mountains lives one a thousand times more beautiful than you. the mirror shows what is, not unsparingly but lightly. it shows the moving image, blurred traces of colour, a notation of the surroundings. surfaces dissolve, heavy becomes light, light floats in space. you see the garden's yellow flowers — now displaced and living, bizarrely, inside the house. you see strange shadows. cut in half, as if by magic, they float above the fireplace, pursuing you like marionettes on strings. the small room becomes big, the dark corner bright, the deep space compact. the mirror is a friendly echo in the room.

four-sided duo

the forum takes on visible form, a square setting reveals what this is all about: a public space; a forum for an exchange of views circling around a topic like the four constituent parts of the wordmark. the logo speaks about the dialogue taking place in the forum. a geometrically simple, readily recalled sign, it draws its uniqueness and visual appeal from being rotated through 15 degrees and from the offset positioning of the two squares.

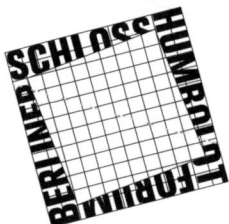

**berliner schloss foundation – humboldt forum
visual identity
berlin, 2009**

SCHLOSS
HUMBOLDT
FORUM
BERLINER

zigzag

the new logo for leather goods manufacturer müller & meirer has the heart-warming appeal of a scribbled love letter – the kind of handwriting it's always a pleasure to decipher. the initials resemble a monogram stitched in zigzag on a sewing machine – subtly referencing the company's long tradition of craftsmanship. yet at the same time the design responds to customary contemporary demands for simplicity, clarity and scalability. not only that but it's invertible, too. our client gave us carte blanche – and we took them at their word, playfully mixing and matching the contrasts of white, silver and black. sometimes the brand name appears white on black, sometimes shimmering silver on white, or even black on black. overall these variations speak of balance and diversity – an impression judiciously supplemented by woodcut-style illustrations to endow the brand with a rounded and distinctive character. the drawings – plants, elves, animals and fairies – provide atavistic, quirky accents that encourage the eye to linger.

müller & meirer
visual identity
kirn an der nahe, 2015

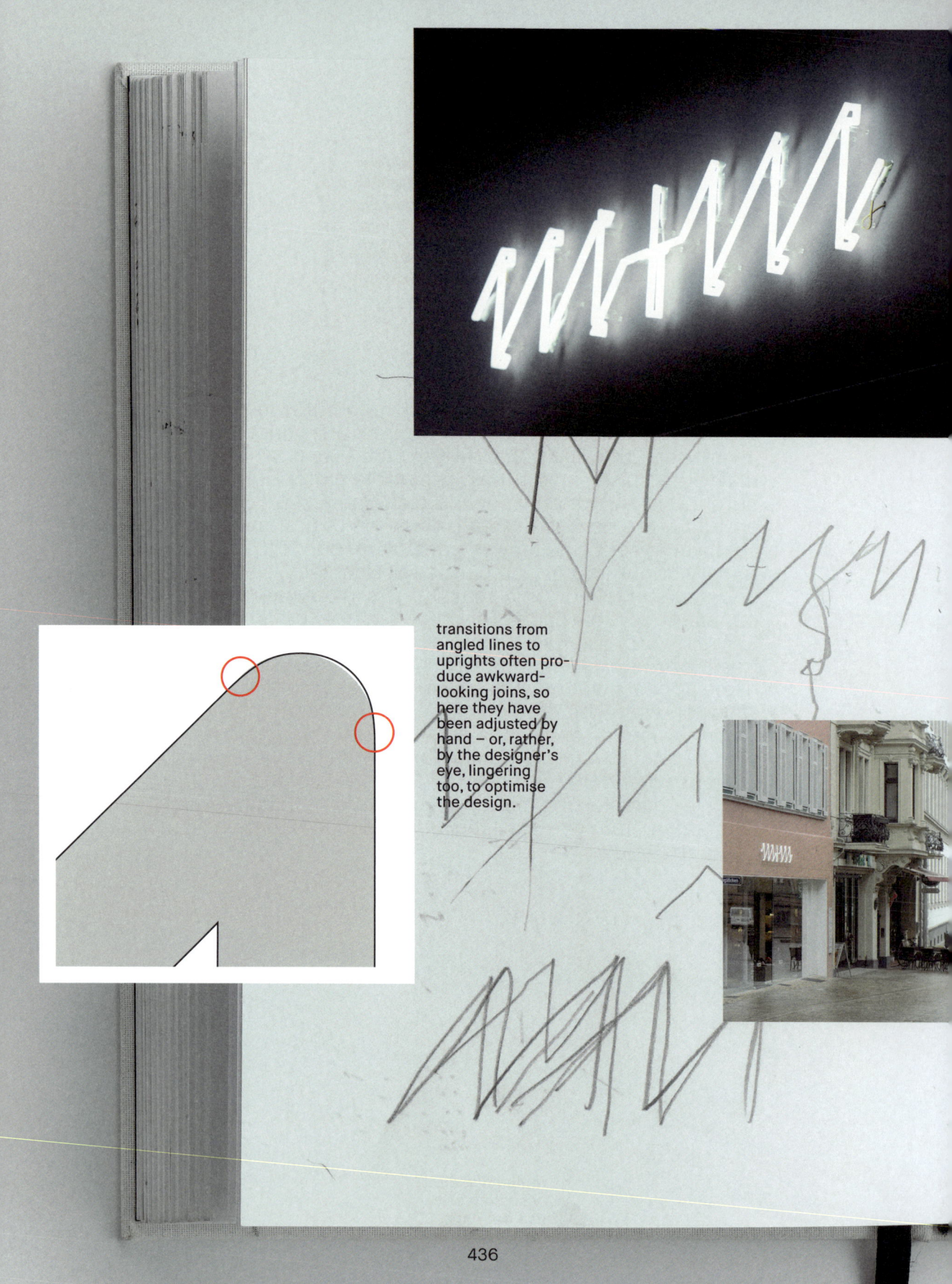

transitions from angled lines to uprights often produce awkward-looking joins, so here they have been adjusted by hand – or, rather, by the designer's eye, lingering too, to optimise the design.

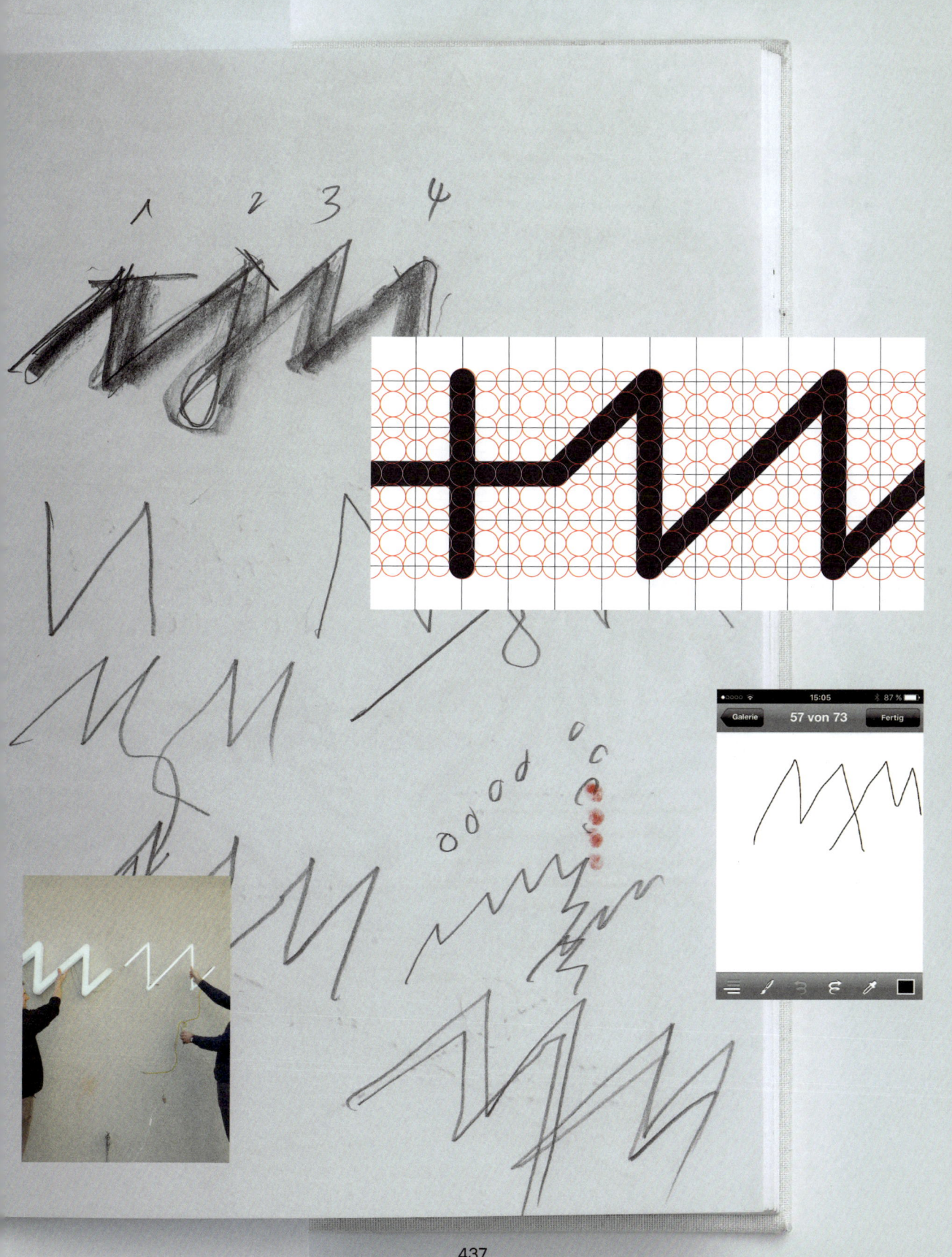

green

fern green, moss green, fir green, pine green, grass green, spring green, leaf green, rush green, mint green: green is the go-to metaphor for nature. the green of an unripe apple or new birch leaves — fresh and full of promise — heightens, in the 1970s, into the shrill, offbeat green of a noisy swabian sports car. the light-coloured paint is volatile, shading into yellow, as zippy as the car itself. mix this colour with blue, though, and the tone becomes distinctly grown-up. deep and dark like heavy water, british racing green has been the livery of british racing cars — and classic sports cars everywhere — since 1929. olive green is beautiful, too — a shadowy, indeterminate colour which in sunlight becomes a notation of pine, moss and movement, calm and soft against the play of dark shadows. a colour tone that's too slow and peaceful for the automotive industry. thankfully.

white

white is chalk, bone, is floury and wan, is greyish, bluish, yellowish, can be delicate, with a pink shimmer, or soft, with a green tone. matte white makes you want to touch it: mmmh, must be soft as velvet. brilliant white is a mirror for bright colours. reality comes in black and white; mix them and enter the grey zone, shades of grey, nuances. a white surface throws back the light, leaving no room for doubt: everything is visible, tangible, immediate.

ornamental promise

the lettering itself reveals what's so special: the latin and cyrillic characters not only communicate sofia's geographical position within europe; the use of two alphabets also underlines the city's exceptional cultural melange whose richness is reflected in the diverse typographic forms. the underlying shapes of the letters forming the two word marks are derived from historical ornaments and motifs that can be found in the bulgarian capital. thanks to the geometrical rendering of the lettering, based on a graphic matrix, the various letters of the two alphabets form a visual unit. moreover, these shapes can also be used to generate a happy, festive mood which, in line with the occasion, can be simple and understated or powerful and large scale.

the bilingual claim for sofia's bid appears on green and red rectangles playfully integrated into the overall pattern. in more formal contexts, on a letterhead for example, these are aligned with the wordmark. the complementary colours are small vibrant splashes in a monochrome setting that echo the country's national colours. the absence of colour reinforces the creative contrast with the dynamic patterns that arise out of the typography, forming a graphic decor that sends out a clear message far and wide: sofia! celebrate! culture!

sofia/city candidate for european capital of culture 2019
visual identity, not realised
2011

anassociation

the company is a non-profit association – the logo an association of initials. the association for the promotion of architecture, engineering and design in stuttgart is a private initiative. it provides a framework for lectures, exhibitions and publications, which holds these three creative disciplines together. the wordmark is a graphic rendering of this bond.

aed
visual identity
stuttgart, 2006

æd

the amalgamation of three letters: a ligature of a and e is contained in the typeset. but as the "artificial" ligature of e and d creates a visual thickening which reduces the legibility of the e, the counters of e and d are enlarged. the oblique thin stroke initializing the bowl of the a turns horizontal at its vertical stem in order to enable its extension to the right to cut the bowl of the d vertically. this measure renders the e legible. the vertical stem of the d is shortened to visually balance the logo.

**eva-maria schön
gebiet geknittert**

andreas cukrowicz

your works recall images of my hike to cape nordkinn. pushing the boundaries with no room for compromise. no trail and nothing but rock fields on the day-long hike to the northernmost point in mainland europe. the only wayfinding system is a large letter t painted at long intervals. clear, precise and self-evident, its bold red is clearly visible amidst the omnipresent grey of the landscape. a subtle explosion. and tense calm.

finals

chance is a good designer if you give it some space. the idea of creating a poster announcing our guest adjudicators from a company called "studio sport", playing with the motif of the football scarf, had its origins in a fashion accessory belonging to the author. this bright red and yellow comme des garçons scarf (see this page) tends to create confusion because it looks like a football scarf without clearly referencing any particular league or club. our first attempt to turn this idea into a design didn't work – we threw it out. but we still wanted to have a scarf specially produced as a welcome gift for our swiss colleagues, bearing the name of their design studio. we examined the ten variants of the layout – by chance! – on our smartphones, while travelling. the narrow-format designs were all displayed at once, stacked up on the screen (see p. 451, right), making them – by chance! – look like a single image, which became the basis for a poster.

flags! fouls! football scarves! the coincidence of the euro 2012 finals, the end-of-semester student show and the visit by guest critics from studio sport is given visual expression here: the carefree gameplan of the typography draws inspiration from the design of football scarves – words extended into extra time, type lined up like defenders in a wall.

end-of-semester presentation
event poster
düsseldorf, 2012

MARTIN & RONNIE
ANDY & DANIEL
VENUS & APOLL
S)

LIVE:
MARTIN & RONNIE
STUDIO
SPORT
AM 3. JULI
2012.

Aktuelles
Sport-Studio
Live mit
RONNIE
MARTIN

orient-ation

the most significant religious location in the muslim world, the largest building in the world, the second tallest building in the world, the biggest clock in the world ... the signage system makes a modest contribution to this world of superlatives. the colours are quiet and defer to the exhibits. arabic and latin types are set in an optical balance and the pictograms are matched with the cultural, social and religious characteristics of the country. the wayfinding system responds to the need of millions of people to find their way around within a short period. the information accompanies them, with pictograms and texts helping them locate the main sights and reach them quickly, reducing the time they spend waiting.

**king abdullah center for crescent observation and astronomy
signage system, visual identity**
mecca, 2015

can the choice of a particular font have ideological implications?

the font choice says a lot about a designer. any typeface contains within it what its designer thinks. at the same time, according to philosopher hannes böhringer, the form "always contains more than the designer intended. and this added element is decisive."

the choice of a font is determined by our own preferences or by what we think we see of them in a particular typeface. these might be formal attributes — one person prefers smooth fonts, another likes them angular, rugged — or technical aspects. much more than the choice, though, it's the way the font is used that determines what kind of signals reach the recipient. when fonts are selected carelessly and set in a sloppy, thoughtless way, this shows a despicable lack of diligence on the part of both designer and client.

the tricky question is: can a bad person create something that's beautiful, in formal terms? can we view the work independently of its creator? are wagner's operas, heidegger's writings or gill's typefaces contaminated, because these individuals had human weaknesses? gill's supposed sexual aberrations might lead to the choice of a different typeface for a children's day centre. but why? is the gill sans typeface, which is absolutely excellent, somehow at fault? gill's design is technically immaculate and visually striking — why shouldn't it be used for a children's day centre, too? good design is always possible — perhaps indeed especially possible — with 'bad' typefaces. perhaps a naïve belief in the goodness of form itself can prevent us getting lost in moral quagmires?

do outstanding designers also have to be morally exemplary people? "why all the bellyache when the life and the work don't harmonise?" (hannes böhringer). it's probably a consequence of political correctness, that we're all supposed to be morally irreprehensible, an implacable and inhuman attitude in which deviations, from whatever norm, are viewed with disapproval. wagner's dubious views, though, didn't stop daniel barenboim insisting on playing a wagner opera in israel, despite fierce opposition.

i'm convinced that form is inextricably linked with inner essence and that every product manifests the spirit of its designer. so let's ask again: how bad does someone have to be for their badness to be expressed in a form designed by them? can people who think and act in deeply reprehensible ways create anything of genuine beauty? are leni riefenstahl's films beautiful? even those who don't find them beautiful have to acknowledge their outstanding quality. and yet i think that this kind of beauty is something that worships the heroic, the powerful, the absolute, which — for me personally — is artistically questionable. from a designer's perspective it becomes clear that while power isn't a bad thing in itself, beauty needs something fragile in it, something non-compliant to give it power.

back to the — perhaps simplistic — question of whether fonts can be morally good or bad. or can we only distinguish between bad and good fonts on aesthetic grounds? after all, someone else might think a font i personally value is a bad one. so surely it's different aesthetic judgements that come into play when a typeface is chosen? as a designer, i find it easier to make aesthetic value judgements than moral ones, and so i'll avoid answering with the insight that good and bad things — including fonts — only come into the world when someone helps to make this happen. these individuals, clients and designers, bring something into the world from which we all benefit. if they also happen to have human weaknesses, that's forgivable. "for the 19th century this was less problematic: genius was in a category of its own." (hannes böhringer).

when massimo vignelli visited our office a few years ago, he said that the melior font by herman zapf was a fitting choice for the german parliament's corporate design because zapf was german. in fact we hadn't given this aspect the slightest consideration. in retrospect i find this rather worrying. perhaps, as "german designers", we also subconsciously chose a german font? we certainly did choose this type for its formal aspects, but by these criteria we might also have considered a swiss typeface, because fonts of a constructivist character — which suits the parliament logo — are more likely to be found in germany and switzerland than in — for example — the netherlands or france. a different choice of font might have given the corporate design a rather cold look — more reminiscent of a (german!) administrative authority. to that extent the choice of font might well reflect different ideologies — but there are no moral strings attached.

457

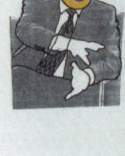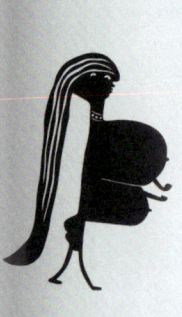

painting by numbers

"when something is not preconceived, when there is no artifice to it, when it is unexpected, it is 'schlump' – sheer serendipity" (grimm's german dictionary). the company works with disabled people. the idea of having them illustrate its annual report is fascinating. the group of artists "die schlumper" set up by the alsterdorf evangelical foundation helped us put this into practice. where the experiment has succeeded is in the portraits created for the report, where the artists respond to the contents. on other pages it becomes clear that art does not lend itself readily to other purposes. l'art, quite simply, is pour l'art.

**alsterdorf evangelical foundation
annual report
hamburg, 2004**

the blue ribbon

a brand has to win hearts. it has to be simple, and it has to go straight to the point. its job is to embody the essence of the company. and the essence is not a picture of a material thing – the elemental nature isn't seen materially, but figuratively. it's a distillation, a translation into visual language. the image must be open to different interpretations. the openness of the drawing lets different readers draw close to the essence of the company through their own different readings. the logo is a ribbon fluttering joyously in the breeze. it calls to mind wind-swept coastal regions; it leads us on board a ship where the sails flap and snap in the wind and odysseus, tied to the mast, listens longingly to the sirens' song. all kinds of things can be read into this ribbon: a sail, a pennant, the ribbon on a sailor's cap, the rocking of a ship in the wind. it's a familiar and easily accessible image, one that everyone understands and yet is open to interpretation. and of course a blue ribbon also builds an elegant bridge to the "blue riband", the great traditional competition for the fastest crossing of the atlantic. thanks to its clear-cut form, even fractions of the logo are easily identified. the fluttering blue ribbon is an appealing sign that can be adapted for a wide variety of applications, effectively transforming it into a brand.

german maritime museum
visual identity, signage system, not realised
bremerhaven, 2006

USEUM

the blue ribbon is a strong image that can be adapted to different purposes. as part of the signage system that guides visitors around the building, important information is written along its length. the narrow blue ribbon is like ariadne's thread, leading people through the labyrinthine architecture created by hans scharoun. you can wander off course, marvel, look, read – the blue ribbon will always take you back to the exit or the café. outside the building, masts hung with fluttering blue ribbons greet the guests and signal the special nature of the place.

what is required of a corporate design?

authenticity

an organisation's corporate design is more than its visual identity. it is a visual language through which a company communicates — about itself, with customers and partners. the language is an expression of the individual company and the product. the designer's task is to give this language a credible, authentic grammar: appropriate photographs instead of pretentious images, precise lettering instead of vague formulations, selected tones instead of random colour noise.

what was your worst project – the one that went wrong?

badly designed projects happen when you don't listen to your inner voice. the lesson they teach you is to listen: to yourself, to others and to the client.

DEUTSCHES SCHIFFAHRTSMUSEUM

A B C D E F G H I R S T

the free-flowing, looping shape of the ribbon calls for a calm and stable typeface. the linear nature of the wordmark lays the foundations for its open form. the unusual length of the german word is shortened with a striking, condensed font to become a wordmark. the font was developed by an unknown italian artist in 1930 and was digitalised for the competition. the character of the font harks back to the 1920s, recalling in particular the year 1929 when the s.s. bremen brought the blue riband to germany. in 1933 the riband was then captured by the s.s. rex, an italian vessel, which neatly closes the loop.

art meets logo

a logo designed to work for art isn't art. it's a typeface. what makes it special is a simple graphic sleight of hand that facilitates the creation of distinctive wordmarks for any number of institutions, while at the same time signposting their relationship to their artistic siblings. the tie that binds together the disparate members of this particular family is a coloured stripe. it nestles behind the black top half of the capital letters that make up the wordmark. the bottom half of the letters resonates in the same colour. the shift of colours in the lettering plays a chord. together with the other colour tones of the gallery, school, museum, café and association, a technicolour concert takes shape, but one in which each instrument can still be readily distinguished from the others. a number of different variations on the theme of those coloured stripes have been composed. the stripes play their way through the different spaces in a variety of rhythms and keys. a distinctive, easily recognised visual language is born, characteristic of the gallery and the school. the striped motif transposes the architectural language of transparency into visual form. the linear graphic elements allow the painting and drawing to be seen as if through half-open drapes, merging art and information into a single unit.

stihl gallery waiblingen/lower remstal school of art
visual identity, signage system, not realised
2006

GALERIE
STIHL WAIBLIN

MUSEUM
STADT WAIBLIN

KUNSTSCHULE
UNTERES REM

FOERDERVER
FREUNDE DER
STIHL WAIBLIN

MUSEUMSCAFÉ

809
810
811
812
813

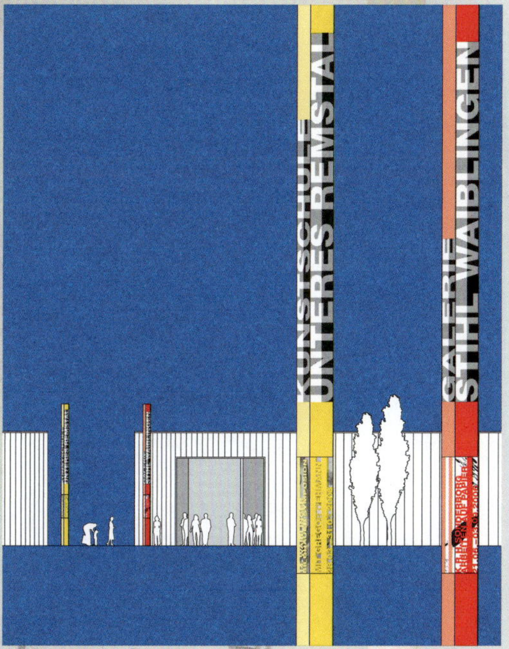

to match the brilliant and transparent nature of the façade, the external name plates take the shape of freestanding translucent pillars. structured like the façade, these are internally lit. the inner layer has a coloured, translucent skin. the pillars with the wordmarks of the gallery and school are located in such a way that they obviously relate to the relevant building. they also act as notice boards for information about events. lettering and posters are applied across the corners, while the tall red and yellow strips send out poetic signals by day and by night. art communicates.

Aperol
Spritz
Friulano
Dolce
Gelato

barbarian black letters

Accademia Tedesca Roma
Villa Massimo
Largo di Villa Massimo 1-2
00161 Roma
Italy

writing letters is one of the author's passions. on the one hand because messages are more likely to be well received when they're beautifully wrapped, on the other because this mode of communication may be more distant but is all the deeper for that. confronted with the luxurious gift of a seven-week scholarship at villa massimo in rome (which can be a challenge: "bloody rome, bloody villa massimo" raged author marie-luise kaschnitz), he faced the question of what to do with it – without needing to call on the support of his office team (seven weeks of dolce far niente being proscribed by his swabian-pietist work ethic). simply writing letters was not perhaps the most obvious idea but it was a good one nevertheless: at long last, time to do something pleasurable (drawing letters on paper) particularly for those clients and friends to whom missives were long overdue. from these 250 roman letters a typeface has been distilled – a powerful brew, capturing the essence of those freehand envelopes and letters and now available as a font with six weights to savour at your pleasure. but be careful, it's strong stuff: for every character there are at least five alternative glyphs.

aaaaaa

massimo
font design
stuttgart, 2016

klaus schmiedek
andreas uebele – playfully serious, seriously playful

every now and then in my post i find a large envelope, its surface entirely covered with big black letters in what looks like a first-grader's clumsy attempt at writing. with a little patience and imagination i manage to decipher my address. as the envelope is correctly stamped and the postal service tries to do things properly – it could be a child's wish-list for santa, they don't want to be killjoys – they convey the letter to its destination and deliver it. hats off to them, i say – who'd have thought they'd take the trouble? and who'd imagine that the author of this scrawl – exemplary in its sheer disdain for standard address formats and text design rules, indeed in its apparent contempt for "beautiful design" – who'd have thought that behind this was a renowned design company, were it not for the clearly printed sender information: büro uebele/ visuelle kommunikation?

only andreas uebele with his proven expertise, winner of countless prizes and awards, can make fun out of the whole business, happily sending up his own profession. or maybe this isn't clowning about, but serious play? an early-morning workout for cortex and synapses before duty calls? a deliberate departure from the familiar, the perfect, a disregard of standard repertoire, a willingness to leave safe ground behind and be open to surprises and chance encounters? to drift, to float, to fly – to learn to see things anew? this is training creativity through play. ibsen said the most sensible thing anyone can do in this world is play. it's a theme we encounter in all kinds of places: "except ye become as little children ...". we are as free as we allow ourselves to be. the only way to discover new terrain is to leave the old, the familiar behind – to look beyond the horizon.

my collaboration with "uba" developed back in the early years of his studio and had its origins in his friendship with michael held, the district head of planning. the two knew each other from university, where they shared the same attitude to designing and making: what's essential? what's the heart of the matter here? re-thinking everything, again and again, looking for intelligent, credible, surprising solutions. both suffered at the banality of things, at the neglect and disfigurement of the environment, the widespread lack of culture. the only remedy for this – to do things better, themselves.

in the early 1990s we were working on new designs for university buildings. one of the driving factors here was a widespread discontent among users at the typical institutional architecture of the times. and to signal our arrival, representing a new generation of planners who were looking for new ways of doing things rather than following standard practices, we wanted a new look for our business documents. this was our first small assignment for andreas uebele. it was followed by larger ones – for wayfinding systems and signage in the new institutions.

alongside the affinity of our attitudes we also shared a mutual understanding of our different roles. having trained as an architect he quickly grasped our architectural intentions, enabling him to respond to them appropriately in his own way. yet surely it's no surprise that while this approach remained consistent, the outcomes looked different every time. any designer knows that there are always alternative options. and nothing is so good now that it couldn't be made still better. again and again, too, we experience how perceptions alter over time.

the twin pleasures of inventing new ideas and designing them, giving them form, are the driving forces of creativity. and when these new ideas are a clear and captivating improvement – delivering a sharp dose of surprise into the bargain: well, that's what you can expect from büro uebele.

we didn't get to enjoy "our" new visual identity for long. around that time everyone started to want corporate identities, mission statements and so on and the state government decided it wanted something of the kind for its administration, too. since then they've used garamond as their house typeface: classical, serious. which put an end to our adventure with the simplicity of univers: clear and objective, light and light-filled – as indeed our buildings aimed to be.

what remained in retrospect: insights from our working conversations, about seeing and feeling, content and message, dignity and value. about the weight of nuances and the significance of details. business cards, for example, and their function as the first tactile encounter with a new person or organisation: how does the material feel between your fingers, even or textured, hard or soft, do you get a sense of a barrier: please keep your distance, or an invitation: let's talk.

everything was open to question and remained so. there was never any finality to the end product, so that, like an encore, thoughts and their after-thoughts enriched the assignment itself and continued to reverberate in a delightful, boundless, creative game of words and ideas, open to beginners and experts alike.

AAAAAAAAAAAAAaaaaaaaaBBBBBB
bbbbbbbCCCCCCCcccccDDDDDD
ddddddddEEEEEEEEEEEEeeeeeeee
FFFFFFFfffffFGGGGGGGggggggg
HHHHHHHHHHhhhhhhIIIIiiiiiiiMJJJJJJ
jjjjjjjjKKKKKKKKKKKkkkkkLLLL
LLLLLLMMMMMMMMMMMmmmmmmm
NNNNNNNNNnnnnnnnOOOOOO
oooooooPPPPPPppppppQQQQQqq
qqppRRRRRRRRRRRrrrrrSSSSS
SSSSSSssssssTTTTTttttttUUUU
UUUUUUUUuuuuuuunuVVVVvvv
vvvvWWWWWWwwwwwwXXXXXXX
xxxxxxxxYYYYYYYyyyyyyyZZZZZz
ʒʒzßßßßßßßÆÆÆÆÆÆÆææææææ
ŒŒŒŒŒœœœœœœðððððððð
ÞÞÞÞÞÞÞ00000011111122222
3333334444444555555566666
7777778888889999∞€$£¥₵&
→↑↞↔↰↲←<>«»,'',""/\(){}§@¶
?¿!¡;.,:;...---

breedesign

a visual identity can draw on the full vocabulary of design. there are all the elements, laid out side by side, clear as day: the grammar of visual language. all you have to do is form the words and shape the sentences. and as with written language it's the writer who decides what is said. it can be engaging and bright or vague and dull. the rules are like building blocks. together they create a house with many different rooms, large and small, intimate boudoirs and prestigious lounges. the plans are laid by the designer who, as with a foreign language, can only become fluent and settled when the grammatical rules have been fully grasped. bagmaker bree's logo dates back to the 1970s. because of its high recognition value the logo was carefully reworked in such a way as to retain its strong characteristic appeal, while at the same time the design weaknesses were eliminated by rounding the stroke endings and the corners of the characters. the outcome is a contemporary image of the company that says: the brand changes, but the traditional values stay the same.

**bree
visual identity
isernhagen, 2004–2011**

the bree brand stands for design at its purest. the motifs selected for the photos in this campaign reveal that fact: a model, a bag, and that's that. no backdrop, no accessories to distract the observer. the product takes centre stage, accompanied only by the woman who wears it. totally naked, she looks straight at the camera. her expression is entirely natural and relaxed; her posture is no adopted pose and bears not a trace of cliché. she faces the observer with self-confidence. her nudity is disarming. the outcome is a calm, cool eroticism, seductive and not in the least vulgar.

what is quality?

what makes a particular font exceptional? and when can a character, logo or sign be regarded as high quality? why is one attractive and the other ugly? can quality be qualified? does beauty have anything to do with quality, and can something ever have quality without being beautiful? by asking more questions, we can get closer to the challenging question of what quality is.

couldn't a sturdy teapot that is unbreakable, durable and shows no signs of wear also be considered attractive because we are pleased with its robustness and longevity? or is it possible that, despite its many other valuable qualities, we wouldn't tolerate its presence because of its abysmal unattractiveness? and is it not also possible – or even probable – that some of us might deem the teapot ugly and therefore worthless, and others might deem it an object of value and therefore of beauty? when we turn away from teapots and apply this approach to items that have no measurable indicators of quality, things get more difficult – fonts and logos can't be washed and ironed, but there are a number of standards of craftsmanship that enable the quality of a font to be assessed. well-balanced pairs of letters and clean typefaces are aspects of quality, although they don't automatically make the font beautiful. but isn't beauty also a mark of the quality of a thing?

if we consider only the functionality of an object, we reduce it to just a few of its attributes. but an object consists of the sum of all its qualities. things tell us how they were created. an object reveals how it was manufactured, who ordered its creation, and who designed it. it feels hot or cold to the touch or is easy to grip. it smells of plastic or metal. it is expensive or broadly affordable. some objects inspire affection, others arouse aversion. whether an object's surface is matte or shiny depends, like all else, on the will of its makers. things also tell us whether they were made carelessly or unquestioningly, whether priority was placed on creating profit or on creating beauty, or whether all efforts were focused on finding an appealing form rather than an effective solution to the problems in hand. the design of an object also reveals whether the designer hastened to comply with the client's directives and point of view, or resisted them. it is the attitude which dwells within a piece of work that gives it a voice.

the stories told by objects endow them with beauty or reveal what is lacking. if careful attention has been paid to even the smallest details, the essential nature of things becomes obvious. the object has character and is beautiful. all the care and attention that go into a thing add up to a pleasing impression, making it good. beauty and quality go hand in hand.

**what's important for you?
what's the essence?**

depth and surface
beauty and fragility

what does a brand sound like, what's the right tone for it? bree produces the right bag for every purpose and for every person. the corporate colours reflect this diversity. the primary bree colour is red – a soft red tone with a touch of blue which removes any hint of aggression and makes it very distinctive. the combination of brown, pink and white allows the company to adopt different ways of addressing the customer.

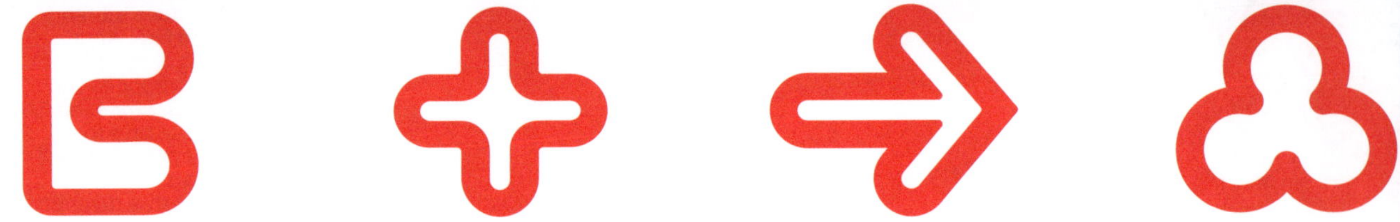

the construction of the logo only appears to be grid-based: in fact various design strategies are used to create a balanced optical effect. the stroke thicknesses vary as they do with handwriting: because horizontal strokes look thicker than upright strokes, the horizontals and diagonals are thinner and the verticals are thicker. with – mathematically accurate – quadrant-shaped transitions between the horizontal and vertical straight lines, irritatingly the thickness of the strokes would appear wider between the circle segments and the straight lines ("bone effect"). that's why the transitions are softly shaped to create a smooth, even shift from straight to curve. the close parallel lines at the centre of the letters b and e are drawn thinner than the other straight lines so that they don't seem to merge with one another. as the mathematical centre of these lines is too low in optical terms, they are raised a little to create a balanced effect. the upper arch of the letters b and e is shifted slightly inwards compared with the lower arch, because otherwise the upper halves of the letters would appear too wide. like all the lines, the upright and the diagonal of the r have rounded endings. for the letter to stand optically on the base line, the vertical and the diagonal need to end just below that line. a similar phenomenon is apparent in the horizontals of the letter e and so an optical correction was made to the upper and lower lines, which are now longer than the middle ones. the letters of the logo vary in breadth. their positive and negative shapes have been adjusted in relation to each other and to the form of the logo as a whole. the distances between the letters have also been optically adjusted for balance. the wordmark is so striking that mere sections of it or individual letters invariably call to mind the full logo of the brand.

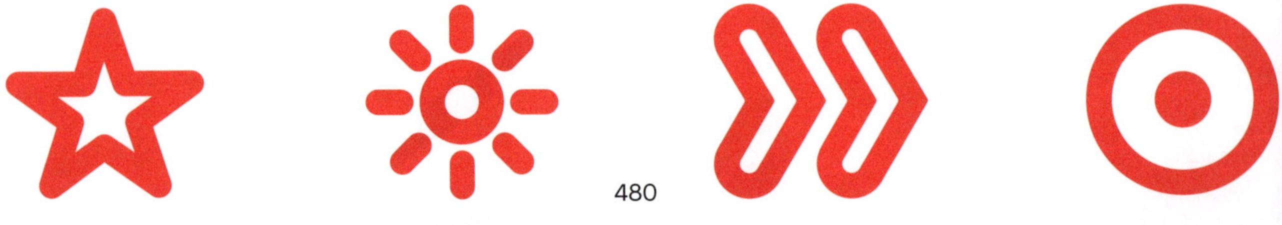

BREE

Vika 6: Damentasche. Reißverschluss; Schutzfüße; innen Handy- und Reißverschlussfach, Schlüsselschlange. Naturleder. 32 × 21 × 9,5 cm. 219 Euro.

the collection takes centre stage, in several acts. the stars of the show are capricious divas, presenting their handles, straps and loops with playful gestures. now and then they dance out of line, disrupting the order of the design. otherwise they stay neatly in place, following the choreography of shadowless light. the rest of the company keeps to clear structures, frozen in place – solo or corps de ballet – with every minute detail in sharp focus. all the members of the collection are displayed with a scientific objectivity, free of background clutter – all of them coming up bright and fresh every time.

38/39

what is the attraction of designing identities for you?

it's a process of resolution. finding a simple, visual interpretation of the complex identity of a client or company is a purifying process. it's like zen meditation — if the visual identity suits the object, everyone involved is happy.
and incidentally, the process of finding an identity reveals all points of conflict between the partners and weaknesses of the company. it takes sensitivity to develop an identity: a suitable logo needs to have the right amount of power, a touch of silence, and the ideal balance between impact and timelessness.

in the future, what will be the key challenges for brand development in terms of content and/or design?

a brand must be beautiful:
fewer vision statements, more form;
fewer pitches, more trust;
fewer workshops, more honesty;
fewer flipcharts, more typography.

when other people's kids start whining and your own abandon their usual angelic demeanour to join in, this brilliantly simple and cleverly educational book is pretty much guaranteed to restore peace, harmony and happiness forthwith.

just three clicks to the product. full, fast, unfussy information on the page about the company and its products. a 12-column grid is the perfect structure for organising information in a way that's unpretentious but interesting and attractive. the navigation is self-explanatory and the typography helps users by displaying the path they've taken through the site. on the home page a random generator shows a different group of bags each time – a surprise factor that's echoed at the next level by varying product combinations.

making the rounds

a tour to turn your world upside down? or a yellow ring that forges a link between architecture and communications design? the ragged type forms a safety net for this typographical balancing act.

**faculty tour, düsseldorf university of applied sciences
event poster
2008**

the ring, a hexalogy

the building is a glazed structure that twists and turns around courtyards and pathways. all the external walls and the internal walls facing the atrium are glazed. graphic symbols cover the internal glass walls like a curtain, not only identifying the location with a different motif on each floor, but also incorporating the information of the wayfinding system. the material of these curtains is "woven" from a grid-style pattern of rings which is different on each storey. the spacing of the rings varies in two directions, creating gaps, clusters and distinctive formations. the codes for different rooms, levels and sections of the building are displayed within these circles. the pattern shapes are non-prescriptive and can be extended at will in any direction. they overlay the glazed walls like a transparent net curtain or a shimmering breeze, varying the look of the façades and also helping to prevent people walking into the glass. the material used in the design has an incorporeal quality: the architecture and its environment are mirrored in the highly reflective film, appearing as a light, mobile and ever-changing image in the slender rings and circle shapes.

new building, drägerwerk ag & co. kgaa
signage system
lübeck, 2009

the circle is a strong shape: self-delimiting, self-referential. it has no straight lines to connect it with other edges or lines. dealing with it becomes challenging when other, non-circular elements come into play. text within a circle cannot be set in the normal way. flush-left is easy to read but in a circle it produces odd shapes around the text. a clear margin becomes apparent only when several lines can be seen together – which is the exception rather than the rule. the system provides a typographic solution to this problem: the text is arranged symmetrically about the central axis of the circle. the capital letters generate a monodimensional image, keeping the residual black space in balance.

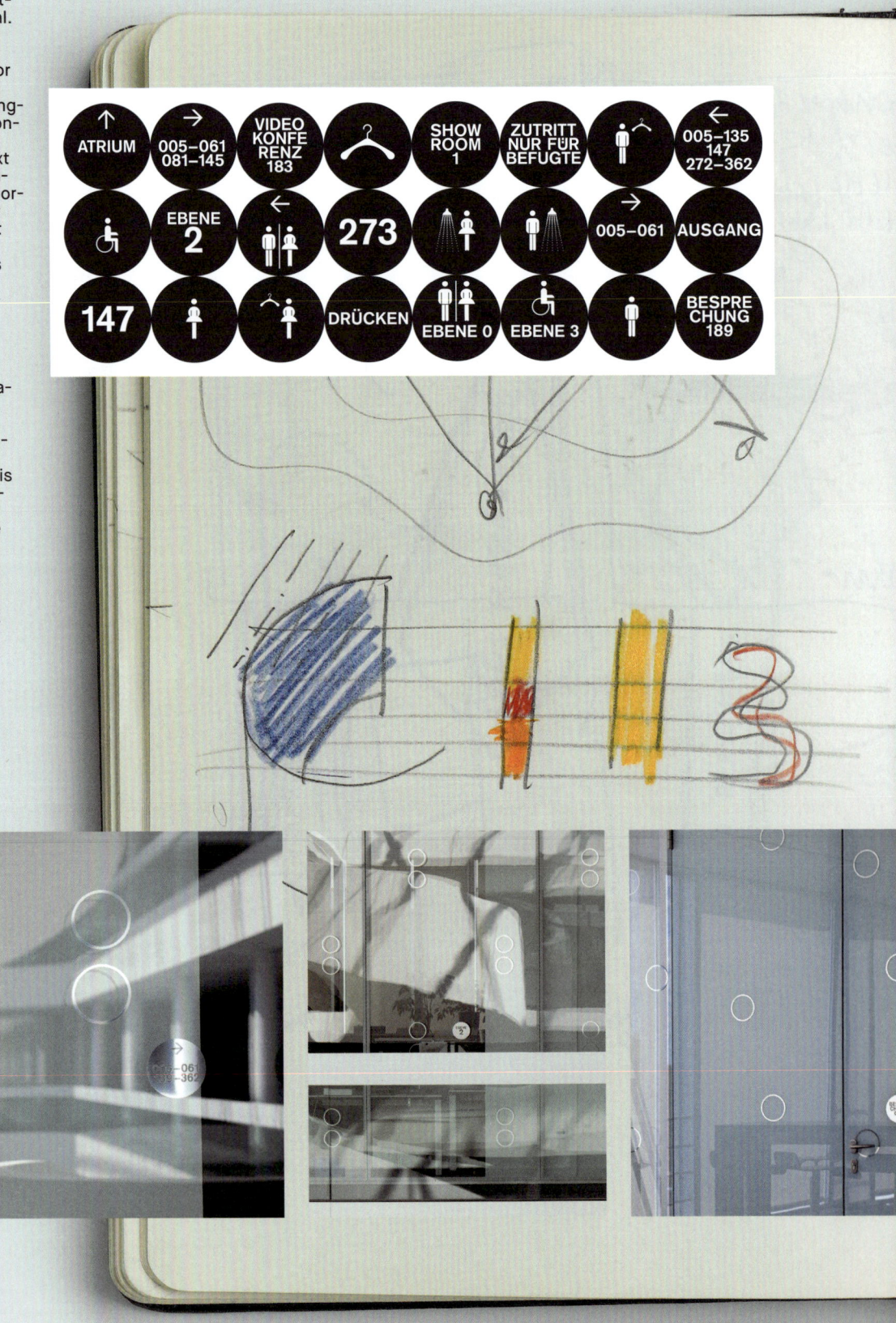

what do you do when a client's threatening to dilute your design?

a)
throw a fit and scream and bite
(party version)

b)
win them over, with fine words and factual arguments
(planned version)

c)
apply a mixture of a and b
(real-world version)

are budgets in the cultural sector generally the same as/lower than/higher than in other sectors?

artist = god = everything
designer = whatever = not a lot

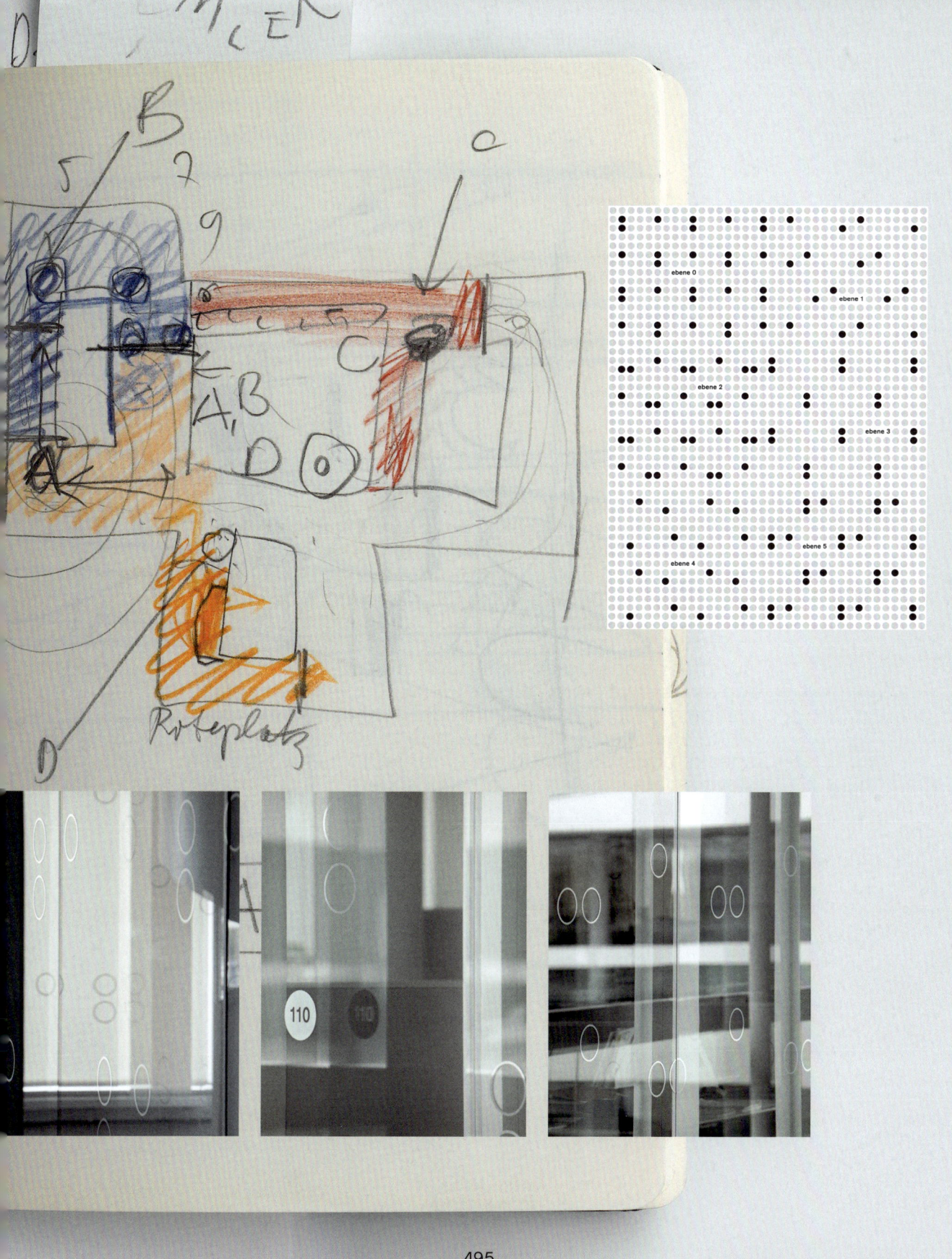

lifting the spirits

this is not a happy place. the people who live here are trapped in themselves, in space, in time. visitors and staff in places like this also feel the sense of pressure, suffering and pain. colour may not be able to heal but it can help to make the place more bearable. strong colour tones give the spaces an individual note. the ceiling is transformed into a fantastic play of colour that opens up an otherwise closed-in situation: the eye strays from canary yellow to mint green and wanders on further, from midnight blue to cotton-wool white speckled with orange. this minor intervention speaks of care – loving care, not just for the people staying here but also for the atmosphere of the spaces they inhabit.

station lukas 01
spatial design
meckenbeuren, 2012

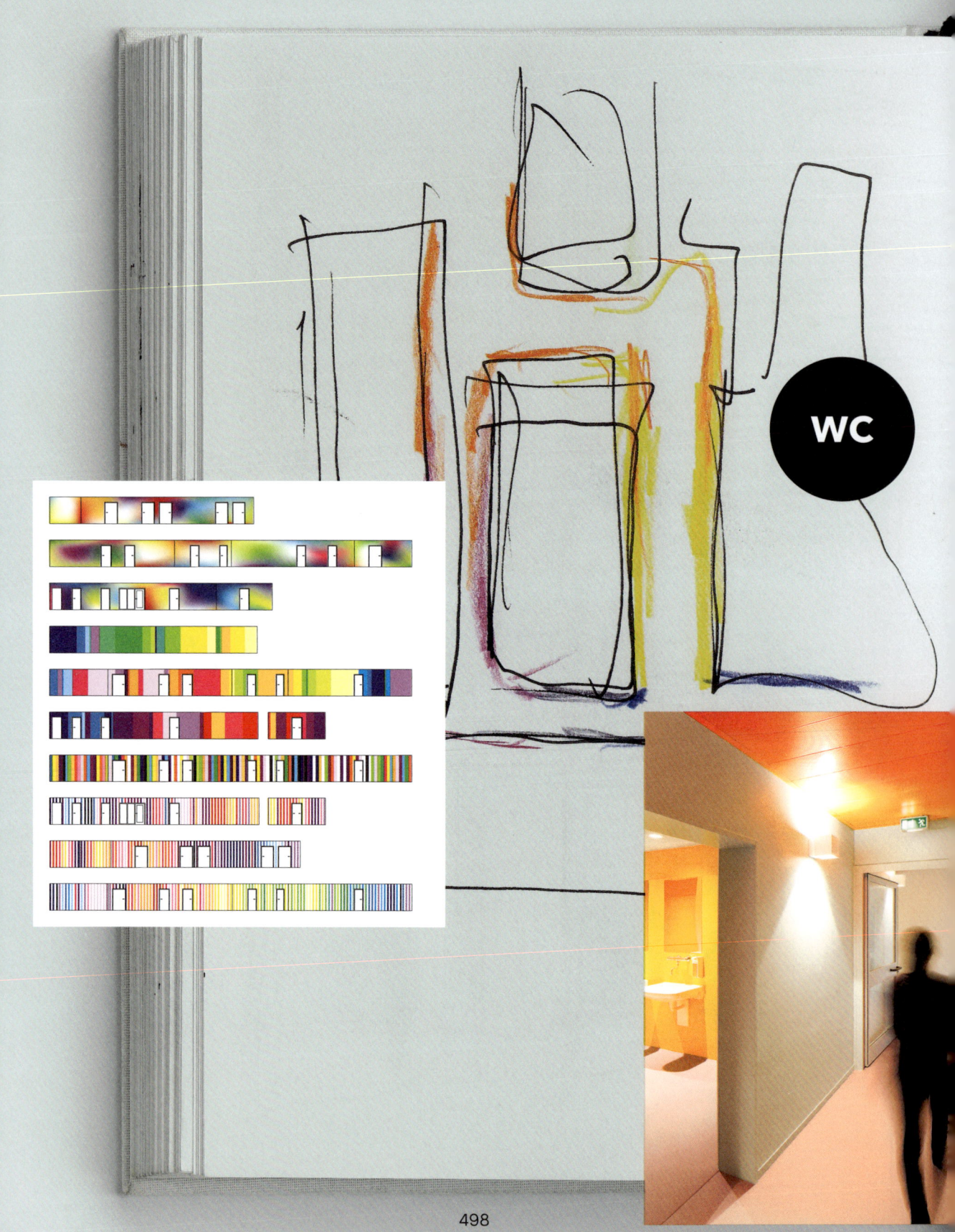

colours of nowhere

motorway toilets are inhospitable places. so it's all the more welcome when this unworthy state of affairs is brought to an end. the new pilot plan involves gradually tearing down the old conveniences and replacing them with their architectural and technological antithesis. the stylish architecture is accompanied by self-cleansing toilet seats. the problem of vandalism and particularly of graffiti on the outside walls has been tackled by means of a graphic façade design that is so high-contrast that the creators of tags and other significant scrawl find they have little desire to leave their mark on the walls. which illustrates how a key financial consideration in terms of building maintenance can give rise to a transformational design measure.

oker, drachenberg and schunter: places in germany. normally you pay them no heed as you drive by, rushing through space and time. but sometimes nature calls and you just have to stop – and then, what do you find? landscape, hills and valleys, visualised as a map, a different colour for each altitude level. at each of these places the design depicts the specific location – in a way that also renders graffiti redundant. these redesigned motorway toilets are gradually becoming a regular sight.

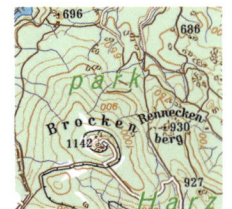

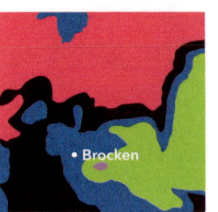

motorway toilets
façade design, standard planning
lower saxony, since 2012

does design have to be beautiful?

design should delight. it should look good, it should be surprising — and also disturbing. that's the role of design: making beautiful things. if it's good and intelligent then it's always beautiful, even if the beauty isn't evident at first sight, because beauty has its own time-out setting. when things aren't obviously beautiful at first sight, when they have something ugly about them and it takes time to appreciate their qualities, they stay beautiful for longer.

tip for creatives

read

index

164	academy of visual arts (hgb) leipzig hgb grau (büro uebele)	260	landesbank baden-württemberg, pariser platz futura
10	adidas gym adihaus, own (büro uebele)	306	la ville d'yverdon-les-bains neue helvetica
362	adidas laces adihaus	208	lederer ragnarsdóttir oei ff din
444	aed akzidenz grotesk	468	massimo massimo (gabriel richter and andreas uebele)
34	alphabet innsbruck akzidenz grotesk	84	mercedes-benz w 194 corporate
458	alsterdorf evangelical foundation frutiger next	172	monument to freedom and unity futura
410	architectural award for exemplary accessible building avenir	50	morgenstelle cafeteria, tübingen university grouch
416	armed forces memorial gill sans, own (luc[as] de groot)	500	motorway toilets avenir next
264	ask klaus! americana, avenir next, britannic bold, chaparral pro, clarendon, clearface, cushing, dutch 801, gedau gothic, glypha, goudy heavyface, iowan old style, korinna, new baskerville, noe display, raleigh, schadow, schneidler, sectra display, serifa, souvenir, stymie, zapf book	434	müller & meirer walsheim
		492	new building, drägerwerk ag & co. kgaa dräger sans
		400	no detail, michael held, 27 houses akzidenz grotesk
		88	notos quartett itc franklin gothic
		184	offenbach hospital avenir next
154	bächlemeid 2×7 (büro uebele), akkurat	272	out the box akzidenz grotesk
236	baden-württemberg space center neue helvetica	60	parrotta contemporary art akzidenz grotesk
		424	radiological practice dr. heinrich avenir next
276	bauhaus museum weimar neuzeit grotesk	104	reuter & kucher tax consultants avenir
146	bazon brock speaks replica	196	schmuque by julia münzing akzidenz grotesk, boutique
432	berliner schloss foundation – humboldt forum akzidenz grotesk	292	silcher school, heidenheim avenir next
		442	sofia/city candidate for european capital of culture 2019 akzidenz grotesk
472	bree avenir next	340	stadtmuseum stuttgart gotham
248	car dealer pappas akzidenz grotesk	496	station lukas 01 avenir next
202	cdu/csu parliamentary party neue helvetica	204	st. damiano, residential community for the mentally disabled own (büro uebele)
396	community of rechberghausen avenir	464	stihl gallery waiblingen/lower remstal school of art neue helvetica
42	daimler corporate	
28	deutsche werkbund exhibition akzidenz grotesk	282	stuttgart region chamber of commerce and industry ff din
448	end-of-semester presentation balloon, banco, bello, cooper, futura, impact, keep on truckin', lubalin graph, walsheim	64	stuttgart trade fair centre avenir
		48	the end by print akzidenz grotesk, ff din
		330	transsolar climate engineering akzidenz grotesk
312	e.on headquarters polo	332	tu berlin brezel grotesk
324	eth zurich science city benton sans	116	university of applied sciences osnabrück ff din
490	faculty tour, düsseldorf university of applied sciences, 2008 neue helvetica	244	viavai winebar bauhaus
240	faculty tour, düsseldorf university of applied sciences, 2012 neue helvetica	304	vilson hardt construtora e incorporadora pressura
100	gastroenterology and oncology at st. anna's clinic avenir	346	vitra campus monospace 821
		160	"vorn" magazine, 2010 akzidenz grotesk
460	german maritime museum itc franklin gothic, fregio mecano	106	"vorn" magazine, 2014 own (büro uebele)
212	german parliament georgia, melior	300	walter knoll frutiger
268	goethe institute goethe titel	180	welcome center stuttgart frutiger
92	gutenberg campus alte schwabacher, neue helvetica, textura	122	werner sobek futura
		148	würzburg university interstate
412	harald f. müller monotype grotesque	178	x/u itc franklin gothic
356	hardt itc franklin gothic	56	"zeigen. an audio tour of berlin by karin sander." akzidenz grotesk
394	html-polka monaco	
426	hypovereinsbank board building frutiger	336	zieglerbürg büro für gestaltung helvetica
128	innsbruck exhibition center akzidenz grotesk	258	72h without art din next
96	institute of electrical engineering, building 2, stuttgart university neue helvetica		
320	interior things circular		
114	karin sander app akzidenz grotesk		
170	karin sander, hans thoma prize 2011 akzidenz grotesk		
296	kinderwelt avenir next, simplon		
452	king abdullah center for crescent observation and astronomy din next, din next arabic		
344	künstlerhaus stuttgart itc franklin gothic		

10
adidas gym
spatial design,
herzogenaurach, 2014
in cooperation with:
zieglerbürg büro für gestaltung, *client:* adidas ag, *team:* carolin himmel (project manager), andreas uebele, *architect:* agps architecture ltd., *invited competition, 1st prize, realised*

28
deutsche werkbund exhibition
exhibition poster, venice, 2014
client: deutscher werkbund berlin, *team:* carolin himmel (project manager), andreas uebele

34
alphabet innsbruck
typographic installation, exhibition catalogue, 2009
client: aut: architektur und tirol, arno ritter, *team:* stefan becker, katrin dittmann (project manager), andreas uebele, *exhibition design in cooperation with:* zieglerbürg büro für gestaltung, *text:* gretl köfler, georg salden, andreas uebele

42
daimler
visual identity, stuttgart, 2007
client: daimler ag, *team:* angela klasar (project manager), silke sabow (project manager), andreas uebele, *invited competition, not realised*

48
the end by print
poster, düsseldorf, 2012
client: düsseldorf university of applied sciences, faculty of design, *design:* elena bergen (project manager), andreas uebele

50
morgenstelle cafeteria, tübingen university
spatial design, 2009
developer: baden-württemberg office for assets and construction management, tübingen office, *client and architect:* zieglerbürg büro für gestaltung, *user:* tübingen/hohenheim student union, *team:* anja klein (project manager), andreas uebele, *text:* hannes böhringer

56
"zeigen. an audio tour of berlin by karin sander."
visual identity, 2009
client: temporary art gallery berlin, *team:* jan filek (project manager), andreas uebele, *edition:* karin sander, andreas uebele

60
parrotta contemporary art
visual identity, stuttgart, berlin, since 2006
client: parrotta contemporary art, *team:* beate kapprell (project manager 2007–2011), angela klasar (project manager 2011–2015), nadja schoch (project manager since 2015), andreas uebele

64
stuttgart trade fair centre
signage system, 2007
client: projektgesellschaft neue messe gmbh & co. kg, *team:* katrin dittmann (project manager), benedikt haid, beate kapprell, katrin theile, andreas uebele, *architect:* wulf architekten, *product design:* zieglerbürg büro für gestaltung

84
mercedes-benz w 194
historical documentation, stuttgart, 2012
client: daimler ag, *team:* daniel fels (project manager), philipp schäfer, andreas uebele, *with contributions from:* harald f. müller, thomas ruff, karin sander, eva-maria schön, *invited competition, not realised*

88
notos quartett
visual identity, berlin, 2012
client: notos quartett, *team:* alexandra gövert (project manager), hendrike nagel, andreas uebele, *programming:* petr pščolka

92
gutenberg campus
typographic design for public spaces, mainz, 2010
in cooperation with: landschaftdrei. dipl.-ing. michael f. heintze, franz hendrikx, *client:* ministry of finance of rhineland-palatinate represented by landesbetrieb lbb, the estate and construction management agency of rhineland-palatinate, *team:* beate kapprell (project manager), andreas uebele, *light planning:* day & light. frank vetter, *open international competition, not realised*

96
institute of electrical engineering, building 2, stuttgart university
signage system, redesign, 2012
client: baden-württemberg office for assets and construction management, stuttgart/hohenheim university building office, *team:* katharina moritzen (project manager 2010–2011), felix rabe (project manager 2011), katrin theile, andreas uebele

100
gastroenterology and oncology at st. anna's clinic
visual identity, stuttgart, 2010
client: prof. dr. med. bodo klump, *team:* angela klasar (project manager), andreas uebele

104
reuter & kucher tax consultants
visual identity, stuttgart, 2004
client: reuter & kucher tax consultants, *team:* beate kapprell (project manager), andreas uebele

106
"vorn" magazine
typographic contribution, berlin, 2014
client: "vorn" magazine, joachim baldauf, *team:* yanik hauschild (project manager), andreas uebele

114
karin sander app
icon design, berlin, 2014
client: karin sander, *team:* petr pščolka (project manager)

116
university of applied sciences osnabrück
signage system, 2004
client: osnabrück office of construction management, *team:* gerd häußler (project manager), andreas uebele, *architect:* jockers architekten bda

122
werner sobek
visual identity, stuttgart, 2007
client: werner sobek ingenieure gmbh & co. kg, *team:* beate kapprell (project manager), maja mory, silke sabow, andreas uebele

128
innsbruck exhibition center
signage system, 2012
client: congress und messe innsbruck gmbh, *team:* carolin himmel (project manager), andreas uebele, *architect:* arge cukrowicz nachbaur bechter zaffignani marte

146
bazon brock speaks
event poster, düsseldorf, 2013
client: düsseldorf university of applied sciences, faculty of design, *design:* andreas uebele, franziska virgili (project manager), *text:* bazon brock

148
würzburg university
signage system, 2010
client: würzburg planning
authority, *user:* würzburg
university, *team:* tino
grass (project manager),
andreas uebele, *product
design:* zieglerbürg büro
für gestaltung, *invited
competition, 1st prize,
not realised*

154
bächlemeid
visual identity,
constance, 2015
client: bächlemeid architekten stadtplaner bda,
team: petr pščolka (project
manager for website),
andreas steinbrecher
(project manager for visual
identity), tobias textor,
andreas uebele

160
"vorn" magazine
typographic contribution,
berlin, 2010
client: "vorn" magazine,
joachim baldauf, *team:*
katharina moritzen (project
manager), andreas uebele

164
academy of visual arts
(hgb) leipzig
visual identity, 2015
client: academy of visual arts
leipzig, *team:* daniel fels,
charlotte lengersdorf, petr
pščolka, gabriel richter
(project manager), nadja
schoch, andreas uebele,
*invited competition,
not realised*

170
karin sander,
hans thoma prize 2011
exhibition poster, bernau
client: karin sander, *team:*
felix rabe (project manager),
andreas uebele

172
monument to
freedom and unity
typographic canopy,
berlin, 2010
in cooperation with:
meck architekten, *client:*
federal government
commissioner for culture and
the media in cooperation
with federal ministry of
transport, building and urban
affairs, *team:* daniel fels
(project manager), andreas
uebele, *text:* hannes
böhringer, *invited
competition, 1st prize,
not realised*

178
x/u
exhibition poster,
düsseldorf, 2009
client: düsseldorf university
of applied sciences,
faculty of design, *design:*
andreas uebele

180
welcome center stuttgart
visual identity,
spatial design, 2014
developer: welthaus
stuttgart e.v., weltladen an
der planie, *architect and
client:* kühfuß architekten in
cooperation with zieglerbürg
büro für gestaltung, *team:*
sven eul (project manager),
andreas uebele

184
offenbach hospital
signage system, 2010
developer: klinikum
offenbach gmbh, *client
and architect:* wörner traxler
richter, *team:* katrin theile
(project manager), andreas
uebele, *product design:*
zieglerbürg büro für
gestaltung

196
schmuque by julia münzing
visual identity, stuttgart,
2015
client: julia münzing, *team:*
carolin himmel, charlotte
lengersdorf (project
manager), petr pščolka,
andreas uebele, franziska
virgili

202
cdu/csu parliamentary party
visual identity, berlin, 2012
client: cdu/csu parliamentary party, *team:* carolin
himmel (project manager),
felix rabe, andreas uebele,
*invited competition,
not realised*

204
st. damiano,
residential community
for the mentally disabled
signage system,
stuttgart, 2010
client and interior designer:
zieglerbürg büro für
gestaltung, *team:* andreas
uebele, svenja voß
(project manager)

208
lederer ragnarsdóttir oei
visual identity,
stuttgart, 2012
client: lro lederer
ragnarsdóttir oei gmbh &
co.kg, *team:* petr pščolka
(project manager), andreas
uebele, *programming:*
petr pščolka

212
german parliament
visual identity, berlin, 2009
client: deutscher bundestag,
public relations division,
team: katrin dittmann, daniel
fels, angela klasar (project
manager 2008–2009), tristan
schmitz (project manager
2008), andreas uebele,
*invited competition, 1st prize,
realised*

236
baden-württemberg
space center
signage system,
stuttgart, 2012
client: baden-württemberg
office for assets and
construction management,
stuttgart/hohenheim
university building office,
team: katrin theile (project
manager), andreas uebele,
product design: zieglerbürg
büro für gestaltung

240
faculty tour,
düsseldorf university of
applied sciences
event poster, 2012
client: düsseldorf university
of applied sciences, faculty
of design, *design:* alexandra
gövert (project manager),
andreas uebele

244
viavai winebar
visual identity,
stuttgart, 2004
client: maurizio estrano,
team: beate kapprell
(project manager), andreas
uebele, *architect:* lamott
architekten bda

248
car dealer pappas
signage system,
salzburg, 2006
client: pappas gruppe,
team: beate kapprell (project
manager), andreas uebele,
architect: kadawittfeld-
architektur, *product design:*
zieglerbürg büro für
gestaltung, *invited
competition, 1st prize,
realised*

258
72h without art
exhibition poster,
mannheim, 2012
client: mannheim university
of applied sciences, faculty
of design, prof. veruschka
von goetz, *team:* elena
bergen (project manager),
andreas uebele

260
landesbank baden-
württemberg, pariser platz
level designation,
stuttgart, 2005
client: landesbank baden-
württemberg, *team:* birgit
lorinser (project manager),
andreas uebele

264
ask klaus!
visual identity,
stuttgart, 2015
client: klaus haasis, *team:*
sven eul (project manager
for preliminary design),
petr pščolka (project manager for website), andreas
uebele, franziska virgili
(project manager for design)

268
goethe institute
structural corporate design, berlin, 2009
client: goethe-institut e. v., *team:* anja klein (project manager), andreas uebele, *product and interior design:* zieglerbürg büro für gestaltung, *invited competition, not realised*

272
out of the box
event poster, hanover, 2013
client: edelstall, hardy seiler, *team:* mona matejic (project manager), andreas uebele

276
bauhaus museum weimar
visual identity, 2015
client: klassik stiftung weimar, *team:* nadja schoch (project manager since 2015), andreas steinbrecher (project manager 2014), andreas uebele, *illustration:* andreas steinbrecher, *open competition, 1st prize, realised*

282
stuttgart region chamber of commerce and industry
signage system, 2014
client: ihk region stuttgart, *team:* angela klasar (project manager), andreas uebele, *architect:* wulf architekten, *colour consulting:* harald f. müller

292
silcher school, heidenheim
signage system, 2012
client: city of heidenheim, *team:* elena bergen, alexandra gövert (project manager 2011–2012), mona matejic, philipp schäfer (project manager 2012), andreas uebele, *interior designer:* zieglerbürg büro für gestaltung, *illustration:* daniela sonntag, andreas uebele

296
kinderwelt
visual identity, heidenheim, 2012
client: city of heidenheim, *team:* philipp schäfer (project manager), andreas uebele

300
walter knoll
signage system, brand world, herrenberg 2007
client: walter knoll herrenberg, represented by markus benz, *team:* andrea bauer, katrin dittmann, marc engenhart (project manager), andreas uebele, *architect:* hansulrich benz

304
vilson hardt construtora e incorporadora
visual identity, curitiba, 2013
client: vilson hardt construtora e incorporadora, *team:* lena drießen, thanh-thao tran (project manager), andreas uebele

306
la ville d'yverdon-les-bains
signage system, 2009
client: la ville d'yverdon-les-bains, *team:* beate kapprell (project manager), andreas uebele, *product design:* zieglerbürg büro für gestaltung, *invited international competition, not realised*

312
e.on headquarters
signage system, munich, 2014
client: e.on energie ag, *team:* frank geiger (project manager), beate kapprell, andreas uebele, *architect:* asp albert speer & partner, *interior designer:* zieglerbürg büro für gestaltung

320
interior things
visual identity, holzminden, 2015
client: wolfgang hartauer, *team:* daniel fels (project manager), petr pščolka, andreas uebele

324
eth zurich science city
signage system, 2010
in cooperation with: zieglerbürg büro für gestaltung, *client:* eth zürich, *team:* nora hug, angela klasar (project manager for phase 1), tristan schmitz (project manager for phase 2), katrin theile (project manager), andreas uebele, *invited international competition, 1st prize, not realised*

330
transsolar
climate engineering monograph, stuttgart, 2004
client: transsolar energietechnik gmbh, *team:* katrin theile, andreas uebele, christine voshage (project manager), *photo:* anja thierfelder, *text:* wilfried korfmacher

332
tu berlin
signage system, 2016
client: tu berlin, *team:* elena bergen (project manager for competition), daniel fels (project manager), yanik hauschild, carolin himmel, tobias hönow, andreas steinbrecher, andreas uebele, lea wenzel, *invited competition, 1st prize, realised*

336
zieglerbürg büro für gestaltung
website, stuttgart, 2012
client: zieglerbürg büro für gestaltung, *team:* petr pščolka (project manager), andreas uebele

340
stadtmuseum stuttgart
visual identity, 2011
client: city of stuttgart office of cultural affairs, *team:* petr pščolka (project manager), andreas uebele, *invited competition, not realised*

344
künstlerhaus stuttgart
poster, leaflet, 2004
client: künstlerhaus stuttgart, *team:* ralph burkhardt (project manager), andreas uebele

346
vitra campus
signage system, weil am rhein, 2011
client: vitra, *team:* carolin himmel (project manager), petr pščolka, andreas uebele, *product design:* zieglerbürg büro für gestaltung, *invited international competition, not realised*

356
hardt
visual identity, curitiba, 2014
client: hardt importadora e distribuidora ltda., *team:* mats kubiak (project manager), andreas uebele

362
adidas laces
signage system, spatial design, herzogenaurach, 2011
in cooperation with: zieglerbürg büro für gestaltung, *client:* adidas ag, *team:* carolin himmel (project manager), andreas uebele, *architect:* kadawittfeld-architektur, *invited international competition, 1st prize, realised*

394
html-polka
event poster, düsseldorf, 2012
client: düsseldorf university of applied sciences, faculty of design, *design:* andreas uebele

396
community of rechberghausen
visual identity, 2004
client: gemeinde rechberghausen, *team:* gerd häußler (project manager), andreas uebele, *open competition, 1st prize, realised*

400
no detail,
michael held, 27 houses
monograph, stuttgart, 2011
client: andreas uebele, baden-württemberg office for assets and construction management, stuttgart/hohenheim university building office, *team:* carolin himmel, katharina moritzen (project manager 2010–2011), felix rabe (project manager 2011), andreas uebele, max uebele

410
architectural award for exemplary accessible building
certificate, plaque, stuttgart, 2003
client: dachverband integratives planen und bauen e. v., dr. ursula broermann †, *team:* frank geiger (project manager), andreas uebele

412
**harald f. müller
visual identity,
öhningen, 2012**
client: harald f. müller,
team: carolin himmel (project manager), angela klasar, andreas uebele

416
**armed forces memorial
spatial design, berlin 2009**
in cooperation with: meck architekten, *client:* federal office for building and regional planning, *team:* katrin theile (project manager), andreas uebele, *led lettering:* own (luc[as] de groot)

424
**radiological
practice dr. heinrich
signage system,
stuttgart, 2007**
client and architect: zieglerbürg büro für gestaltung, *team:* daniel fels, benedikt haid (project manager), andreas uebele

426
**hypovereinsbank
board building
signage system,
munich, 2005**
client: hvb immobilien ag, *team:* alexandra busse (project manager), andreas uebele, *architect:* prof. guido canali, prof. gilberto botti

432
**berliner schloss
foundation – humboldt forum
visual identity, berlin, 2009**
client: federal ministry of transport, building and urban affairs, *team:* jan filek (project manager), andreas uebele, *invited competition, 1st prize, realised*

434
**müller & meirer
visual identity,
kirn an der nahe, 2015**
client: müller & meirer lederwarenfabrik gmbh, *team:* carolin himmel (project manager), angela klasar (project manager), petr pščolka, andreas uebele, *interior designer:* zieglerbürg büro für gestaltung, *illustration:* andreas steinbrecher

442
**sofia/city candidate
for european capital
of culture 2019
visual identity, 2011**
client: sofia municipality and sofia development association, *team:* petr pščolka (project manager), andreas uebele, *international competition, not realised*

444
**aed
visual identity,
stuttgart, 2006**
client: verein zur förderung von architektur, engineering und design in stuttgart e.v., *team:* claudia burtscher (project manager), andreas uebele

448
**end-of-semester
presentation
event poster,
düsseldorf, 2012**
client: düsseldorf university of applied sciences, faculty of design, *design:* philipp schäfer (project manager), andreas uebele

452
**king abdullah
center for crescent
observation and astronomy
signage system, visual
identity, mecca, 2015**
developer: king abdullah bin abdulaziz al saud, represented by bin ladin group, *client:* sl-rasch gmbh special and lightweight structures, *team:* daniel fels (project manager), angela klasar (project manager), andreas uebele

458
**alsterdorf
evangelical foundation
annual report,
hamburg, 2004**
client: evangelische stiftung alsterdorf, pastor rolf baumbach †, *team:* alexandra busse (project manager), andreas uebele, *illustration:* die schlumper

460
**german maritime museum
visual identity, signage
system, bremerhaven, 2006**
client: german maritime museum, *team:* gerd häußler, carolin himmel (project manager), andreas uebele, *invited competition, not realised*

464
**stihl gallery
waiblingen/lower remstal
school of art
visual identity, signage
system, 2006**
client: city of waiblingen, *team:* gerd häußler, carolin himmel (project manager), andreas uebele, *open competition, not realised*

468
**massimo
font design, stuttgart, 2016**
client: büro uebele, *team:* gabriel richter (project manager), andreas uebele

472
**bree
visual identity,
isernhagen, 2004–2011**
client: bree collection gmbh & co. kg, *team:* tino graß, andreas gregor, benedikt haid, gerd häußler (project manager 2004–2008), beate kapprell (project manager 2008–2010), angela klasar (project manager 2010–2011), silke sabow, sabine schönhaar, andreas uebele, *illustration:* andreas uebele, willi uebele, *photo:* joachim baldauf (advertisements), hans hansen (product)

490
**faculty tour,
düsseldorf university of
applied sciences
event poster, 2008**
client: düsseldorf university of applied sciences, faculty of design, *design:* tristan schmitz (project manager), andreas uebele

492
**new building,
drägerwerk ag & co. kgaa
signage system,
lübeck, 2009**
developer and client: molvina vermietungsgesellschaft mbh & co. objekt finkenstraße kg, *general contractor:* commerzleasing und immobilien commerz real baucontract gmbh, *user:* drägerwerk ag & co. kgaa, *team:* rebecca benz (project manager 2007), katrin dittmann, katrin theile (project manager 2007–2009), andreas uebele, *architect:* goetz hootz castorph architekten und stadtplaner gmbh

496
**station lukas 01
spatial design,
meckenbeuren, 2012**
client and interior designer: zieglerbürg büro für gestaltung, *team:* angela klasar (project manager), andreas uebele

500
**motorway toilets
façade design, standard
planning, lower saxony,
since 2012**
client: staatliches baumanagement weser-leine, *team:* benjamin brinkmann (project manager), jan paul gaugler, angela klasar, philipp schäfer, katrin theile, thanh-thao tran, andreas uebele, *architect:* gruppeomp architektengesellschaft mbh bda

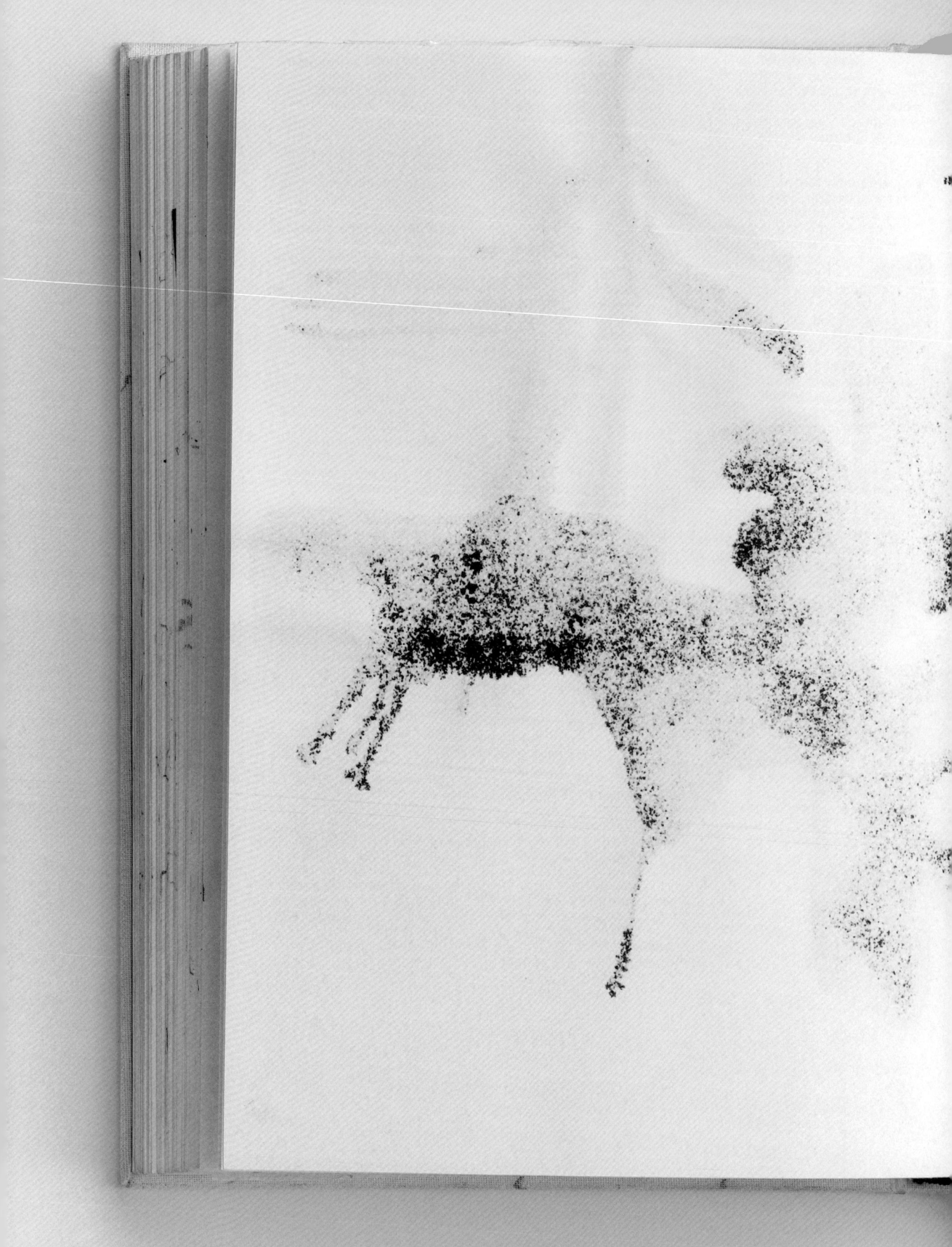

i
origin unknown, 2010

ii
"die kunst des findens von etwas", interview by karolina rosina, bachelor's thesis, design akademie berlin srh hochschule für kommunikation und design, communication design programme, 2012

iii
interview by katharina moritzen, bachelor's thesis, düsseldorf university of applied sciences, faculty of design, 2013

iv
text in new year's cards for zieglerbürg büro für gestaltung, stuttgart, 2000 – 2014

v – vi
"die ideenfindung ist ein mythos", interview by sophie degenfeld, horizont journal, frankfurt am main, 2013

vii
"beauty's transience", stuttgart, 2015

viii
"alphabet métro", adrian frutiger, bremgarten (bern), 2004

ix – x
origin unknown

xi
terms for "das lesikon" by juli gudehus, verlag hermann schmidt, 2007

xii
"beeinflusst design die gesellschaft?", interview by stephanie passul, düsseldorf university of applied sciences, faculty of design, 2014

xiii
interview by bahar türkay, www.xoxothemag.net, 2015

xiv
"codierungen der visuellen kommunikation", interview by mario simon and nadja slave, bachelor's thesis, schwaebisch gmuend university of design, communication design, 2014

xv
interview by max niederschick, www.greller-propeller.at, 2013

xvi
"relevanz gestalterischer regeln", interview by marie-christine bock and anne john, schwaebisch gmuend university of design, communication design, 2014

xvii
"what designers do" (www.whatdesignersdo.info), interview by karin fischnaller, bachelor's thesis, munich university of applied sciences, faculty of design, 2014

xviii
"über design", interview by lisa jacob, master's thesis, düsseldorf university of applied sciences, faculty of design, 2010

xix – xx
contribution by thomas ruff to "mercedes-benz w 194", düsseldorf, 2012

xxi
interview by mimi palermo, hamburg, 2017

xxii
programme text for talk held at typo berlin, conference topic was sustainability, 2012

xxiii → xvi

xxiv
contribution to the journal of the society for experimental graphic design (segd), washington, 2013

xxv → iv
xxvi → xvi
xxvii → xiv

xxviii
"schreiben als gestalter", interview by simon renner and joshua rudolf, bachelor's thesis, schwaebisch gmuend university of design, communication design, 2014

xxix → xvi
xxx → xi
xxxi → iv

xxxii
"barrierefreiheit in leitsystemen für sehbeeinträchtigte und blinde menschen", interview by anne hofmann, bachelor's thesis, potsdam university of applied sciences, design programme, 2014

xxxiii – xxxiv
"views on pictograms", interview by fiona dodd, final project, university of sunderland, faculty of graphic communication and design, 2013

xxxv
interview by sabrina bauer, edda bohnet, katrin brüggemann and judith kalicki for the "schrift/macht/welten" typography symposium at the gutenberg museum in mainz, 2012

xxxvi → xvi

xxxvii, xxxviii
contribution to the domus magazine (sandra hofmeister), german edition, july/august 2013

xxxix
"kitchen pieces", contribution by karin sander, rome, 2015

xl
contribution by hans hansen, hamburg, 2016

xli → xvi

xlii
"die falle der gestaltung", origin unknown, 2004

xliii, xliv → xvi

xlv
interview in connection with talk at the 2011 segd conference, society for environmental graphic design (segd), montreal, 2011

xlvi → iv
xlvii, xlviii → xlv
xlix, l → iv
li → xv
lii → xvi

liii – liv
"melior antiqua", contribution by hermann zapf, darmstadt, 2009

lv
"verdana and georgia", contribution by matthew carter, london, 2009

lvi
contribution by norbert lammert, berlin, 2016

lvii → v
lviii → xvi

lix – lx
"akd – antikommunikationsdesign", interview by benedikt haid, master's thesis, northwestern switzerland university of applied sciences, design master studio, 2010

lxi – lxii
contribution to the kulturaustausch journal (timo berger), 01/2014

contributions / interviews

lxiii → iv
lxiv → xv

lxv
contribution by manfred schmalriede, quotation from the opening remarks at the one-man show "andreas uebele: schrift im raum", galerie parrotta contemporary art, stuttgart, 2009

lxvi
"natural beauty and artificial beauty", contribution by jórunn ragnarsdóttir, stuttgart, 2016

lxvii – lxx
talk for the exhibition "72h ohne kunst" at the mannheim art association, mannheim university of applied sciences, faculty for design, prof. veruschka von goetz, 2012

lxxi → xi
lxxii → xvi

lxxiii – lxxiv
foreword to the book "read/ability" by jan filek, niggli verlag, 2013, revised version

lxxv
interview by andy butler, www.designboom.com, 2013

lxxvi → ii

lxxvii
contribution by peter zizka, frankfurt am main, 2015

lxxviii
"typography becomes architecture and more", contribution by klaus klemp, frankfurt am main, 2017

lxxix
origin unknown

lxxx
"culture and identity", interview by mia stevanovic, bachelor's thesis, munich university of applied sciences, media design programme, 2015

lxxxi → xvi
lxxxii → lxxx

lxxxiii
interview by ebru aytoğ in conjunction with a talk given at grafist 19, 19th istanbul graphic design week, 2015

lxxxiv
origin unknown

lxxxv
"sweeping", contribution by hannes böhringer, berlin, 2015

lxxxvi
"andreas uebele on a 2015 scholarship at villa massimo", contribution by joachim blüher, rome, 2016

lxxxvii → lxxx
lxxxviii → ii
lxxxix → iv
xc → xi
xci → lxxx

xcii
"design city", interview by kimberly lloyd in conjunction with a talk given in the mudam, luxembourg, 2010

xciii → xii
xciv, xcv → lxxx
xcvi → xviii
xcvii → lxxx
xcviii → xvi
xcix → xxviii
c → xvi

ci
interview by jessica sauter, school of colour and design, academy of advertising design, stuttgart, 2015

cii → xlv
ciii → lxxx

civ
"what about sarah?", interview by sarah cleeremans, master's thesis, la cambre art school, brussels, 2015

cv
contribution by massimo vignelli for the master's thesis "deutsche gestalten" by caroline hentschel, düsseldorf university of applied sciences, faculty of design, 2006

cvi
contribution by durs grünbein, a response to the question "ist verdichten besser als auflösen?", rome, 2015

cvii → xxviii
cviii – cx → iv

cxi
"gebiet geknittert", contribution by eva-maria schön, berlin, 2015

cxii
"cape nordkinn", contribution by andreas cukrowicz, bregenz, 2015

cxiii – cxiv → v

cxv
interview with page magazine, july 2006

cxvi
origin unknown, 2012

cxvii – cxviii
"andreas uebele – playfully serious, seriously playful", contribution by klaus schmiedek, stuttgart, 2016

cxix
interview by frank hildebrandt, julia kranick, marie longjaloux, marie-christin schlang und paul schoemaker, düsseldorf university of applied sciences, faculty of design, 2013

cxx → lxxx
cxxi → lxxv

cxxii
interview with page magazine for the cd/ci ranking booklet, may 2015

cxxiii, cxxiv → lxxx
cxxv → xviii
cxxvi → xv

* ix
published by phaidon press limited
© phaidon press limited, www.phaidon.com

** xxxiii
charles trueheart: "sign language: at their best, pictograms tell us clearly where to go and what to do; at their worst, things can get interesting", the american scholar, issue 1/2008, vol. 77, p. 18

*** xxxvii
www.edding.com/de

**** lxxiii
in "wie man's liest" (niggli 2009) gerard unger quotes the font designer walter tracy, who distinguishes between legibility and readability in his book "letters of credit" (1986)

editorial note
our thanks to all interviewers and interview participants. quotations have been edited slightly for this publication. in some cases, we were unable to identify the interviewer, the year, or the context. we apologize for these omissions and would be pleased to hear from the persons involved.

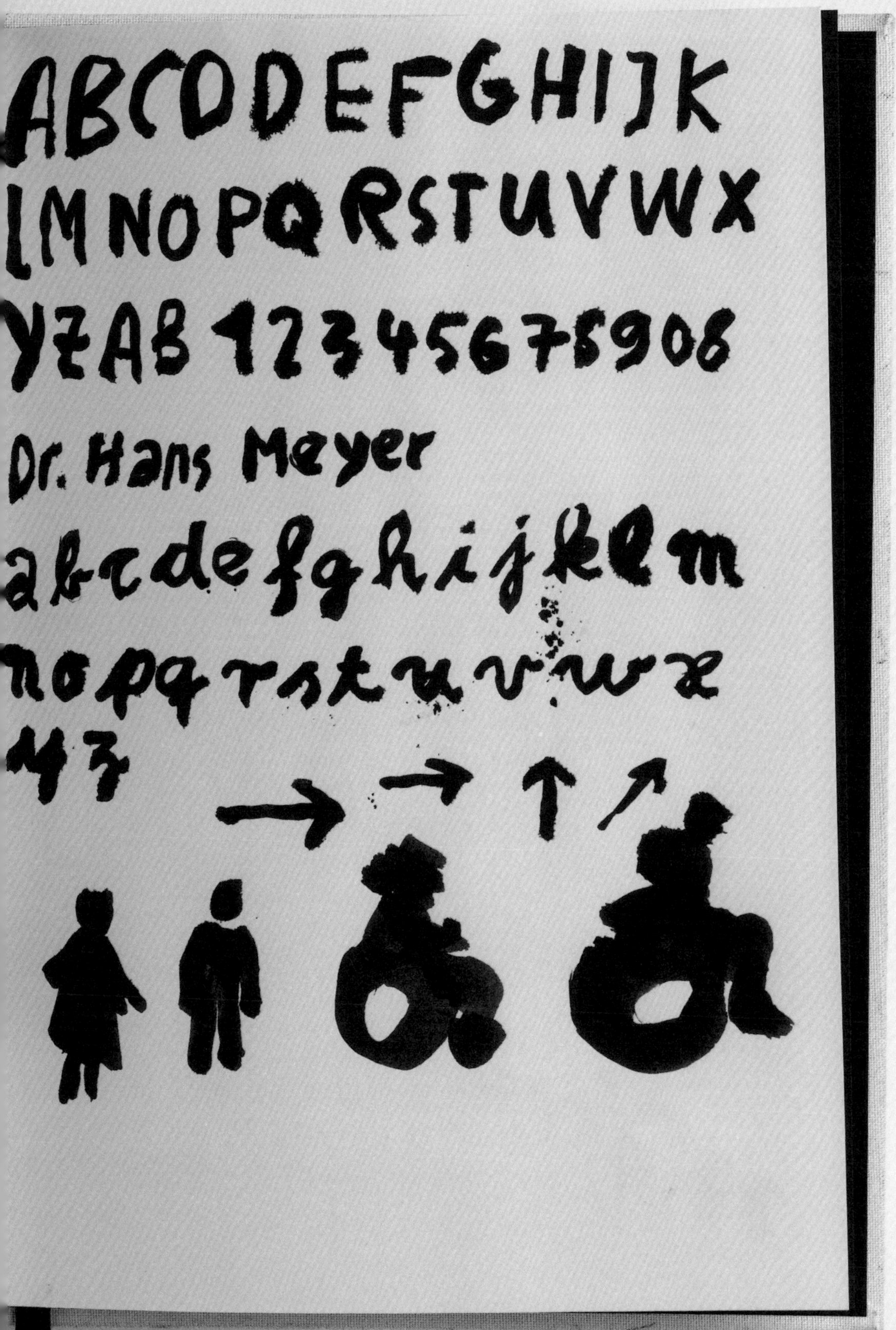

ABCDEFGHIJK
LMNOPQRSTUVWX
YZAB 1234567890

Dr. Hans Meyer

abcdefghijklm
nopqrstuvwx
yz

architect KAI BIERICH doesn't look down on designers from on high, grudgingly admitting them as partners in his work – he positively encourages their interventions. he sees architectural and design values on an equal footing. this, paired with his unwavering solidarity, lays a sure foundation for producing good work (page 5).

JOACHIM BLÜHER is a man of the arts and as director of villa massimo he has expanded the concept of what art is by creating a practitioner scholarship for the applied arts, too. in his text on page lxxxvi he brilliantly outlines what makes art and design different – or, rather, what they have in common.

language and design are natural allies. which is why we turn to the philosopher HANNES BÖHRINGER on a regular basis, seeking his input – including a contribution for this book. in some of our projects his words are literally inscribed in the design space, an integral component of the work (page lxxxv).

MATTHEW CARTER describes the special attributes of his font georgia, created for digital applications, on page lv. this typeface exhibits similar formal characteristics to melior, which we used as the house typeface for the german parliament, making it – in our view – an excellent substitute font for email communications (page lv).

how does an architect view our work? ANDREAS CUKROWICZ offers a succinct, striking description in a very personal text (page cxii) which also explains how life and work – my life and work, at any rate – relate to each other.

typeface designer ADRIAN FRUTIGER, whose work is of paramount importance in my view, permitted me – generously and unfussily – to use the typeface i had enquired after, which was no longer being used for its original application (page viii).

by chance the postal address of poet DURS GRÜNBEIN, resident in rome, fell into my hands. in a letter to him i posed the question "poetry – composition or decomposition?"; he answered with a postcard whose inscription you can read on page cvi.

just as we compete for clients, so we also compete for the services of the best craftspeople, printers and photographers: HANS HANSEN, master of object photography, was my no.1 choice for one of my very early commissions. twice he turned me down, citing a conflict of interests with a client of his own. my client was much, much smaller – but this didn't stop me (cheekily) approaching him for a third time. this time he said yes. you can see his contribution on page xl.

KLAUS KLEMP disagreed with me – and won me over with his humane, endearing manner and with the power of his arguments. his clear opinion and his discerning eye prompted me to ask him for a contribution to this book, see page lxxviii.

NORBERT LAMMERT is a client who has an opinion, who takes time, who listens and who can reach a decision swiftly. what more can you ask for? in the bundestag president we had a partner who was always approachable – available for consultation on the tiniest of issues ("left-justified?" we asked; "centred" he proposed). the outcome of the thirteen-minute discussion: excellent. (page lvi)

JÓRUNN RAGNARSDÓTTIR asked for an appointment at our office and didn't beat about the bush: she ordered a corporate design from us, asking – pretty much on her way out of the door – if we could let her know what it would cost. she would be commissioning us anyway, she added: she wanted us and nobody else to do her design. how to fall in love with my client. her touching text is on page lxvi.

photographer THOMAS RUFF is someone i admire hugely and so i wrote to him personally, by hand, to request a photographic contribution for the competition to document the w 194. even though we didn't know each other his reply, by email, came with just what we'd hoped for – not one but two amazing "messed up" images of the classic racing car, one of which can be admired on pages xix–xx (says ruff: "sadly i can't photograph cars, i can only mess them up").

the limp lettuce on page xxxix was slipped between the leaves of the book by the artist KARIN SANDER, my long-time friend and collaborator – it's an image that beautifully captures our relationship, akin to the interaction between design and art.

art and design theorist MANFRED SCHMALRIEDE (page lxv) uses the term "correspondence" in his text, written for the opening of an exhibition of our works in galerie parrotta. his choice of word connects – by chance? – with my own letter-writing habit, ingrained over many years and indeed the starting point of my career as a graphic designer.

we have designed many projects for the stuttgart and hohenheim university building authority (now the baden-württemberg state office for property and construction). its former director KLAUS SCHMIEDEK (pages cxvii–cxviii) hired me when i was still a relatively inexperienced graphic designer and graciously stood up for me in a tricky situation.

"gebiet geknittert" (page cxi) has its origins in a box of walking maps inherited from my father – which i couldn't bear simply to throw out. i sent them to my friend the artist EVA-MARIA SCHÖN, who transformed this mundane material into art.

i met the new-york-based graphic designer MASSIMO VIGNELLI at a competition presentation in london. the encounter was brief but friendly (i hope you get the job, i don't need it, i have done so much, i wish you good luck). in subsequent years he was consistently appreciative of our work and visited our office. the quotation on page cv is from an article he wrote for caroline hentschel's master's dissertation on german graphic design, supervised by myself.

it was massimo vignelli who said melior was an outstanding font choice for the bundestag corporate design because its designer – the famous typeface designer HERMANN ZAPF – was german: a coincidence that hadn't even occurred to me. i had chosen melior purely on the basis of its formal rigour, which the designer himself discusses on pages liii–liv.

PETER ZIZKA (page lxxvii) has long been a friendly fellow designer and a fellow designer friend, something that's all the more valuable when you're in competition with each other.

kai bierich
*1957 in hamburg, two children. studied architecture at darmstadt technical university 1977–1985. visited the usa 1981–1982. worked at behnisch & partner, stuttgart 1986–1987 and independently 1986–1992. lecturer in design at stuttgart university 1989–1996. worked with the architect tobias wulf 1992–1996. partner of wulf & partner freie architekten bda 1996–2011. lecturer at the stuttgart academy of art and design 1997–2001. director of the *landesmesse stuttgart* project 2001–2007. wulf & ass. architekten gmbh 2001–2011. visiting professor nankai university, tianjin, und cafa beijing in china 2006–2009. managing partner, wulf architekten gmbh, since 2011.

joachim blüher
lives in rome and is director of villa massimo.

hannes böhringer
*1948 in the rhineland; spent his youth in düsseldorf; attended a secondary school specialising in classics; studied philosophy and history at münster, heidelberg and bochum universities; gained his doctorate in 1975; taught at kunstakademie düsseldorf (düsseldorf arts academy); research assistant at the pädagogische hochschule (college of education) in münster; assistant lecturer at the institute of philosophy, freie universität berlin, 1979; post-doctoral lecturing qualification, 1984; professor of philosophy at freie universität berlin from 1986, in the art department of kassel university 1989, and at braunschweig university of art 1995 to 2012; guest professorships in budapest, paris and madison (wisconsin); co-editor of the journal daidalos from 1986 to 1990; co-founder of kunstverein giannozzo art association, berlin, 1987; president of the german society for 19th-century research from 2005 to 2010; awarded the maholy-nagy prize by maholy-nagy university of art and design, budapest, 2009. collaborations with hans hansen, axel kufus, eva-maria schön, jozsef tillmann, andreas uebele and walter zimmermann.

matthew carter
*1937, is a type designer with 60 years' experience in typographic technologies, ranging from hand-cut punches to computer fonts. after a long association with the linotype companies he was a co-founder of bitstream inc. in 1981, a digital type foundry where he worked for ten years. carter is now a principal of carter & cone type inc., designers and producers of original typefaces, in cambridge, massachusetts.

andreas cukrowicz
*1969 in bregenz, austria. studied architecture at tu wien (vienna university of technology) 1988–1993 and in professor penttilä's masterclass at the academy of fine arts vienna 1993–1996. has worked with anton nachbaur-sturm since 1992, founding their joint architecture practice cukrowicz nachbaur architekten in 1996 – which subsequently became cukrowicz nachbaur architekten zt gmbh, based in bregenz, in 2008. member of various architecture advisory boards (in hittisau 1998–2011, in lochau since 2007, in konstanz 2009–2013). president of the vorarlberg branch of the austrian architects association (zentralvereinigung der architekten österreichs) 2005–2011. deputy member of vorarlberg's panel of independent experts since 2011. lecturer at linz university of the arts and spittal university of applied sciences 2010. visiting professor on design master's programme at technical university of munich 2012–2013. lives with sabine and paulus in bregenz.

adrian frutiger
1928–2015, was one of the most important typeface designers of the 20th century. apprenticeship as a compositor in interlaken, 1944–1948. training in lettering and graphic design under alfred willimann and walter käch at the kunstgewerbeschule (school of applied arts) in zurich 1949–1951. moved to paris, 1952. typeface designer and artistic director with deberny & peignot. established his own studio with bruno pfäffli and andré gürtler in arcueil, paris, 1962. frutiger designed many famous typefaces, including *univers*. he taught at école estienne, paris, for ten years and at école nationale supérieure des arts décoratifs, paris, for eight years, as well as lecturing and teaching in other institutions, nationally and internationally. many exhibitions of his work. major honours: chevalier de l'ordre des arts et lettres; 1968 city of mainz gutenberg prize; 1987 tdc medal of the type directors club new york; 1990 officier de l'ordre des arts et des lettres de france; 2006 sota typography award boston (usa); 2007 designer award, swiss federal office of culture, bern; 2013 volkswirtschaft berner oberland culture prize for his lifetime achievement.

durs grünbein
*1962 in dresden, lives in berlin and rome. poet, translator, essayist, librettist. his work has been translated into many languages and has won many awards, including the georg büchner prize in 1995, the friedrich nietzsche prize in 2004, the friedrich hölderlin prize in 2005, the pier paolo pasolini prize, awarded in rome, in 2006, and sweden's tomas tranströmer prize in 2012. he is professor of poetics at kunstakademie düsseldorf (düsseldorf arts academy) and a member of the order pour le mérite and several academies, including the deutsche akademie für sprache und dichtung in darmstadt and the akademie der künste in berlin. durs grünbein has written many books of poetry and several volumes of prose and essays. recent works published by suhrkamp verlag include *der cartesische taucher. drei meditationen* (essays, 2008), *die bars von atlantis* (essays, 2009), *aroma. ein römisches zeichenbuch* (poetry and prose, 2010), *vom stellenwert der worte* (frankfurt poetry lecture, 2010), *limbische akte* (2011), *koloss im nebel* (poems, 2012), *cyrano oder die rückkehr vom mond* (poems, 2014) and *die jahre im zoo* (prose, 2015).

hans hansen
*1940 in bielefeld. lithography training with reprographics firm thomas & kurzberg, studied applied graphic design under prof. walter breker at kunstakademie düsseldorf (düsseldorf arts academy). independent graphic designer and (primarily) photographer from 1962 onwards; first assignment producing photographs of tapio wirkkala's glassware pieces. photography assignments worldwide for germany's lufthansa airline 1963–1967. moved to hamburg 1967. 1968 onwards: assignments for volkswagen and other automakers in germany, france, italy and the usa. own studio in hamburg-hochkamp from 1970; increasing focus on product photography. since 1980: independent projects plus advertising, industry and editorial assignments. studio on hamburg's fleetinsel island since 1993.

klaus klemp
*1954, studied design, art history and history at dortmund, münster and marburg. director of frankfurt am main's culture department and of the city's karmeliterkloster and leinwandhaus galleries 1989–2006. committee member of the german design council 1995–2005. lecturer on design history and theory and public design at various german universities since 1998, honorary professor at hochschule rheinmain (rheinmain university of applied sciences) in wiesbaden since 2008. exhibition manager (2006), deputy director (2013) and currently curator for design at frankfurt's museum angewandte kunst. professor of design theory and design history at hfg offenbach university of art and design since 2014. member of the ddc (german designer club), board member of the dieter and ingeborg rams foundation and council member of the gesellschaft für designgeschichte (design history society). numerous exhibitions and publications on architecture, design and visual art.

norbert lammert
*1948 in bochum. studied social sciences, graduating in 1972 and gaining his doctorate in 1975. member of the cdu (christian democratic union) since 1966; member of the executive committee for cdu north rhine-westphalia since 1986, chair of the cdu regional association for the ruhr district 1986–2008. member of the bundestag (german parliament) since 1980. parliamentary state secretary 1989–1998. vice-president 2002–2005 and since 18 october 2005 president of the german bundestag.

jórunn ragnarsdóttir
*1957 in akureyri. degree in architecture at stuttgart university 1976–1982. worked for arno lederer's architecture practice 1982–1985; co-owner of joint practice büro lederer ragnarsdóttir from 1985; joint practice with marc oei (lederer ragnarsdóttir oei) since 1992. lecturer at stuttgart university, working with prof. boris podrecca, 1992–1993. stage sets and costumes for reykjavik city theatre 1998–2000. member of the design advisory board for the city of lübeck 2009–2015. member of the design advisory board for the city of mannheim 2010–2012. professor at kunstakademie düsseldorf (düsseldorf arts academy) 2010–2012. since 2012 managing partner of lro lederer ragnarsdóttir oei gmbh & co. kg. since 2012 member of the committee for city planning in munich. since 2014 chair of the design advisory board in freiburg. since 2014 member of the state monuments council of berlin's senate department for urban development and the environment. since december 2015 member of the advisory board for the stuttgart academy of art and design. since 2016 member of the design advisory board for the city of regensburg.

thomas ruff
*1958 in zell am harmersbach, lives and works in düsseldorf. studied fine art photography under bernd becher at kunstakademie düsseldorf (düsseldorf arts academy) 1977–1985 (awarded "master student" status 1982). professor at kunstakademie düsseldorf 2000–2006. selected solo exhibitions: 2016: *object relations*, art gallery of toronto; *thomas ruff*, national museum of modern art, tokyo; 21st century museum of contemporary art, kanazawa. 2014: *lichten*, s.m.a.k., ghent and kunsthalle düsseldorf. 2012: *thomas ruff*, haus der kunst, munich. 2009: *oberflächen, tiefen*, kunsthalle wien (vienna). 2001–2003: *photographs 1979 to present*, kunsthalle baden-baden, lenbachhaus munich, irish museum of modern art dublin, tate liverpool and other locations. 1995: german pavilion, venice biennale. 1990: *porträts, häuser, sterne*, stedelijk museum, amsterdam, le magasin, grenoble, kunsthalle zürich.

karin sander
*in bensberg, north rhine-westphalia, studied fine art and art history at stuttgart academy of art and design and on the independent study program at whitney museum, new york. multiple awards including a daad (german academic exchange service) scholarship in new york, a stiftung kunstfonds award, the villa romana award (florence), cité internationale des arts residency (paris), akademie schloss solitude residency (stuttgart), the hans thoma award – the grand state prize for fine arts (federal state of baden-württemberg) – and a fellowship at the villa massimo german academy in rome. karin sander's work is represented in many public exhibitions and collections including moma new york, the san francisco museum of modern art, new york's metropolitan museum of art, osaka's national museum of art, staatsgalerie stuttgart and the hirshhorn museum in washington, d.c. karin sander is professor of architecture and art at eth zurich (the swiss federal institute of technology in zurich). she lives and works in berlin and zurich.

manfred schmalriede
*1937 in oldenburg. studied painting, photography, history, art history and philosophy. professor of art and design theory at hochschule pforzheim university of applied sciences 1971–2002. lecturer in history and theory of photography at essen university 1979–1991. lecturer at berlin's neue schule für fotografie (new photography school) since 2001. member of the deutsche gesellschaft für photographie (german photographic association) and the deutsche fotografische akademie (german academy of photography). curator of photography and design exhibitions.

klaus schmiedek

*1940, studied architecture in hanover and stuttgart, specialising in residential and urban development and graduating in 1969. after three years working on land-use planning and residential development with dbe-architekten in stuttgart, moved into the building authority sector in 1973. internship with stuttgart university building authority. following completion of state planning qualifications, became head of planning for the state building department of schwäbisch gmünd, 1975–1980. advisor on university buildings for the finance ministry 1980–1986. deputy head 1986–1990 and head 1990–2005 of the stuttgart and hohenheim university building authority.

eva-maria schön

*1948 in dresden, photographic training with lore bermbach in düsseldorf, then studied graphic design at düsseldorf university of applied sciences, continuing her studies with klaus rinke at kunstakademie düsseldorf (düsseldorf arts academy). based in berlin since 1980. prizes and awards: villa romana award, karl-schmidt-rottluff award, art/omi-residency in new york, djerassi resident artists program in california, residencies in guernsey, in shenzhen, china, and at fondazione casa atelier bedigliora, switzerland.

andreas uebele

*1960, studied architecture and urban planning at stuttgart university and art at the stuttgart state academy of art and design. in 1996 he founded his own visual communications agency in stuttgart and since 1998 has been a professor for communications design at düsseldorf university of applied sciences and a member of forum typografie. member of the type directors club of new york and of the art directors club of new york since 2002. member of agi, alliance graphique internationale, since 2007 and of bdg, the association of german communication designers, since 2009. awarded a scholarship for practitioners at villa massimo, rome, in 2015.

massimo vignelli

1931–2014, studied architecture in milan and venice. established the vignelli office of design and architecture in milan, with leila vignelli, in 1960. became co-founder and design director of unimark international corporation in 1965. with leila vignelli, established vignelli associates in 1971 and vignelli designs in 1978. his work includes graphic and corporate identity programmes, publication designs, architectural graphics and exhibition, interior, furniture and consumer product designs for many leading american and european companies and institutions. vignelli's work has been published and exhibited worldwide and is represented in the permanent collections of several museums, notably the museum of modern art, the metropolitan museum of art, the brooklyn museum and the cooper-hewitt museum in new york, the musée des arts decoratifs in montreal and die neue sammlung in munich. he was president of the alliance graphique internationale (agi) and the american institute of graphic arts (aiga), a vice-president of the architectural league, and a member of the industrial designers society of america (idsa).

hermann zapf

1918–2015. apprentice retoucher with the printing firm karl ulrich & co. in nuremberg 1934–1938. independent typeface designer from 1938. artistic director at the type foundry d. stempel ag in frankfurt am main 1947–1956. taught calligraphy at offenbach's werkkunstschule (applied arts college) 1948–1950. advisor to mergenthaler linotype company in brooklyn and berlin 1956–1974. worked for publishers including suhrkamp and s. fischer. professor of graphic design at the carnegie institute of technology in pittsburgh, pennsylvania, 1960. advisor to hallmark cards 1967–1972. received the f. w. goudy award from rochester institute of technology in rochester, new york, in 1969. lecturer in calligraphy and typography at darmstadt technical university 1972–1981. awarded the mainz gutenberg prize 1974. vice-president of design processing international inc., new york, 1977–1987. professor of typographic computer programs at rochester institute of technology in rochester, new york, 1977–1987. president of zapf, burns & co., based in new york – a business dedicated to the development of typographic software 1987–1991. appointed honorary royal designer for industry by the royal society of arts, london, 1985. awarded the leipzig book fair gold medal 1989. awarded the german federal cross of merit (first class) 2010.

peter zizka

*1961, trained as an art restorer and studied visual communication at hfg offenbach university of art and design, as well as studying under bruce mclean at frankfurt's städelschule (fine art academy). founded the heine/lenz/zizka design practice with achim heine and michael lenz 1989. his socially-relevant design work includes projects like the floor-based installation *virtual minefield*, exhibited in galleries including kunsthal rotterdam and (in 2013) the main gallery of the united nations, new york. the second designer, after konstantin grcic, to receive a scholarship for practitioners at villa massimo in rome, 2011. large-scale typographic installation, *wortfusion* (word fusion) on the façade of frankfurt's paulskirche, marking the 25th anniversary of german reunification, 2015. columnist on design for the magazine bilanz and freelance curator for frankfurt's museum angewandte kunst (applied arts museum).

for many years PAUL BOOTHROYD has been producing translations for us that are better than like wot the original oughta have bin. by expanding his maison neue font with different widths and 52 weights, font designer TIMO GAESSNER has enabled us to achieve perfectly balanced (otherwise much loathed) justified text – applying a method developed by johannes gutenberg for using letters of different widths in his 42-line bible. photographer HANS HANSEN, who we have worked with for over 20 years, didn't turn up his nose at the task of setting our sketchbooks and other odds and ends in the best possible light. YANIK HAUSCHILD not only spent almost three years working his way through our not-always-entirely-tidy archives, but also took this book and its design firmly in hand; without him, it would still be a haphazard stack of scraps. superhero MIRIAM HOLZAPFEL lovingly and mercilessly robbed me of the cherished illusion that i could write well, which was both painful and salutary. thanks for that – and for the proofreading. for more than twenty years ASTRID RABIN has been cutting, blow-drying and styling the author's texts, including all those that appear on these pages. we have been working hand in hand with ARCHITEKTURBÜRO ZIEGLERBÜRG for twenty years and more; many of the projects shown here were conceived, developed and realised together.

thanks

aaaaaaaaaaaaaaaaaaaaaaaaaaaa
bbbbbbbbbbbbbbbbbbbbbbbbbbbb
cccccccccccccccccccccccccccc
dddddddddddddddddddddddddddd
eeeeeeeeeeeeeeeeeeeeeeeeeeee
ffffffffffffffffffffffffffff
gggggggggggggggggggggggggggg
hhhhhhhhhhhhhhhhhhhhhhhhhhhh
iiiiiiiiiiiiiiiiiiiiiiiiiiii
jjjjjjjjjjjjjjjjjjjjjjjjjjjj
kkkkkkkkkkkkkkkkkkkkkkkkkkkk
llllllllllllllllllllllllllll
mmmmmmmmmmmmmmmmmmmmmmmmmmmm
nnnnnnnnnnnnnnnnnnnnnnnnnnnn
oooooooooooooooooooooooooooo
pppppppppppppppppppppppppppp
qqqqqqqqqqqqqqqqqqqqqqqqqqqq
rrrrrrrrrrrrrrrrrrrrrrrrrrrr
ssssssssssssssssssssssssssss
tttttttttttttttttttttttttttt
uuuuuuuuuuuuuuuuuuuuuuuuuuuu
vvvvvvvvvvvvvvvvvvvvvvvvvvvv
wwwwwwwwwwwwwwwwwwwwwwwwwwww
xxxxxxxxxxxxxxxxxxxxxxxxxxxx
yyyyyyyyyyyyyyyyyyyyyyyyyyyy
zzzzzzzzzzzzzzzzzzzzzzzzzzzz

the 52 additional weights of the maison neue font by timo gaessner,
an adapted version developed specially for this book

members of staff since 1985

henrike bansemer
lisa bansemer
andrea bauer
stefan becker
rebecca benz
elena bergen
marc t. bernauer
jutta boxheimer
lili brenner
benjamin brinkmann
ralph burkhardt
claudia burtscher
jakob buse
alexandra busse
katrin dittmann
lena drießen
marc engenhart
sven eul
daniel fels
jan filek
markus fischer
marian fitz
susanne fritsch
jan paul gaugler
frank geiger
sibylle geiger
marc-oliver gern
raoul gottschling
alexandra gövert
tino graß
andreas gregor
natalie de gregorio
tove günter
benedikt haid
ludwig haslberger
yanik hauschild
gerd häußler
vanessa heepen
céline hermel
matthias herzogenrath
carolin himmel
judith hinel
tobias hönow
nora hug
ilona jablonski
beate kapprell
angela klasar
anja kathrin klein
kristof knauer
svenja knödler
till köhler
jessica krier
mats kubiak
manja kurzak

charlotte lengersdorf
cecile leufgen
christian lindermann
birgit lorinser
bettina maier
mona matejic
helena mayer
claus mihm
katharina moritzen
maja mory
hendrike nagel
anne marie de paola
jonas pelzer
daniel perraudin
imke plinta
caroline pöll
julien pommé
petr pščolka
felix rabe
weronika rafa
simon renner
kristina reuter
thomas reuter
gabriel richter
norbert riedelsheimer
petra rudloff
silke sabow
margarethe saxler
philipp schäfer
nick schmidt
tristan schmitz
matthias schnabel
sabine schönhaar
nadja schoch
sabrina sigle
daniela sonntag
laura staib
andreas steinbrecher
tobias textor
katrin theile
thanh-thao tran
rené ulrich
lika valentien
franziska virgili
christine voshage
svenja voß
silvia wasner
lea wenzel
peter wilhelm
burkhard wittemeier
corinna ziemann

concept, layout and composition
büro uebele visuelle kommunikation
yanik hauschild, andreas uebele

text
andreas uebele

images
ad architectural digest, 10/2010, noshe (56), arge lederer ragnarsdóttir oei, jangled nerves, visualisation renderstüble (342), joachim baldauf (160·477), andreas cukrowicz (cxii) vanessa daldegan (359), ddp images (218), digitalglobe, google (173), stefan dimitrov, süddeutsche zeitung (234), sven eul (125·154·278·281·413), daniel fels (34·36–37·51·54–59·97–99·103·160·167·204·206–07·237·292–93·344·400·412·418–19·422–23·478·497–98), frankfurter allgemeine zeitung (420), german parliament [junophoto, julia nowak-katz (232) lichtblick, achim melde (233), werner schuering (224), rolf unterberg (220)], brigida gonzález (11–17·20–27·282·284–85·289–91), hadid90 (457), fritz and sibylle haase (460), roland halbe (78), hans hansen (sketchbooks·39–41·107–09·112–13·127·xl·321·331·401–09·458·482–83), tamara hansen (49·179·448), yanik hauschild (72·106·115·126·147·215), michael heinrich (493–95), carolin himmel (143), florian holzherr (417·420), gerhardt kellermann (434·438·440–41), claudia klein (213·216·223·228·235·273·297·472·487), frank kleinbach (183) steffen knöll (234), andreas körner (66–67·79·117–19·121·185–87·190–91·194–95·245–46·249–51·254–57·262–63·300–01·303·313–19·330·344·410–11·424–25·427–31), mats kubiak (111·358·360–61·394·415·486·491), eva-lotta lamm (234), landschaftdrei. dipl.-ing. michael f. heintze, franz hendrikx (93–94) julien lanoo, vitra (347·351), markus malcher (398), meck architekten (174–75·177), mercedes-benz classic (85–86·original image xix–xx), miriam migliazzi & mart klein, die zeit (234), rené müller (124–25), julia münzing (201), notos quartett (88), chrigel ott (xxxiii), studio panorama (234), parrotta contemporary art (62–63), jórunn ragnarsdóttir (lxvi), paul rand (ix), christian richters (65·69–71·74–75·80–81·83·363–69·372–75·379–85·388–93·501–02·504–07), thomas ruff (xix–xx), karin sander (xxxix), hanspeter schiess (128·130–31·134–37·140–41·144–45) schlecker (lx), berit schneidereit (85–86·101·197–99·218–19·247·265·305·323·439·447·474–75·479·484–85), eva-maria schön (cxi), anton stankowski "konstruktion und intuition. 40 varianten", stankowski-stiftung (357), rené staud (86), tobias textor (155–56·158), andreas uebele (2·18–19·28·30·61·100·110·116·146·xxxvii–xxxviii·170–71·192·242–43·253·259·lxvii–lxx·279·286·329·357·414·449·470·488·523), büro uebele (18–19·91·96·132–33·150–53·188–89·192–93·238–39·286·309·325·348–49·370–71·386–87·421·436–37·450·457·460·499), verlag hermann schmidt "abz. im bann der buchstaben" (462), vista rasch gmbh (456–57), steffen vogt (312), peter zizka (lxxvii)

fonts
adapted version of maison neue book,
maison neue italic/medium/bold (timo gaessner)
antwerp regular/semibold/bold (henrik kubel)
massimo bold (gabriel richter and andreas uebele)

paper
maxiscript 100 g/150 g, profigloss 115 g

copy editing
miriam holzapfel, astrid rabin

german proofreading
joachim straßburger

translation
paul boothroyd, susan mackervoy, alyssa schmitt

english proofreading
andrew leslie

repro
immedia23

printing
offsetdruckerei karl grammlich

binding
josef spinner

unit 32, isbn 978-0-9956664-2-9
copies of this book can be ordered from
www.unitedtions.com

© 2017 andreas uebele
büro uebele visuelle kommunikation
www.uebele.com